It's All for the Kids

It's All for the Kids

GENDER, FAMILIES, AND
YOUTH SPORTS

MICHAEL A. MESSNER

UNIVERSITY OF CALIFORNIA PRESS
Berkeley   Los Angeles   London

University of California Press, one of the most distinguished university presses in the United States, enriches lives around the world by advancing scholarship in the humanities, social sciences, and natural sciences. Its activities are supported by the UC Press Foundation and by philanthropic contributions from individuals and institutions. For more information, visit www.ucpress.edu.

University of California Press
Berkeley and Los Angeles, California

University of California Press, Ltd.
London, England

An earlier version of Chapter 2 appeared as Michael A. Messner and Suzel Bozada-Deas. 2009. "Separating the men from the moms: The making of adult sex segregation in youth sports." *Gender & Society* 23 (1).

Library of Congress Cataloging-in-Publication Data

Messner, Michael A.

   It's all for the kids : gender, families, and youth sports / Michael A. Messner.
       p.   cm.
   Includes bibliographical references and index.
   ISBN 978-0-520-25708-5 (cloth : alk. paper)
   ISBN 978-0-520-25710-8 (pbk. : alk. paper)
   1. Sports for children.   2. Sports for children—Coaching.   3. Sports for children—Psychological aspects.   4. Sports—Sex differences.
   5. Parent and child.   I. Title.

GV709.2.M465   2009
796.083—dc22   2008036052

Manufactured in the United States of America
18   17   16   15   14   13   12   11   10   09
10   9   8   7   6   5   4   3   2   1

This book is printed on Natures Book, which contains 30% post-consumer waste and meets the minimum requirements of ANSI/NISO Z39.48–1992 (R 1997) (*Permanence of Paper*).

For the many adult volunteers who work to make youth sports a healthy, life-affirming, and equitable experience for all of our kids

Contents

Illustrations

Preface

When I tell people that I'm writing a book on adults' involvement in youth sports, they frequently raise their eyebrows, chuckle, and mutter something about how "crazy" parents are getting these days. Then they rub their hands together and wait expectantly to hear my horror stories: a bat-wielding dad who attacks his son's baseball coach; a coach's artery-bursting tirade at a soccer referee; a dad publicly humiliating his child, who has failed to lay down a sacrifice bunt. But the thing is, during my seven years of observing youth sports, I never saw any physical violence from adults, and I very rarely witnessed a parent or a coach verbally "losing it." Instead, most of what I witnessed was adults behaving in respectful and civil ways toward each other, and in supportive and constructive ways with the kids. The moments when a coach "lost it" after a bad play, or after an umpire's call, stood out as memorable because they were so unusual.

The image of adults-behaving-badly at youth sports events is now a common part of our cultural lexicon. According to sociologists Stan

Eitzen and George Sage, many people believe that adults' "sideline rage" in youth sports has recently grown to "epidemic" proportions. The National Alliance for Youth Sports claims that 15 percent of youth sports matches are marked by verbal or physical abuse from parents or coaches.[1] To be sure, some highly publicized cases of adult violence in youth sports have occurred, and a recent study of participants in youth sports indicated low but significant levels of coaches arguing with referees, verbally abusing an opponent, displaying bad sportsmanship, and even encouraging their kids to cheat or to intentionally injure an opponent.[2]

It is important to illuminate—and to eliminate—these kinds of damaging moments in youth sports. But I am not so much interested in these infrequent incidents of rage and violence as I am in the normal, day-to-day organization and dynamics of youth sports. The research I conducted for this book was prompted by a desire to understand the role youth sports plays in the social organization of gender and other forms of inequality in an era of social change. Does youth sports contribute to breaking down gender inequalities, or to reinforcing them? Is youth sports a site of healthy empowerment for boys and for girls? Or does sex segregation, combined with informal rituals and beliefs, tend to reinforce gender inequalities? Under what conditions is youth sports progressive or regressive—or some combination of the two—in terms of gender relations?

I have spent much of my academic career studying and writing about gender and sports. Fifteen years ago, when I was being reviewed for tenure and promotion at my university, I confessed to my senior colleague Jon Miller that I was worried that perhaps one or more of our colleagues—especially the international demographers or the criminologists—might vote against me, perhaps seeing sport as a trivial matter for a scholar to study. "Don't worry," he reassured me. "If anyone suggests that sports are unimportant, I'm prepared to say that 'There are a hell of a lot more sports fans out there than there are juvenile delinquents. And they're a lot more dangerous.' "

Jon was right about one thing: sports matter. For most of the past century, organized sports have held a position of honored centrality in American high schools and colleges. Professional and college sport has become a huge, multibillion dollar business that occupies an enormous amount of space in the print media and even more airtime in the electronic media. These are aspects of sport that have been studied extensively by scholars. But, curiously, there have been very few book-length studies of youth sports—despite the fact that this is where we find the largest number of participants at any level of organized sports (excepting spectatorship, which is also under-studied). In the United States, organized team sports—especially soccer, baseball, softball, basketball, football, and in some parts of the U.S. and in Canada, ice hockey—are among the most frequent and important activities in the lives of kids. And youth sports is a major site of volunteer activity by adults—often, but not always, with their own children's teams. As such, youth sports participation is habitually woven into the daily routines of millions of families.

For the past dozen years or so, this has certainly been the case for my family. My son Miles played AYSO soccer, Little League Baseball, and YMCA basketball between the ages of six and eight. By the time he was eight or nine, he decided that sports were not for him, and he has since poured his creative energies into making electric guitars scream and cry. Miles's younger brother Sasha dabbled in soccer, basketball, and flag football, but stayed the course with Little League Baseball, playing his final season last summer at the age of fourteen. During these years, there were moments when it seemed to my wife Pierrette and I that our sons' involvements in sports had taken over our lives. As sports seasons ended and new ones approached, decisions had to be made about which sports to play, whether to quit or continue. During baseball seasons, we continually had to juggle priorities: Should Sasha skip his baseball practice, or attend a music lesson? Should he go to his baseball game, or to the middle school play practice? Family vacations were planned with baseball season in mind, and there were countless hurried family dinners and many Saturday schedules that were sandwiched around a baseball game.

Youth sports are fueled almost entirely by adult volunteerism. When their kids join a team, parents have to decide at what level they will be involved. Some parents prefer simply to drive their kids to practices or games, perhaps staying to watch the games. Other parents want to be as involved as possible and volunteer to be head coaches, while some contribute as assistant coaches. Others may take on less visible volunteer jobs, such as "team parent" (the person who organizes snacks for the kids' games, keeps communication flowing between coaches and parents, and organizes social events for the team, such as a team party). When I noticed that these tasks were largely divided by gender—the coaches were almost all men, while team parents (often called "team moms") were all women—my sociological imagination was ignited. I asked myself: Why is this? How is this gendered division of labor created? Is it changing?

When my sons started playing sports, I wanted to be involved, but never as the head coach or manager. On more than one occasion over the years, Sasha asked if I would volunteer to coach his team. My own father had been a very successful high school coach, and I have always been reluctant to take on that role (I won't dive into a psychoanalytic analysis of this aversion here). So, instead, when my kids played youth sports I volunteered to assist the coach at the beginning of each season. In the early years, this usually resulted in my being an assistant coach. In Sasha's final three years of Little League Baseball, I settled in to the role of official scorekeeper during games. These helping roles allowed me to feel that I was contributing something without having to take on the much larger responsibility of running a team. And holding these marginal volunteer positions for several years also gave me a wonderful vantage point for participant-observation research.

I grew up playing sports, but my experience as a kid was mostly with sports organized by my friends and me, not by huge national organizations (the exception being Little League Baseball). I loved sports, and at least when I was young, I was pretty good at them. As I was growing up, I believed with almost religious fervor that playing sports was unequivocally good for people ("people," in my day, meant *boys*), and that sports contributed positive things to schools, communities, and the nation. Later, in college, I learned from feminism how sport had excluded girls and women, thus reinforcing commonsense notions of natural male superiority. And I started listening to the voices of men who, as boys, had been hurt or humiliated while participating in sports. It was then that I started to develop a critical perspective on sport.

Consequently, much of my research and writing for the past two decades has explored the ways that sport helps to create social inequality (particularly of gender, race, social class, and sexual orientation), and how sport too often rewards and glorifies violence. However, I never entirely lost my love for sport, nor my enthusiasm for the positive potential of sport to enhance lifelong physical activity, health, friendship, and cooperation. So when my sons began to get involved in youth sports, I entered into the activities along with them, hoping that these would be positive, life-enhancing experiences. I wanted youth sports to be places where my sons would have fun, while learning healthy attitudes and practices and experiencing respectful and cooperative relations with others.

For the most part, I believe playing youth sports was a positive thing for my sons. They were fortunate usually to have wonderful coaches and teammates. However, Miles brought the emotional underside of youth sport back into focus for me one evening, perhaps four years ago. He had long since quit playing sports, but on this evening he had gone to the baseball park with me to watch one of Sasha's games. "This place brings back memories," he said as he looked out on to the baseball field. "What memories?" I asked. "Striking out," he said. "Striking out *again*, and having to walk back to the dugout." Ouch.

I immediately remembered from my own Little League days how that felt. The walk back from home plate to the dugout after striking out—after striking out *again*—under the eyes of your teammates, the opposing players, your family, and a few score spectators in the grandstands, can be one of the longest walks of your life. How your coaches and teammates greet you when you get back to the dugout can make all the difference. Sasha started his final season of baseball with a terrible slump—frequently striking out, and going many games before finally getting his first base hit. After each strikeout, I would cast my eyes down to my scorebook to record the "K" (strikeout), as Sasha walked away from the batter's box. But it warmed my heart to see that his teammate waiting on deck would give him a "fist" (this generation's version of the "high five") and a word of encouragement as he made his way back the dugout. There, Sasha would invariably be met by his manager or coach, who would complement his "good cuts," tell him to hang in there, maybe give him a tip on his stance or swing. Toward the end of the season, Sasha suddenly started slashing base hits and doubles all over the field, helping his team win some important late-season games. His teammates joked that perhaps he had started to take steroids.

The lesson of that final season of Little League for Sasha was to always keep trying, and to mutually support your teammates, even during tough times. Eventually, if you persevere, you will make contributions to the team—maybe even have a moment or two of glory. Sport participation holds this positive pedagogical potential for all kids, but there are other aspects of sport—often less visible—that create or perpetuate problems, particularly those related to social inequalities. And it is these problems associated with sport that have preoccupied much of my research. My friend and colleague Don Sabo has often told me that the "critical" orientation I take in my research has too often resulted in my failing to point out the many positive aspects of sport participation. I believe this is true, and I hope that as people read this book they will hold in their minds the fact that my critical orientation to sport is fueled by optimism—optimism based on my understanding of the potential of sport to contribute to shaping healthy, equitable, cooperative, and peaceful individuals and communities. This potential is rarely fully realized, but I believe it can be.

National surveys reveal that large majorities of adults expect sport participation to have a positive impact on their kids. Those studies, and the fact that every year tens of thousands of adults volunteer in youth sports, shed light on one interpretation of this book's title: It's all for the kids. But a deeper look at adults' involvement in youth sports reveals the irony in my title: in fact, it's not always *all* about the kids, not entirely. As this book will show, it's also about adults, and about how volunteering in youth sports defines their identities and shapes their families, workplaces, and communities.

Acknowledgments

The research for this book spanned seven years, so I apologize if I forget to thank some of the many people who have encouraged me and offered assistance with this project. For most of the time I was doing research for this book, I was serving as Chair of the Department of Sociology at the University of Southern California. During a two-year stretch of that time, I was fortunate to work with Suzel Bozada Deas, who served as my able research assistant and conducted three-fourths of the interviews for this study. During those two years, when I was often preoccupied with administrative tasks, the research would have seemed dead in the water if not for Suzel's efforts. Two other graduate students provided valuable assistance: Celeste Atkins transcribed most of the interviews, and I am grateful for her work. And thanks to Kristen Barber for her detective work in helping me find data on Little League and AYSO leagues in surrounding communities. Sasha Hondagneu-Messner served on occasion as a valuable research assistant with my fieldwork.

I completed the writing of this book blissfully, while on sabbatical. It has never before struck me so deeply what a privilege it is to be supported by one's institution to simply sit at home and write. I thank my colleagues in the Department of Sociology and in the Gender Studies program at USC for allowing me the time to complete this work. Thanks also to my many wonderful graduate students who so thoughtfully kept their demands on my time to a minimum during this sabbatical break. And many thanks to my physical therapist Lori Montgomery: when I began writing this book, it was a pain in the back; as I finish writing, it's not.

Several scholars helped me with my background research on youth sports, gender, volunteer work, and coaching. Many of these peoples' works are cited in my bibliography, but I will note here a few who went beyond, helping me find articles, books, or research reports that broadened my understanding: thanks to Mo Weiss, Nancy Theberge, Faye Wachs, Jay Coakley, Stan Eitzen, George Sage, Nicole LaVoi, Annelies Knoppers, Sally Raskoff, Sherri Grasmuck, and Jennifer Ring. As always, my friend and collaborator Don Sabo provided encouragement and concrete ideas. I've appreciated our ongoing back-and-forth e-mails during my writing, and especially Don's sharing with me the invaluable national survey research on youth sports conducted by him and his colleagues. That research has allowed me to broadly contextualize my local study with national survey data.

My editor at the University of California Press, Naomi Schneider, was encouraging and helpful throughout the process. A handful of generous souls read early drafts of some of my chapters. Thanks to Erin Moore, Alison Bell Rainey, Laurie Narro, Pierrette Hondagneu-Sotelo, and Don Sabo for their encouragement and suggestions. Jennifer Ring and three anonymous reviewers for UC Press offered helpful suggestions for revision. Just as important during the writing process was the daily connection I had via e-mail with my always supportive mom, Anita Messner-Voth, my sister Melinda Messner-Rios, and my e-mail group of childhood friends: Donnie Hallstone, Jon Scattini, Jim Clark, and Maureen Parton. Pierrette Hondagneu-Sotelo continues to be the greatest colleague and partner I could possibly hope for. I am grateful for how our love continues to deepen, and for the many levels of our supportive connection, not the least of which is our ritual morning coffee that in recent months included my daily recital of "what I will write today." The last time I wrote a book while on sabbatical, our two sons were little boys. Now, seven years later, they are two huge teenagers who are rapidly morphing into young men. I have to say, given Miles's and Sasha's growing independence, it's been easier for me to focus on my writing this time around. But it strikes me that the topic of this book would never have occurred to me if I had not been blessed to have two such wonderful sons. Their presence has enriched my life in numerous ways, one small part of which is how their very different engagements with youth sports broadened my understanding of this topic.

This book is dedicated to the many adults who volunteer to make youth sports a good experience for kids. My family has benefited from the caring and generous women and men who have combined to make South Pasadena youth sports a positive experience. I especially appreciate the willingness of fifty individuals who agreed to be interviewed for this study, to the coaches on my son's teams who tolerated having me at games and practices as a researcher, and to several league officials in South Pasadena AYSO and Little League Baseball/Softball who facilitated my research. I have also had the opportunity to meet youth sports coaches from other communities and states, and have consistently been impressed with their dedication to kids and communities. Youth sports coaches always express interest in my research, and it is my hope that they will find insights in this book that will contribute to some reflection and discussion about ways to improve youth sports.

ONE "It's All for the Kids"

GENDER, FAMILIES, AND YOUTH SPORTS

Back in 1995, when we arrived at our six-year-old son Miles's first soccer practice, I was delighted to learn that his coach was a woman. Coach Karen, a mother in her mid-thirties, had grown up playing lots of sports. She was tall, confident, and athletic, and the kids responded well to her leadership. "Great, a woman coach!" I observed cheerily. "It's a new and different world than the one that I grew up in." But over the next twelve years, as I traversed with Miles, and eventually with his younger brother Sasha, a few more seasons of AYSO (American Youth Soccer Organization), a couple of years of YMCA youth basketball, and over decade of Little League baseball, we never had another woman head coach. It's not that women weren't contributing to the kids' teams. All of the "team parents" (often called "team moms")—parent volunteers who did the behind-the-scenes work of phone-calling, organizing weekly snack schedules and team parties, collecting money for a gift for the coaches—were women. And occasionally I would notice a team that had a woman assistant coach. But women head coaches were very few and far between.

I started keeping track of the numbers of women and men head coaches in the annual AYSO and LLB/S (Little League Baseball/Softball) yearbooks that we would receive at the end of each season, and I found that my hunches were true.[1] There just weren't very many women head coaches. The yearbooks reveal that from 1999 to 2007, only 13 percent of the 1,280 AYSO teams have had women head coaches. The numbers are even lower for LLB/S teams; between 1999 and 2007, only 5.9 percent of the 538 teams have been managed by women. These low numbers were surprising to me, for several reasons. First, unlike during my childhood in the 1950s and 1960s, when there were almost no opportunities for girls to play sports, today, millions of girls participate in organized soccer, baseball, softball, basketball, and other sports. With this radical demographic shift in youth sports, I expected that the gender division of labor among parents would have shifted as well. Second, today's mothers of young children in the United States came of age during and after the 1972 institution of Title IX, and are part of the generation that ignited the booming growth of female athletic participation. It stood to reason to me that many of these women would see it as a natural transition to move from their own active sports participation into coaching their own kids. Third, women outnumber men significantly in every volunteer activity having to do with kids in my town, such as the PTA, Scouts, and school special events. Coaching youth sports seems to be the great exception to this rule.

Sport has changed over the past thirty years or so, from a world set up almost exclusively by and for boys and men to one that is moving substantially (though incompletely) toward sex equity. Yet, men dominate the very public on-field leadership positions. This paradox tweaked my sociological interest. When I first began informally to ask longtime coaches and league officials why most teams are coached by men, they were often surprised to hear how few women coaches there were. Several people told me that they believed that the number of women coaches is rising. But though the numbers have risen modestly in recent years for soccer, they have not risen for baseball and softball, as figure 1 shows.

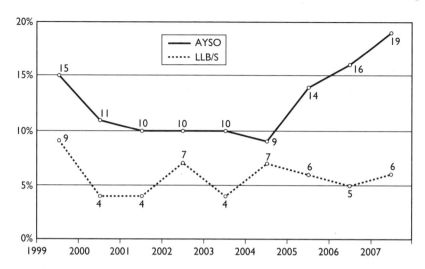

Fig. 1. Percentage of women coaches in South Pasadena AYSO and LLB-S, 1999–2007.

The proportion of baseball and softball teams headed by women has stayed remarkably flat between 1999 and 2007. In fact, the proportion of LLB/S teams headed by women was higher in 1999 than in any other year of my study. In soccer, there was an increase in the number of women coaches for the 2005, 2006, and 2007 seasons, nudging the numbers above the 15 percent that they reached in 1999, before they dipped to the 10 percent range for the next five years. An older AYSO yearbook that I came across, from 1994–95, revealed that women coached 17.6 percent of the teams that season. It appears that, despite some year-to-year fluctuations, the proportion of baseball and softball teams headed by women has plateaued, while there is reason to think that there is a modest upward trend in soccer.

As I began more systematically to analyze the annual yearbooks, to observe, and to talk with coaches and parents, I noticed some other patterns. Not only are women coaches low in number, they tend to be placed differently than men. As figure 1 shows, soccer teams are twice as likely as Little League Baseball/Softball teams to be coached by women. Boys' teams are coached almost exclusively by men, and this is especially true of boys' baseball teams, only slightly more than 2 percent of which are coached by women. Additionally, there is clearly a kind of "glass ceiling" on women coaching in the leagues for kids more than 10 or 12 years old. Nearly all of the women coaches were coaching kids between the ages of 4 and 10 . The statistical picture is clear: women head coaches are very few in number. Most of the women who do coach do not move up the ranks to coach teams with kids past the age of 8 or 10 years old; they either quit coaching after one or two years, or they "cycle back" to coach a younger son's or daughter's team made up of 6- or 8-year-olds. Of the very few women who do go on to coach age 10, 12, or older kids' teams, nearly all of them coach girls' teams.

When I shared these statistics with league officials, they expressed disappointment with the low numbers of women head coaches. Early in the study, I spoke with Bill Munson,[2] a longtime AYSO coach and one of the main organizers in the league. Munson expressed support for my research, saying that he hoped it might be helpful to him and others in figuring out how to get more women to coach. He said that he is "really frustrated," after spending the last two years "looking for ways to beg, cajole, wheedle women to become coaches." He said that he has a "hunch" that the women coaches that they have had thus far "were athletes in the '70s and '80s, and they have that confidence." But women who never played soccer lack confidence in their abilities to learn how to coach. "It's easier to take a man who doesn't know the first thing about soccer, and convince him that he can learn everything he needs to know in one training session, than it is to convince a woman that she can do it." Besides men's greater apparent confidence, he said, he's not sure what it is that makes it an experience that's so much more likely "to discourage women."

Munson's words were echoed by other league officials in AYSO and LLB/S, who told me that, in their view, they are making an effort to recruit and to encourage women coaches, and that they really don't understand why there aren't more. I wanted to understand this too. The low numbers of women coaches gave me a picture of persistent sex segregation, but simply trotting out these numbers couldn't explain *how* this picture is drawn. I wanted to know: *what are the social processes that sustain this sex segregation?* And by extension, I wanted to explore another question: *what might be happening that might serve to destabilize and possibly change this sex segregation?*

Questions about social processes—how people, in their routine daily interactions, reproduce (and occasionally challenge) patterned social relations—are best answered through a combination of qualitative methods. Between 2003 and 2007, I systematically explored the gender dynamics of volunteer coaches in South Pasadena by deploying several methods of data collection. For a two-year stretch of this longer study, I was fortunate to have the able assistance of a graduate student research assistant, Suzel Bozada-Deas. First, I continued to conduct an ongoing content analysis of eight years (1999–2007) of South Pasadena's AYSO and LLB/S yearbooks. This data provides the statistical backdrop for my study of the social processes of gender and coaching that I have introduced in this chapter. Second, I conducted field observations of numerous soccer, baseball, and softball practices and games. I participated in a clinic set up to train Little League baseball coaches, and observed annual baseball and softball tryouts as well as several annual opening ceremonies for AYSO and LLB/S. A key dimension of this field work was my several seasons of participant observation—for a few years as a volunteer assistant coach, and for the last three years as the official scorekeeper of my son's Little League Baseball teams, ranging in age from T-ball teams made up of 6- and 7-year olds, to Juniors baseball teams of 13- and 14-year-olds. And third, Suzel and I conducted fifty in-depth interviews with women and men volunteers, nearly all of whom were head soccer coaches and baseball or softball managers. Appendix 1 is a demographic overview of the interview subjects, and Appendix 2 shows the racial-ethnic composition of the coaches and of the city of South Pasadena. Appendix 3 compares the proportion of women coaches in South Pasadena youth sports with some surrounding communities. And in Appendix 4, I discuss some of the issues I faced in conducting the research—especially the field observations and the interviews.

The research findings stretched me beyond a simple study of sex segregation in youth sports coaching. My observations and interviews led me to explore how youth sports fit into families and communities. I gained insights into how peoples' beliefs about natural differences between boys and girls (what sociologists call "gender essentialism") help to shape men's and women's apparently "free" choices to volunteer (or not) for their children's activities. I discovered ways in which gender divisions of labor in families relate to more public displays of masculinity and femininity in activities like youth sports. And the study gave me provocative hints about how gender beliefs, family structure, and youth sports are key elements in constructing symbolic boundaries in a community that is defined (often covertly) as "white" and "upper middle class." In the rest of this chapter, I will briefly discuss the context of this study—first, in terms of the community, and second, in terms of youth sports in general, with a focus on the organizations of AYSO and LLB/S.

A COMMUNITY "FOR THE KIDS"

"It's all for the kids," said a smiling dad with an ironic wink as he displayed his son's team banner on the opening day of the South Pasadena AYSO soccer season. Held on a bright and warm Saturday morning in September, the AYSO opening ceremony is an autumn rite, a major community event that takes hundreds of volunteer hours to pull off.[3] On this day, nearly 2,000 kids gathered wearing their new soccer uniforms at the high school track and football field, accompanied by nearly 200 head coaches and roughly 400 assistant coaches. Several hundred more parents and others sat in the stands, as each team marched around the track with their coaches and behind their team banners, which had been painstakingly and often very artistically handmade by parents (nearly always moms). As each team marched by the stands, the team's name and sponsor were announced over the loudspeaker system and the crowd gave them a warm round of applause. The mood of the day was celebratory. On the platform, the local AYSO commissioner sat with various honored guests and dignitaries, including coaches and kids from South Pasadena championship teams from the previous season, soccer referees, representatives of the local police and fire departments, city council members, and U.S. congressman Adam Schiff. Following the national anthem, Schiff gave a short speech in which he praised the growth and prosperity of South

Pasadena's twenty-five-year tradition of youth soccer, and spoke approvingly of how the league reflects the values of a community that so cares about its children.

Indeed, over the years, I had often heard South Pasadena parents saying, "It's all for the kids"—while in the midst a school fundraiser, a Cub Scouts event, or a Little League or AYSO event that had taken hundreds of volunteer hours to pull off. The tone of "It's all for the kids" is often mildly sarcastic, and sometimes self-mocking, especially when uttered by a professional-class parent who has moved his or her family to South Pasadena precisely because of its "kid friendly" reputation and good public schools. This belief that "our town" is "safe" and "kid friendly" makes sense due to the (usually) unspoken comparison with much of the Greater Los Angeles area, which is assumed to be much *less* safe, *less* kid friendly, with substandard or deteriorating public schools. But simply buying in to the expensive housing market of South Pasadena does not itself ensure a "kid friendly" community. It's part of the community belief system that what makes South Pasadena "special" for kids is the widespread volunteer ethic. And youth sports is one of the most public expressions of this community volunteerism for our kids. At the 2003 opening ceremony, AYSO commissioner Janet Braun stated that the ceremony is "really a celebration [of] our community spirit of volunteerism—all the values that we're teaching our kids. . . . [The ceremony is] a reminder that we can do a lot of great things when we work together, that children are our greatest asset and we need to help guide them, that we live in a great community, the greatest country in the world."[4]

A community of about 25,000 people, South Pasadena is a town characterized by distinctive early-twentieth-century Craftsman homes on streets lined with beautiful mature trees. The entertainment industry frequently shoots movies, music videos, television shows, and commercials in this town, especially when it wants to create a "Middle America" mood. Nestled between Los Angeles's neighborhoods of El Sereno and Highland Park on the west, and the cities of Pasadena on the north, Alhambra on the south, and San Marino on the east, South Pasadena has a reputation for its good public schools (one high school, one middle school, and three elementary schools). Indeed, much of the gentrification of South Pasadena in recent decades results from an influx of educated professionals who moved to town to take advantage of these schools. Over the past decade, South Pasadena home prices have soared at a rate faster even than most surrounding communities. By 2008, one would be hard-pressed to find a home in South Pasadena for less than $700,000. Even relatively modest-seeming homes were going for $1 million, and the larger "estate area" homes for several million. South Pasadena is clearly a more affluent town than neighboring Alhambra (the 2000 median household income in South Pasadena was nearly $60,000, compared with Alhambra's $39,000; half of South Pasadena's adult residents held a bachelors degree or higher, while less than a quarter of Alhambra's residents did). However, this apparent affluence is deceptive: there is a substantial working-class and lower-middle-class population in South Pasadena. Nearly one-third of South Pasadena's households had annual incomes of $35,000 or less in the year 2000. More telling than that statistic, perhaps, is the fact that 55.6 percent of the town's population lives in rental units. Less obvious than the expensive craftsman homes (and apparently unnoticed by the film industry) are several large apartment complexes within the community. By contrast, in the more affluent neighboring community of San Marino, 91.6 percent of residents live in owner-occupied homes, and the median family income is $139,000.[5]

South Pasadena's reputation as a "white" town also runs against a statistical reality that reveals considerable diversity: the 2000 Census found 44.2 percent of South Pasadena residents as white, 25.6 percent Asian American, 16.1 percent Hispanic, 3.4 percent black, 5.2 percent Pacific Islander/Hawaiian, and 4.5 percent claiming "two or more" racial/ethnic categories. While the racial/ethnic breakdown of South Pasadena differs dramatically from that of its immediate neighboring communities, it is a far cry from being a "white" town.[6] This paradox—the reputation of South Pasadena as a wealthy and white enclave, versus the reality of substantial economic and racial/ethnic diversity—became increasingly interesting to me as I conducted this study of youth coaching. How, I wondered, does the very *public*—indeed, very *communal*—organization of youth soccer, baseball, and softball fit in with the now commonly seen as a safer alternative to letting children run and play freely in parks and neighborhoods. As softball coach and mother of two, Rosa Ramirez, said, "Now you do sports for your kids so they'll have something to do. When I was growing up you didn't have to worry about kids running outside and playing with their friends. So I don't think it was as important as it is now." The parents in South Pasadena often expressed sorrow that their kids aren't able to experience the kind of "carefree" childhood that they did, but they were usually quick to sigh and add that "Things have changed"—that "It's a more dangerous world for kids out there than it was when we were kids." In such a context of fear for kids' safety, organized sports seem a safe alternative.

Accompanying this rising culture of fear that sees our children as needing protection in an increasingly dangerous world is a third trend that underlies the growth of youth sports: changes in family structure, especially among the middle classes. Since the 1970s, fueled by feminism, middle-class women have surged into colleges, professional schools, and, ultimately, into the workforce. Although working-class women were present in the labor force in great numbers in the 1950s and 1960s, the middle-class postwar ideal family consisted of a male family breadwinner and a stay-at-home wife and mother. Starting in the 1970s, and continuing today, this "Leave it to Beaver" family-type is no longer the statistical norm, nor is it the cultural ideal among most professional-class families. But women's movement into the professions has been accompanied by strains and tensions in the lives of families. Men do some more housework and childcare than did their own fathers, but women—even those with full-time jobs—still do far more than their share of this family labor, resulting in what sociologist Arlie Hochschild called women's "second shift."[12] Thus, career women who are also mothers are subjected to a set of cultural double standards and paradoxes around and through which they must navigate.[13] One of these contradictions is that today, even when both parents have careers, it is believed that children need *more*, not less attention from adults. Parents believe that educational and career success for their kids is far more difficult to achieve than it used to be, so that it becomes their responsibility to give their kids as many enriching experiences and advantages as they can. In response, the ascendant philosophy of childrearing for middle-class parents is what sociologist Annette Lareau calls "concerted cultivation," which involves a carefully controlled scheduling of children's educational, cultural, artistic, and athletic experiences. According to Lareau, middle-class parents see concerted cultivation as a way of giving their children advantages through extracurricular activities, tutors, private music lessons, private athletic coaches, and by spending time with their kids doing enriching activities. "Parents usually enjoy this involvement, but they also see it as part of their *obligation* to their children. Parental involvement is a key component of the child-rearing strategy of concerted cultivation."[14] And part of this parental involvement commonly involves ferrying one's children to and from myriad youth sports games and practices, and contributing volunteer time to youth sports as head coaches, assistant coaches, referees, team parents, or league officials.[15]

A fourth trend that helps to fuel the boom in youth sports is, as I discussed above, the feminist-inspired growth in girls' and women's sports. After the passage of Title IX, in 1972, educational institutions were forced to start funding athletic opportunities for girls. And community groups and organizations also responded to growing demands from girls and their parents for opportunities to play. So, as youth sports grew, much of that growth reflected changing cultural attitudes and values about the value of sports for girls.

Today, youth sports in the United States is huge. A 2008 national survey found that two-thirds of American youth are currently involved in at least one organized or team sport, and those who are involved report that, on average, they had played on 2.1 sports teams over the past year.[16] And the more privileged one's family is, the more likely it is that the children will be involved in organized sports. The same national study found that white children are more likely to be participants in sports than are children of color, as are kids who live in suburban (as opposed to rural or urban) areas, those who live in families with two parents at home, and those whose parents are college-educated with higher family incomes. Clearly, class and race privilege make it more likely that families will have access to youth sports, and that they will also have the kinds of resources (such as transportation) necessary to participate.[17] And adults in professional-class families are likely to see sports activities as an important element of the larger package of activities that go into the concerted cultivation of their kids. The survey found that 95 percent of parents in the United States believe that sports participation helps raise their child's self-esteem, and 68 percent of parents believe that participating in sports will help their child get better grades in school.[18] These beliefs translate into high levels of parental involvement in their children's sports activities.[19]

TWO NATIONAL YOUTH SPORTS ORGANIZATIONS

While 81 percent of high school kids who play sports do so on school-based teams, 55 percent of younger kids (those between third grade and middle school) participate in community-based athletic programs, such as YMCA (youth basketball and other sports), USA Hockey, Pop Warner Football, AYSO (soccer), and Little League Baseball and Softball.[20] My study focuses on two youth sports programs in a single community, both of which are local affiliates of massive national and international organizations. Little League Baseball/Softball (LLB/S) and American Youth Soccer League (AYSO) offer an interesting contrast in youth sports organizations, especially with respect to gender. By far the older organization, Little League Baseball began in 1938 and for its first thirty-six years was an organization set up exclusively for boys. When AYSO started, in 1964, it too was exclusively for boys, but by 1971, the time it began to blossom beyond a merely local organization, girls' teams had been introduced. Thus, over the years, the vast majority of people who have participated in AYSO have experienced it as an organization set up for boys *and* for girls.

I began my study with the understanding that this differently gendered history of these two organizations might give us hints at the differences in the gender divisions of labor in coaching (more women head coaches in soccer than in baseball). Sociologist Raewyn Connell argues that every social institution—including the economy, the military, schools, families, or sport—has a "gender regime," which is defined as the current state of play of gender relations in the institution.[21] We can understand an institution's gender regime by measuring and analyzing the gender divisions of labor and power in the organization (i.e., what kinds of jobs are done by women and men, who has the authority, etc.). The idea that a gender regime is characterized by a "state of play" is a way to get beyond static measurements that might result from a quick snapshot of an organizational pyramid, and to understand instead that organizations are always historically shifting entities, subject to gradual—or occasionally even rapid—change. Gender relations are embedded in all organizations, but organizations with deeper patriarchal legacies (like Little League Baseball) are characterized by male-dominated divisions of labor and power that have tremendous historical inertia and are therefore very difficult to disrupt and change. An important part of this inertia might be the continuing sense among adult men that they literally *own* baseball, due to their experience of having played the game as boys and to the deep emotional connection that many U.S. men attach to baseball—a connection that has much to do with nostalgia for their own boyhood, and often with emotional ties to their own fathers.[22] By contrast, we might expect the more recently formed AYSO to be characterized by a more fluid gender regime that is thus more open to incorporating feminist ideals of gender equality. In the United States, youth soccer is a sport so recently institutionalized that many parents—male and female—never played the game as kids. Thus, we might expect that in addition to AYSO having no pre–Title IX patriarchal baggage weighing down its gender regime, today's fathers will also tend to have little or no personal history or emotional connection to the sport. Theoretically, I reasoned, this difference could level the playing field, in terms of adult women's and men's volunteer activities as head coaches in AYSO as compared with LLB/S.

Little League Baseball and Softball

Little League Baseball was founded in 1938 in Williamsport, Pennsylvania, and by 1946 it had expanded to twelve leagues in Pennsylvania.[23] In the postwar years, Little League expanded rapidly throughout the United States, growing to 776 leagues by 1951, the same year that the first non-U.S. league was formed in Canada. By the mid-1950s, Little League Baseball was fully established as a major institution, with 4,000 leagues in the United States and further growth into Mexico and other nations. Little League Baseball continued to expand worldwide through the 1960s and into the 1970s.

In 1974, two years after the passage of Title IX—a statute passed in the United States to ensure gender equity in schools and universities—Little League Baseball was forced to open its game to girl participants. According to an LLB/S online publication, the organization created Little League Softball for girls in 1974, "amid the turmoil of lawsuits to permit girls to play on Little League Baseball Teams."[24] The creation of Little League Softball is consequential in terms of the gender regime of the organization. On the one hand, it represents an organizational response to the rapidly growing demand among girls to play baseball and to the dramatically shifting cultural climate of the early 1970s, brought about by the explosion of feminism and the concomitant growth of girls' and women's sports. On the other hand, the fact that the organization created a niche for girls to play softball, a substantially different game from baseball, meant that the organization was channeling girls and boys into separate and very different athletic tracks.

Starting in 1943, at the outset of the U.S. entry into World War II, and stretching through 1954, there was an impressive burst of professional women's baseball, celebrated in the 1992 film *A League of Their Own*. Despite this moment, baseball in the United States seems almost always to have "belonged" to boys and men.[25] In the early 1970s, when girls began to stake a legal claim to play baseball with the boys, this disrupted the entrenched gender regime of Little League Baseball. A key case cited by sport historians is a civil rights complaint brought against Little League Baseball by the National Organization for Women (NOW) on behalf of a Hoboken, New Jersey, girl, Maria Pepe. In 1972, the twelve-year-old Pepe played in the first three games of the season on an otherwise all boys' team. "By the third game," Pepe recalled many years later, "it started getting more involved. Little League (the national organization) sent letters to my coach that said they had to drop me. My coach said, 'How do I fight this?' He reluctantly said I couldn't play."[26] In that same year, the national Little League headquarters was threatening to revoke the charter of other local leagues who allowed girls to play on baseball teams. The NOW civil rights claim made its way to the New Jersey Superior Court, which in 1974 ruled in favor of Pepe and ordered Little League Baseball to allow 8–12-year-old girls to play baseball. Once forced by law to incorporate girls, the organization responded rapidly to create a track for girls—but a track that was substantially different from the boys' sport: baseball for boys, softball for girls.[27]

The "slash" in the term "LLB/S" is a visible indicator of the current "state of play" of the gender regime of the organization. When the all-male LLB was challenged, from within by girls and their families, and from without by NOW and other organizations, Little League Baseball's initial response was resistance to girls' participation. Resistance to girls occurred in local sites too. In their 1979 book on Little League Baseball, sociologists Lewis Yablonsky and Jonathan Brower noted how a Michigan Little League board of directors passed a rule that all players had to wear jock straps, and then used the rule to try to stop an eight-year-old girl from playing. And when a girl showed up to try out in a previously all-male Los Angeles area Little League, adult men complained that the twelve-year-old girl had " 'infiltrated' their league":

> Remarks about her by two men betrayed feelings unrelated to her athletic abilities. "She's got a good arm, but can't field or hit," asserted the first. "She's got big tits and they don't belong in baseball." A third coach put it more bluntly when he defiantly remarked, "I won't let her play on my team. No girl is to play on my team! I'll give up my team if I have to take her!"[28]

When resistance—both in its local and national organizational forms—ultimately failed, the organization responded by incorporating girls, but along a separate and different track. Girls have been (at first, grudgingly) incorporated, but in a way that reflects a history of what sociologist Nancy Theberge called "adapted rules" for girls' sports—that is, sports for girls and women developed with somewhat, or even dramatically different rules than those developed for boys and men.[29] Today, LLB/S is an organization that boasts 2.7 million children participants worldwide, 2.1 million of them in the United States. There are 176,786 teams in the program—153,422 of them in baseball, 23,364 in softball. Little League stays afloat through the labor about one million volunteers.

I wondered if the South Pasadena numbers on women and men volunteer coaches between 1999 and 2007—numbers that revealed that women coached 11 percent of girls' softball teams, and 2 percent of boys' baseball teams—reflected the general national pattern. When I asked the national media relations manager of LLB/S this question, I was told that the national organization does not keep statistics on either the sex of players or of coaches.[30] In the absence of national data against which to compare my local numbers, I asked several of the communities surrounding South Pasadena for their LLB/S 2006 or 2007 data on coaches. What I found was that South Pasadena LLB/S is, if anything, slightly more liberal than its local neighbors, in terms of how many women are serving as head coaches. Nearby East Altadena had only one woman head coach among its eighteen teams, and she was heading a Challenger Division team that supports the "special needs" kids. Men headed all of the regular East Altadena boys' baseball teams and girls' softball teams, and thirty-four of the thirty-six assistant coaches (94.5 percent) were men. Nearby Santa Anita, which has only baseball and no girls' softball league, demonstrated an almost absolute gender division of labor. Men headed all twenty-five baseball teams; of fifty-five assistant coaches, only one was a woman. And every one of the twenty-two "team mothers" listed in their annual yearbook was a woman. The comparisons with other towns is summarized in appendix 3.[31]

American Youth Soccer Organization

AYSO started in the Los Angeles area in 1964 with nine teams. For the first few years, the teams were entirely for boys. In 1971 in San Fernando, California, Joe Karbus, a father of five who was unhappy with AYSO's all boys' status, organized the first girls' teams. In the mid-1990s, a few AYSO leagues sprouted in Moscow, Trinidad and Tobago, and the U.S. Virgin Islands. But AYSO remains mostly a U.S. organization, with today over 650,000 players on more than 50,000 teams. The national

AYSO office employs fifty paid staff members, but like LLB/S, AYSO is an organization largely driven by volunteer labor. Roughly 250,000 volunteer coaches, team parents, and referees donate their time annually. AYSO has very well-developed and institutionalized coach training and certification programs, as well as a "Safe Haven" training program that focuses on health, safety, and (especially) anti–sexual abuse training, and that is mandatory for all AYSO coaches.

South Pasadena's AYSO began in 1979. Today, the league consists of 163 teams and hundreds of adult volunteers, with an annual 2006–7 operating budget of $326,000.[32] I wondered if the South Pasadena numbers on women and men volunteer coaches between 1999 and 2007— numbers that revealed that women coached 17.1 percent of girls' teams, and 11.1 percent of boys' teams—reflected the general national pattern. When I asked a representative of the national AYSO this question, I was told that the organization does not keep statistics on the sex of coaches. In the absence of national data against which to compare our local numbers, I asked several of the communities surrounding South Pasadena for their AYSO 2006 or 2007 data on coaches. The data that I received from five nearby AYSO regions, summarized in appendix 3, revealed that South Pasadena's proportion of women soccer coaches is higher—often significantly higher—than in these surrounding communities.

ORGANIZATION OF THE BOOK

In this book, I tell a story that illustrates how coaching in South Pasadena youth sports remains a highly sex-segregated activity. I draw from interviews and field observations to illustrate ongoing social processes that create sex segregation, and I draw especially from the interviews to reflect on how peoples' beliefs about gender differences among boys and girls, about families, and about the community create a context in which most people "choose" to participate in public activities in a sex-segregated manner. I begin each chapter with a brief vignette from my field notes, to provide the reader with evocative scenes that illustrate the social processes discussed in the chapters. I was inspired to use these opening vignettes after reading two recent ethnographies that I admire: Ann Arnett Ferguson's *Bad Boys* (2000), a study of black boys in a public school, and Sherri Grasmuck's *Protecting Home* (2005), which looks at the role of Little League Baseball in a Philadelphia neighborhood. Like Ferguson and Grasmuck, I use these field-notes vignettes to create a kind of "feel" for the day-to-day and moment-to-moment social construction of gender and community in youth sports. As Grasmuck notes, many ethnographic studies are written in such a way that they suck the life (and too often the humor) out of everyday life. I hope that these vignettes add analytic depth, as well as keeping some of the life and humor in my story.

My story begins in chapter 2 with a description of the social processes through which women who volunteer to help out with their kids' teams routinely become "team moms" and men become assistant coaches. I show how the term "team mom" persists stubbornly in day-to-day conversations, despite the official gender-neutral terms of "team parent" (in LLB/S) and "team manager" (in AYSO). I discuss the ways that parents' gender ideologies about families and sport come together to create what I call a "sex category sorting process" that channels men predominantly into one activity, women into another.

In the following two chapters, I look at the experiences of women (chapter 3) and men (chapter 4) who become head coaches. I draw from the coaches' stories of how they decided to coach, and contrast their experiences as coaches. Drawing from interviews and from observations, I describe what I call the "gender-sorting process," a concept that helps to explain the glass ceiling on the number of women coaching boys or girls in the older age-groups. In short, I argue that all coaches must navigate their coaching styles between two contradictory sets of knowledge—what I call "kids-knowledge" and "sports-knowledge." Most women and some men coaches in the youngest children's teams begin coaching by emphasizing kids-knowledge, drawing on resources (or "capital") that is culturally defined as "feminine"—that is, defining themselves primarily in affective terms, as nurturing, as caring, as facilitating the kids to have "fun." As the kids rise up into the higher age-groups, their sports activities become defined in more instrumental terms—the coaches' emphasis tips away from fun and equal participation toward sports-knowledge that values and rewards skill acquisition, competition, and winning. Coaches at these higher age-levels are seen as more "serious" (and often more loud and aggressive). Coaches with more affective styles (many of them women, but a few of them men) either drop out of coaching altogether when their kids get to these older age-levels, or they cycle back and coach a younger child's team. The coaches who emphasize sports knowledge, who express more narrowly masculine public styles, remain and coach at the higher levels.

In short, the "sex category sorting process" that I describe in chapter 2 selects most women volunteers into the "team mom" job, and most men volunteers into a coaching job. The "gender-sorting process" that I describe in chapters 3 and 4 selects most women coaches out of the possibility of coaching boys, or of coaching older boys or girls, while selecting out less narrowly masculine men as well. When I talk about "sorting" processes and people being "selected" in or out of certain kinds of positions, I am purposefully deploying language that runs counter to the assumption that people freely "choose" to volunteer in the activities or positions that they end up in. I do not want to deny the clear fact that people in my study are exercising agency, that they are making choices about family, work, parenting, and whether to volunteer as a youth sport leader, and if so, whether to be a head coach, an assistant coach, or a team parent. Instead, what I hope to show is that what people see as individual (or familial) choices are in fact *bounded* and *shaped* by institutional constraints, they are *given meaning* by stubbornly persistent cultural belief systems about gender and families, and they are *given force* by deep emotional commitments to gender difference.

In chapter 5, I focus on how the women's and men's beliefs and actions help to shape a context that engenders the kids they are coaching. Drawing from coaches' comments on how they see and treat boys and girls in sports, I suggest that youth sports today is a key site for the development of what I call "soft essentialism." Adults' views of children and gender commonly oscillate between two apparently contradictory beliefs—that girls and boys should have equal opportunities, and that girls and boys are naturally different. Soft essentialism, as an emergent ideology, negotiates the tension between these two beliefs. Youth sports is an ideal place for the construction of soft essentialism; unlike in most other institutions, ideas and strategies for equal opportunity for girls are being carved out within a kind of "separate-but-equal," sex-segregated context.

In chapter 6, I broaden my scope to consider how sex-segregation among youth sports volunteer coaches and "team moms" connects with families and community. I explore the fact that many South Pasadena head coaches are professional-class men with demanding public careers, while many of the women involved as coaches or as team parents are college-educated women who have opted out of full-time careers. I look at the way that the ongoing creation of South Pasadena as a "kid friendly" and "safe" town for children rests on the volunteer labor of women and on the choices of some highly visible professional-class women and men to create families with male breadwinners and female homemakers who have left full-time careers. I discuss how sex-segregation in youth sports (and the ideology of soft essentialism) articulate with an ideal family form that is grounded in white, professional-class, and hetero-sexual experience, which in turn becomes a key part of the symbolic boundaries that construct South Pasadena's reputation as a "safe town for children and families." Finally, I consider how these class-based gender and family dynamics help to create community-based symbolic bound-aries: from the inside, many South Pasadena residents see themselves as creating a good, safe place for their kids; from the outside, many in neigh-boring communities see South Pasadena as a privileged and exclusive white professional-class enclave that is not particularly open or friendly to "others."

Ultimately, I use the story of volunteer coaches in South Pasadena as a window into understanding broader issues of our time—particularly how peoples' perceptions of their own individual choices with respect to family divisions of labor, paid occupations, and volunteer labor with their children's activities help to construct a world of gender inequalities, and how gender inequality fits into the construction of a certain kind of community. This book tells a story that illustrates the multidimensional dynamics of gender in everyday life. In the past decade or so, gender scholars have moved beyond the notion that masculinity and femininity are "sex roles" that people simply absorb during childhood and then bring to their sports experiences, in the same ways that they might bring different-sized baseball bats or different kinds of soccer shoes. Instead, gender is seen as a multilayered social process that is not simply part of the personality structure of individuals but is also a fundamental aspect of everyday group interactions, divisions of labor and power in organizations, and cultural symbols that swirl around us.

This book will illustrate that people are not passive dupes in gender systems; rather, we are active participants in creating gender. In the language of social theory, people exercise *agency* in the creation of everyday social life. Agency is often *reproductive:* when our actions are consistent with traditions and conventions of existing gender differences and hierarchies, we help to reproduce those existing relations. Sometimes, agency is *resistant:* when our actions contradict or challenge existing gender differences or hierarchies, we contribute to changing existing gender relations. Often, reproductive and resistant agencies are simultaneously evident in contemporary sport. We see this paradoxical simultaneity operating every day: when a heavily muscled woman bodybuilder gets breast implants in order to appear strong *and* conventionally hetero-sexy; when co-ed community softball teams flourish yet informal practices reinforce gender hierarchies (like men cutting in front of women teammates to catch fly balls); when women's college sports grows by leaps and bounds but head coaching shifts from a primarily female profession to one dominated by men.[33]

In short, sport is a "contested terrain" in which gender is being constructed in complex and often contradictory ways. Youth sports, a key part of this contested terrain, is a locus of tension between change and continuity in gender relations. The story I tell here is primarily one of continuity—of how gendered divisions of labor in volunteer youth sports are reproduced by peoples' actions, and of how these gendered divisions of labor help to create a sense of continuity and stability within the context of turbulent historical change in gender, families, and communities. However, even within seemingly stable contexts, there are always points of tension, moments of strain and resistance, and tendencies toward change. I focus my story, when appropriate, also on these moments of strain and tension. In so doing, I hope to make some modest suggestions as to how social change happens, and how social inequalities in families and communities might be confronted and reduced.

TWO "Looking for a Team Mom"

SEPARATING THE MEN FROM THE MOMS

February 14: A winter chill lingers and the field is soggy from recent rains. But here we are at the baseball field, starting another Little League Baseball season, so it must be spring. It's the first practice of the season for this 11- and 12-year-old boys' team. In addition to myself, three more dads have volunteered to assist Coach Dean. The practice drills are all ones that we learned at the coaches' clinic the previous day. I overhear one assistant coach say to Dean, "So, are the women still laying low?" Dean, with a chuckle, replies, "Yes! So far no team mom!" The assistant coach quips, "I guess nobody wants to do it, huh?"

February 23: Coach Dean, in his almost daily e-mails to the team's parents, continues to include a set-off note that reads: "Still looking for a Team Mom . . ."

It strikes me that if it were worded as "team parent," this would at least theoretically expand the potential pool times two!

February 26: At the team's first practice game, I'm standing alone by the dugout, and behind me sitting in the stands are three moms. One of them says, in hushed tones, "I hear they are still looking for a team mom." Another giggles and whispers conspiratorially, "I'm laying low on that one." Another laughs and says, more loudly, "Me too. I'm sure they can find a dad to do it." They all laugh.

By the second game, the "team mom" is Tina, Coach Dean's wife.

When we asked a longtime Little League Softball manager, Albert Riley, why he thinks most of the head coaches are men while nearly all of the team parents are women, he said with a shrug, "They give opportunities to everybody to manage or coach and it just so happens that no women volunteer, you know?" Soccer coach Shelley Parsons saw a certain inevitability to this adult division of labor: "The women always volunteer to be the team moms, the women have always volunteered to make the banners, and the dads have always volunteered to be the refs and the assistant coaches." Riley's and Parsons' statements were typical for head coaches, who generally offered up explanations grounded in individual choice: faced with equal opportunities to volunteer, men just *choose* to be coaches while women *choose* to be team parents.

But as the story that opens this chapter suggests, and as I will illustrate in multiple ways, the gendered division of labor among men and women volunteers in youth coaching results not simply from an accumulation of individual choices; rather, it is produced through a profoundly *social* process. I will draw from interviews with head coaches to illustrate how gender divisions of labor among adult volunteers are shaped by gendered language and belief systems and are seen as "natural" extensions of gendered divisions of labor in families and workplaces. I will also draw from field observations to illustrate how the gendered organizational context of youth sports shapes peoples' expectations, ideas, and choices about men's and women's roles as coaches or team parents.

THE PIPELINE TO HEAD COACHING POSITIONS

When asked how they initially became coaches, most people spoke of having first served as assistant coaches—sometimes for just one season, sometimes for several seasons—before moving into a head coaching position. Drawing from language used by those who study gender and race in occupations, we can describe the assistant coach position as an essential part of the "pipeline" to the head coach position.[1] One of the reasons for this is obvious: many parents—women and men—believe that as a head coach they will be under tremendous critical scrutiny from other parents in the community. Without previous youth coaching experience, many of them lack the confidence they feel they need to take on such a public leadership task. A year or two of assistant coaching affords one that experience and builds confidence, which can lead to the conclusion, "I can do that," and to the decision to take on the responsibility of a head coaching position.

But the pipeline from assistant coaches to head coaches does not operate in a purely individual, voluntarist manner. Longtime Little League manager George Starr, who also served as a member of the league's governing board, gave a glimpse of how the pipeline works when there's a shortage of volunteers for head coaching positions:

> When I first got on the [Little League] board and I was in charge of the minor leagues, one time we had ten teams and only like six or seven applicants that wanted to be strictly manager. So you kinda eyeball the yearbook from the year before, maybe a couple of years [before], and see if the same dad is still listed as a[n assistant] coach, and maybe now it's time he wants his own team. So you make a lot of phone calls. You might make twenty phone calls, and hopefully you are going to get two or three guys that say, "Yes, I'll be a manager."

The assistant coach position is a key part of the pipeline to head coaching positions, both because it makes people more confident about volunteering to be a head coach and, as George Starr's words illustrate, because it makes them visible and thus more likely to be actively recruited by the league to be a head coach. So in order to understand how it is that most head coaches are men, we need to understand how the pipeline operates—how it is that, at the entry level, women's and men's choices to become assistant coaches and/or team parents, are constrained, shaped, or enabled by the social context. This chapter explores this entry-level process.

RECRUITING DADS AND MOMS TO HELP

There is a lot of work involved in organizing a successful youth soccer, baseball, or softball season. A head coach needs help from two, three, even four other parents who will serve as assistant coaches during practices and games. Parents also have to take responsibility for numerous support tasks like organizing snacks, making team banners, working in the snack bar during games, collecting donations for year-end gifts for the coaches, and organizing team events and year-end parties. In AYSO, parents also serve as volunteer referees for games. When we asked head coaches how they determined who would help them with these assistant coaching and other support tasks, a very common story resulted: the coach would call a beginning-of-the-season team meeting, sometimes preceded by a letter or e-mail to parents, and ask for volunteers. Nearly always, they said, they ended up with dads volunteering to help as assistant coaches and moms volunteering to be team parents. Soccer coach Wendy Lytle told a typical story:

> At the beginning of the season I sent a little introductory letter [that said] I really badly need an assistant coach and referee and a team mom. You know anyone that is keen on that, let's talk about it at the first practice. And this year one guy picked up the phone and said, "Please can I be your assistant coach." And I spoke to another one of the mums who I happen to know through school and she said, "Oh, I can do the team mum if you find someone to help me." And by the first practice, they'd already discussed it and it was up and running.

We can see from Lytle's statement how the assistant coach and team-parent positions are sometimes informally set up even before the first team meeting, and how a coach's assumption that the team parent will be a "team mom" might make it more likely that women end up in these positions. When asked how he selected a team parent, Soccer coach Gilbert Morales said, "I just generally leave it to a volunteer issue. I ask for volunteers." When asked who normally volunteers, he replied, "Usually female. Usually female. I've found that most of the team parents are usually team moms." Even coaches who consciously try to emphasize that "team parent" is not necessarily a woman's job, like softball coach Rosa Ramirez, find that only women end up volunteering to do this:

> Before the season started we had a team meeting and I let the parents know that I would need a team parent, and I strongly stressed *parent*, because I don't think it should always be a mother. But we did end up with the mom doing it, and she assigns snacks and stuff like that.

None of the head coaches we interviewed said that they currently had a man as the team parent, but four recalled that they had once had a man as a team parent (though one of these four coaches said, "Now that I think about it, that guy actually volunteered his wife to do it"). When we asked if they had ever had a team parent who was a man, nearly all of the coaches said never. Many of them laughed at the very thought. Soccer coach Joan Ring exclaimed with a chuckle, "I just can't imagine! I wonder if they've *ever* had a team mom who's a dad. I don't know. Same with the banner. That would be funny to see: has a man ever made a banner? I don't know (laughs)." Soccer coach Doug Berger stammered his way through his response, punctuating his words with sarcastic laughter: "Ha! In fact, that whole concept—I don't think I've ever *heard* of a team dad [*laughs*]. Uh—there *is* no team dad. I've never heard of a team dad. But I don't know why that would be." A few coaches, like softball coach Lisette Taylor, resorted to family metaphors to explain why they think there are few if any men volunteering to be team parents: "Oh, it's always a mom [*laughs*]. Team mom. That's why it's called team *mom*. You know, the coach is a male. And the mom—I mean, that's the *housekeeping*—you know: assign the snack."

Gendered Language

In the late 1970s, a popular riddle made the rounds that went something like this:

> A man is driving along in his car when he accidentally hits a boy on a bike. He gets out of the car, looks down and sees the injured boy, and

says, "Oh, God! I've hit my own son!" He rushes the boy to the hospital, and in the emergency room, the doctor walks in, looks at the boy, and exclaims: "Oh God! I can't do surgery on this boy! He's my son!" How is this possible?

The answer, of course, is that the doctor is the boy's *mother*, and the point of the riddle is to illustrate the automatic assumption in the mind of the listener that *doctor* always implies a *man*. Another way to put this is to say that there are gendered assumptions in the language that we link to certain professions, so much so that often, when the person holding the position is in the statistical minority, we attach a modifier, such as *male* nurse, *male* secretary, *woman* judge, *woman* doctor. Or, *woman* head coach.

Over and over, in interviews with coaches, during team meetings, and in interactions during games, practices, and team parties, I noticed this gendered language. Most obvious was the frequent slippage from official term "team parent" to the commonly used term "team mom." But I also noticed that a man coach was normally just called a "coach," while a woman coach was often gender-marked as a "woman coach." As feminist linguists have shown, language is a powerful element of social life—it not only reflects social realities like gender divisions of labor, it also helps to construct our notions of what is "normal" and what is an "aberration."[2] Joan Ring's statement, "I wonder if they've *ever* had a team mom who's a dad," illustrates how gendered language makes this whole idea of a male team parent seem incongruous, even laughable, to many. In youth sports, this gendered language supports the notion that a team is structured very much like a "traditional" heterosexual family: the head coach—nearly always a man—is the leader and the public face of the team; the team parent—nearly always a woman—is working less visibly behind the scenes, doing the "housekeeping" support work; assistant coaches—mostly men, but including the occasional woman—help the coach on the field during practices and games.

Teams are even talked about sometimes as "families," and while we never heard a head coach referred to as a team's "dad," we did often and consistently hear the team parent referred to as the "team mom." This gendered language, drawn from family relations, gives us some good initial hints as to how coach and team-parent roles remain so sex-segregated. Gendered language, in short, helps structure people's thoughts in ways that shape and constrain their actions. Is a man who volunteers to be a team parent now a "team mom?"

Gender Ideology and Gendered Organizations

When we pressed the coaches to consider why it is nearly always women who volunteer to be the team parent, many seemed never to have considered this question before. Some of the men coaches seemed especially befuddled by this question, and appeared to assume that women's team-parenting work is a result of an almost "natural" decision on the part of the woman to volunteer to help in this way. Some men, like soccer coach Carlos Ruiz, made sense of this volunteer division of labor by referring to the ways that it reflected divisions of labor in their own families and in their community: "In this area, we have a lot of stay-at-home moms, so it seems to kind of fall to them to take over those roles." Similarly, baseball coach Albert Riley, whose wife served as the team parent, explained: "I think it's because they probably do it at home. You know, I mean, my wife—even though she can't really commit the time to coach, I don't think she would *want* to coach—uh, she's very good with that [team parent] stuff." Soccer coach Al Evans explained the gender divisions on youth sports teams in terms of people's comfort with a nostalgic notion of "the classical family":

> I suppose unconsciously, on that sort of Freudian level, it's like you got the dad and he's the boss and you got the mom and she's the support, and then you got all the little siblings, so in a sense you're making this picture that, without really drawing too much attention to it—that's sort of the classical family, you know, it's like the Donna Reed family is AYSO, right? They have these assigned gender roles, and people in San Marino and South Pasadena, probably all over the United States, they're fairly comfortable with them, right? It's, uh, maybe insidious, maybe not, [but] framed in the

sort of traditional family role of dad, mom, kids—people are going to be comfortable with that.

Ted Miller, a Little League baseball coach, broadened the explanation, drawing connections to divisions of labor in his workplace:

> It's kinda like in business. I work in real estate and most of your deal makers that are out there on the front lines, so to speak, making the deals, doing the shuckin' and jivin', doing the selling, are men. It's a very good ol' boys' network on the real estate brokerage side. There are a ton a females who are on the property management side, because it's *housekeeping*, it's *managing*, it's like running the *household*, it's behind the scenes, it's like cooking in the kitchen—[*laughs*]—I mean I hate to say that, but it's that kind of role that's secondary. Coach is out in the front leading the squad, mom sitting behind making sure that the snacks are in order and all that. You know, just the way it is.

Having a male coach and a team mom just seemed normal to Evans ("You know, just the way it is") because it seemed to flow naturally from divisions of labor in his household and in his workplace—gendered divisions of labor that have the good ol' boys operating publicly as the leaders, "on the front lines . . . shuckin' and jivin'," while the women are offering support "behind the scenes, . . . like cooking in the kitchen." Echoing this view, soccer coach Paul Leung said, "I hate to use the analogy, but its like a secretary: you got a boss and you've got a secretary, and I think that's where most of the opportunities for women to be active in the sports is, as the secretary."

It was striking to me how several of the men's explanations for divisions of labor between women and men were offered somewhat apologetically—"I hate to say that," "I hate to use the analogy,"—as though they suspected that their beliefs might be considered politically incorrect. When explaining why it is that team parents are almost exclusively women, a small number of women coaches also seemed to see it as natural, like most of the men coaches saw it. Pam Burke, a soccer coach who also served as a "team mom" for her daughter's team, held conservative views on gender. A homemaker, Burke disagreed with the women coaches who, for feminist reasons, disapproved of the gendered nature of the "team mom" position. In her view, women's support and nurturance needs to be respected and valorized, though she too admitted to some ambivalence about these issues:

> I think we have to be careful in making that a negative, because more often than not, at least in this community, the father is the primary breadwinner, so he's working forty to fifty hours a week, and those are his responsibilities. We have lots of stay-at-home moms here in this community, and those are the people who have the time [to serve as a team parent], and these are typically mothering-woman sorts of skills. I mean, you can call it a stereotype and you can call it bad, but its true: if it weren't for me, my daughter's coach would be a disaster. He's doing *soccer* [and] he doesn't want to do this other stuff. And it takes like five minutes, and its not a lot of work, and its what we do as women, and mothers certainly, and for the most part we do it well, so I don't take offense to that. I have a sort of strange view actually of women and men in the world. I don't think women should be in positions of leadership over men, so I'm, I kind of have this struggle inside of me because I recognize the many differences between men and women, and I take kind of a controversial stand over it, because I don't think we should make us equal in ways that I don't think that we are. I don't think we are the same, and I think we should celebrate the differences.

Many women coaches, however, saw the gendering of the "team-parent" position as a problem, and made sense of its persistence, as did many of the men, by referring to the ways that it reflects family- and work-related divisions of labor. But several of the women coaches added an additional dimension to their explanations, by focusing on *why they think the men don't or won't* consider doing team-parent work. Soccer coach Wendy Lytle said, "I think it's because the dads want to be involved with the action. And they are not interested in doing paperwork and collecting money for photos or whatever it is. They are not interested in doing that sort of stuff." Jessica Torres, another soccer coach, extended this point: "I think it's probably, well, identity, which is probably why not many men do it. You know, they think, that is a women's job, like secretary or nurse or, you know." In short, many of the women coaches were cognizant of the ways that the "team-parent" job was viewed by men, like all "women's work," as non-masculine and thus undesirable. Jessica Torres found it ironically funny that her husband, in fact, does most of the cooking and housework at home but won't take on the role of team parent for his daughter's team. When asked if changing the name to "team dad" might get more men to volunteer, she replied with a sigh,

> I don't know. I wish my husband would be a team dad because he's just very much more domesticated than I am [*laughs*]. You know, "Bring all the snacks, honey, hook us up," you know. I think there's a lot of men out there, but they don't want to be perceived as being domesticated.

Torres's comment illustrates how—even for a man who does a substantial amount of the family labor at home—publicly taking on a job that is defined as "feminine" threatens to saddle men with a "domesticated" public image that would be embarrassing or even humiliating to them. That some women coaches speculated as to why men would *not* consider being team parents, while the men coaches relegated their responses to considering merely why women *do* volunteer as team parents, indicates that at least some of the women coaches have a more nuanced (and critical) understanding of gender than do most of the men coaches. As Ellen Lessing observed, her voice dripping with sarcasm, "All the [support] jobs are [done by] women, except for the assistant coach. That's the—the *man's* job." From these explanations, we can see that many coaches—both women and men—believe that men become coaches and women become team parents largely because these public roles fit with their domestic proclivities and skills. But the women add an important dimension to this explanation: women do the team-parent work because it has to be done . . . and because they know that the men won't do it.

FINDING A TEAM MOM

Explanations from interviews are revealing, especially about people's beliefs and underlying values, giving us a window into how people make sense of decisions that they have made. They give us insights into how gendered language and beliefs about men's and women's "roles" help to shape the kinds of decisions that individuals make. Yet asking people to explain how (and especially why) things like gendered divisions of labor persist is not, by itself, the most reliable basis for building an explanation. Rather, watching *how* things happen gives us a deeper understanding of the social construction of gender.[3] My observations from team meetings and early season practices reveal deeper social processes at work—processes that shaped people's apparently individual decisions to volunteer for assistant coach or team-parent positions. This excerpt from field notes from the first team meeting of a boys' baseball team illustrates how men's apparent resistance to even consider taking on the team-parent position ultimately leaves the job in the hands of a woman (who might have been reluctant to do it):

> The boys are on the field playing catch, and Coach Bill stands facing the parents as we sit in the grandstands. Our boys are 13–14 year olds, so we are all old hands at this. The coach doesn't ask for volunteers for assistant coaches; instead, he announces that he has "invited" two of the fathers, "who probably know more about baseball than I do," to serve as his assistants. He then asks for someone to volunteer as the "team mom." He adds, "Now, 'team mom' is not a gendered job: it can be done by a mom or a dad. But we *really need* a team mom." Nobody volunteers immediately. One mom sitting near me mutters to another mom, "I've done this two years in a row, and I'm not gonna do it this year." Coach Bill goes on to ask for a volunteer for scorekeeper. Meanwhile, two other moms have been whispering, and one of them suddenly bursts out with, "Okay! She's volunteered to be team mom!" People applaud. The volunteer seems a bit sheepish about it; her whole body-language suggests someone who has just reluctantly agreed to do something. But she affirms that, yes, she'll do it.

As we have seen, this first team meeting of the year is often the moment at which the division of labor—who will be the assistant coaches, who will be the team parent—is solidified. In this case, the male assistant coaches had been selected previous to the meeting by the head coach, but it apparently took some cajoling from a mother during the team meeting to convince another mother to volunteer to be the team mom. I have seen two occasions when a woman who did not volunteer was drafted by the head coach to be the team mom, even though she was clearly more oriented toward assistant coaching, as the following story from field notes I took over the first few weeks of the season of a 7-year-old boys' baseball team illustrates:

> At the first practice, Coach George takes charge, asks for volunteers. I tell him that I am happy to help out at practice and games and that he should just let me know what he'd like me to do. He appoints me assistant coach. This happens with another dad, too. We get team hats. Elena Rosas, a mother, offers to help out in any way she can. She's appointed "co–team mom" (the coach's wife is the other team mom). She shrugs and says okay, fine. Unlike most team moms, Elena continues to attend all practices. At the fifth practice, Coach George is pitching batting practice to the kids; I'm assigned to first base, the other dad is working with the catcher. Elena (the "team mom") is standing alone on the sidelines, idly tossing a ball up in the air to herself. Coach George's son suddenly has to pee, so as George hustles the boy off to the bathroom, Elena jumps in and starts pitching. She's good, it turns out, and can groove the pitch right where the kids want it. (By contrast, George has recently been plunking the kids with wild pitches.) Things move along well. At one point, when Coach George has returned from the bathroom, with Elena still pitching to the kids, a boy picks up a ball near second base and doesn't know what to do with it. Coach George yells at the kid: "Throw it! Throw it to the team mom!" The kid, confused, says, "Where is she?" I say, "The pitcher, throw it to the pitcher." The coach says, "Yeah, the team mom." I say, "Looks like a coach to me."

A couple of years later, I interviewed Elena Rosas and asked her how it was that she became a team parent and continued in that capacity for five straight years. Her response revealed a great deal about the informal constraints that channel many women away from coaching, toward being team parents:

> I always wanted to help out. I loved the sport, so anything I could do to help out [my son's] baseball, I was more than willing. The first year, when he was in kindergarten, he was on a T-ball team and I volunteered to be manager, and of course the league didn't choose me, but they did allow me to be assistant coach. And I was so excited, and [*laughs*] of course I showed up in heels for the first practice, because it was right after work, and the coach looked at me and I informed him that, "I'm your new assistant." And he looked at me—and I don't know if *distraught* is

the correct word, but he seemed slightly *disappointed,* and he went out of his way to ask the parents who were there watching their children if there was anyone who wanted to volunteer, even though I was there. So there was this male who did kind of rise to the occasion, and so that was the end. He demoted me without informing me of his decision [*laughs*]— I was *really* enthused, because [my son] was in kindergarten, so I *really* wanted to be coach—or assistant coach at least—and it didn't happen. So after that I didn't feel comfortable to volunteer to coach. I just thought, okay, then I can do team mom.

As Elena's story illustrates, women who have the background, skills, and desire to coach are sometimes assigned by head coaches to be team moms. Some baseball teams even have a niche for such moms: a "dugout coach" (sometimes called a "dugout mom") is usually a mom who may help out with on-field instruction during practices, but on game days she is assigned the "indoors" space of the dugout; here, it is her responsibility to keep track of the lineup, to be sure that the boy who is on deck (next up to bat) is ready with his batting gloves and helmet on. The dugout coach also—especially with younger kids' teams—might be assigned to keep order inside the dugout: to keep kids focused on the game, to keep equipment orderly, to help with occasional first aid, and to help see that the dugout is cleaned of empty water bottles and snack containers after the game is over.

PLAYING FIELDS AS GENDERED SPACES

Although most teams don't have "dugout coaches" (they tend to be more common on younger kids' baseball or softball teams), their occasional presence reveals something about the spatial organization of gender. After learning of the existence of dugout coaches through some of our interviews, I started to make sense of something I had observed during the 2005, 2006, and 2007 seasons, during which I served as the official scorekeeper for my son's baseball teams. As scorekeeper, I chose to sit in the corner of the dugout closest to home plate. This gave me a good view of the entire field, and a good vantage point from which to observe coaches.

When our team was batting, the head coach would assign an assistant to coach first base, and would himself coach third base, a place from which he would shout instructions and flash signs (hand signals indicating strategies) to batters, base runners, and the first-base coach. While our team was on defense, for safety reasons the boys were required to be inside the dugout at all times, but I noticed that the coaches nearly always remained standing on the field, immediately outside the dugout. After I became aware of this pattern, I watched it recur in game after game, with team after team. The coaches almost never set foot inside the dugout. Instead, they stood on the field, arms crossed, talking with each other, barking out a few orders to the kids or interacting with an umpire. One notable exception to this pattern is described in this field note:

> It's the first Saturday day game of the season and it's early afternoon and in the low 80s, hotter than we have experienced yet this year. The dugouts this year have green semitransparent screens added to the back and the top, which shade those inside from the sun. Somewhere late in the game, Coach Joe stepped into the shade of the dugout carrying a five-gallon bucket, which he placed upside down just inside the dugout door, and sat down on the bucket. As he was sitting down, he muttered, to nobody in particular, "Whew! I gotta get out of the sun for a minute." But he barely stayed in the dugout for even a minute. Within a couple of pitches, he was back on his feet, standing just outside the dugout in the full sun.

Coach Joe's apology for entering the dugout to sit down, and his quick exit, underlined for me the extent to which coaches may think (though probably not consciously) of the dugout as a kind of no-man's-land. Standing on the field of play, I came to realize, publicly marks the coach as an authority, while sitting in the dugout may diminish his stature. Just as language tends to smuggle in gendered meanings, so too space is often gendered in ways that mark and reinforce divisions of labor and power.[4] In workplaces, bosses and managers (often men) tend to occupy larger spaces than those who do the less-valued and less-rewarded work, such as clerical labor. Bosses have the right to freely move into the spaces of their subordinates, while the subordinates must knock and ask permission before entering their boss's office. In homes, kitchens are often coded as female workspaces, while a man's den or converted garage-workshop are masculine spaces. Sports spaces too are gendered: in public gyms, as sociologist Shari Dworkin has shown, the "cardio" workout area (treadmills, stationary bikes, etc.) is considered a more feminine space, while the "free weights" room is often seen as a male space. Women who want to lift weights as part of their workout need to muster courage to transgress this space.[5] The space of an American football field provides a clear image of dichotomous gender separation, with armored male bodies fighting it out on center stage while women cheer on the sidelines.[6]

My observations suggested that the baseball, softball, and soccer fields on which our children play are also gendered spaces, as the following observation of a "dugout coach" illustrates:

> I'm walking the rounds, briefly visiting and observing the five baseball fields clustered together in the South Pasadena Arroyo, and my observations reaffirm that, yes, I have achieved saturation in my research. It's the same old pattern, over and over: a co-ed T-ball game—all men coaches and assistant coaches; a boys' 10–12-year-olds game—all men coaches and assistant coaches; and finally I settle in to watch a boys' 7–8-year-olds game—all men coaches and assistant coaches. I'm standing behind the gate that leads to the dugout of the team that's currently in the field when the inning ends. As the kids surge toward the dugout, suddenly a woman rushes down from the stands, hurries by me through the gate, and begins meeting the boys as they enter the dugout. She holds a lineup card in one hand, shoos the remaining boys into the dugout with the other hand, and yells out the names of the boys who are coming up to bat: "Tommy, you're leading off; Jose, on deck; Eddie, in the hole! C'mon guys, get your helmets on. Everybody: drink up; keep hydrated. C'mon now, let's get some runs this inning!" I watch her for the whole inning, and she stands literally with one foot in the dugout and one foot on the field, continually shifting her attention from the field, to the kids in the dugout, and back to the field. The male manager stands in the third-base coaching box and is focused for the entire inning on batters and base runners on the field. He never looks toward the dugout, and doesn't need to, because the "dugout coach" has things organized and moving like clockwork. After the third out, she tells the boys, "Okay, good inning, back in the field now. C'mon, get your mitts and take the field! Joey, don't forget your hat." As the boys spill back onto the field, she leaves the dugout and sits back in the stands with the other parents.

The playing field itself is the public space where the (usually male) coach exerts his authority and command. The dugout is like the home— a place of safety from which one emerges to do one's job on the field. Work does happen in the domestic space of the dugout, but it's of the type that is behind-the-scenes, supportive of the "real" work of leadership and competition that is done on the field. In short, even women who have on-field game knowledge and skills are sometimes relegated to the dugout as a liminal space between the (clearly masculine) space of the playing field, occupied by the head coach and the assistant coaches, and the bleachers, occupied by the non-coaching parents and the "team mom." As we will see in the next chapter, women who are head coaches sometimes experience the playing field as a hyper-masculine space. Women who step on to this space as coaches must begin with a certain amount of chutzpah, and in order to survive (and sometimes thrive) in this space, they often consciously develop strategies that allow them to be seen as legitimate leaders.

CHALLENGES AND RESISTANCE

The head coach's common assumption that fathers will volunteer to be assistant coaches and mothers to be team moms creates a context that powerfully channels men and women into these directions. Backed by these "commonsense" understandings of gendered divisions of labor, many men and women just "go with the flow" of this channeling process. Their choices and actions help to reproduce the existing gendered patterns of the organization. But some don't, choosing instead to swim against the tide. Ellen Lessing already had several seasons of experience as a head soccer coach when she attended the first team meeting for her youngest child's team:

> At our first team meeting the coach announced, "I'm looking for a couple of you to help me out as assistant coaches," and he looked directly at the men, and *only* at the men. None of them volunteered. And it was really amazing because he didn't even *look* at me or at any of the other women. So after the meeting I went up to him and said, "Hey, I've coached soccer

for like ten seasons; I can help you out, okay?" And he agreed, so I'm the assistant coach for him.

This first team meeting, as Ellen Lessing described it, is an example of a normal gendered interaction that, if it had gone unchallenged, would have served to reproduce the usual gender divisions of labor on the team. It's likely that many women in these situations notice the ways that men are, to adopt sociologist Pat Martin's term, informally (and probably unconsciously) "mobilizing masculinities" in ways that serve to reproduce men's positions of centrality.[7] But Lessing's ten years of coaching experience gave her the confidence and the "capital" that allowed her not only to see and understand, but also to challenge the very gendered selection process that was taking place at this meeting. Many—perhaps most—mothers do not have this kind of background, and so when faced with this sort of moment, they just go with the flow. On another occasion, as the following story from my field notes describes, I observed a highly athletic and coaching-inclined woman assertively use her abilities in a way that initially *seemed* to transcend this kind of sex-segregation process, only to be relegated symbolically at season's end as a "team mom":

> A new baseball season, the first team meeting of the year; a slew of dads volunteer to be assistant coaches. Coach George combs the women for a team mom, and gets some resistance; at first nobody will do it, but then he finds a volunteer. At the first few practices, few of the fathers who had volunteered to assistant coach actually show up. Sandra, a mom, clearly is into baseball, very knowledgeable and athletic, and takes the field. She pitches to the kids, gives them good advice. On the day when George is passing out forms for assistant coaches to sign, he hands her one too. She accepts it, in a matter-of-fact way. It appears to me that her work with the kids at the practices is being acknowledged by Coach George with assistant coach status.
>
> At a later practice, there are three dads (including me) filling in for Coach George, who had to work. Sandra is there, but hangs on the margins, almost as though she's waiting to be invited to help. As no invitation seems forthcoming, she eventually finds a niche, backing up fielders, giving them pointers. I am struck again at how knowledgeable she is, a good teacher.

Though few dads show up for many of the practices, there never seems to be a shortage of dads to serve as assistant coaches at the games. Coach George invites Sandra to coach third base once, but beyond that she is never included in an on-field coaching role during a game.

End of season, team party. Coach George hands out awards to all the kids. Then he hands out gift certificates to all the assistant coaches, but does not include Sandra. Then he hands out gift certificates to the "team moms," and includes Sandra here, even though I don't recall her doing any team-parent tasks. Amazing! She had clearly been acting as an assistant coach all season long.

This story illustrates how, on the one hand, a woman volunteer can informally circumvent the "sorting process" that pushes her toward the "team mom" role by persistently showing up to practices and assertively doing the work of a coach (and doing it well). As Barrie Thorne showed in her groundbreaking research on children on school playgrounds, when children cross gender boundaries (e.g., a girl who plays football with the boys; a boy who plays jump rope with the girls), "they challenge the oppositional structure of traditional gender arrangements."[8] However, Thorne also points out that individual incidences of gender crossing are often handled informally, in ways that affirm rather than challenge gender boundaries: an individual girl who joins the boys' game gets defined "as a token, a kind of 'fictive boy,' not unlike many women tokens in predominantly male settings, whose presence does little to challenge the existing arrangements."[9] Similarly, Sandra's successful "crossing" led to her becoming accepted as an assistant coach during practices. However, the fact that she was accepted as a practice coach, but rarely recognized as a "real" coach during games, made her (to adapt Thorne's terms) a kind of "token," or "fictive," coach, whose gender transgression was probably unknown to the many adults who never attended practices. So, in the final moment of the season, when adults and children alike were being publicly recognized for their contributions to the team, she was labeled and rewarded for being a "team mom," thus symbolically reaffirming the categorical gender boundaries.

A few coaches whom we interviewed consciously attempted to resist or change this gendered sorting system. Some of the women coaches, especially, saw it as a problem that the team-parent job was always done by a woman. Girls' softball coach Rosa Ramirez was concerned that the designation "team mom" amounted to negative role-modeling for kids, and fed into the disrespect that women coaches experienced:

> I think the way things are right now in Little League, all kids think that the moms should just be team moms. Which means that they don't take the mothers seriously, and I think that's a bad thing. I mean it's a *bad thing.* I think especially I think that's a lack of respect to women, to mothers. There are a lot of mothers who have played, who played softball since they were little, played all the way through high school. Some even played through college, and yet when they come out here, these kids, you know, boys and girls alike, are like, "Whatever, right, what do you know?" But they *do* know.

Ramirez's comments illustrated her understanding that a gender sorting process channeled men to become coaches and women to become team moms, because, she said, many people assume that

> that's all the women are good for. I think that's what the mentality is. [When] we need coaches, we're talking to the dads. [When] we need a team mom—I think that's part of the problem, they always say *team mom.* I think I'm the only one who says *team parent,* and I made it very clear to our parents that it did not have to be a mother, that it could be a father, and that I encourage any dad out there that had time to do what team parents are supposed to do, to sign up and do it. But it didn't happen.

Such coaches find that simply de-gendering the language—by using the term "team parent," and even stressing that it is "not a gendered job"— is unlikely to yield male volunteers. So what some women coaches do is they simply refuse to have a team parent. Soccer coach Joan Ring said, "I do it all. I don't have a team parent." Pam Burke agreed: "I never have a team mom, because I don't want one. I have a way I want things done and I would rather not let go of those things." And June Park said, "I think in general, compared to the men who coach, I do more of that [team-parent work]." This kind of resistance by women coaches is understandable, especially from those who see the "team mom" phenomenon as demeaning to women and who feel that it contributes to a climate of disrespect for women coaches. However, it's also easy to see how this form of resistance ends up creating extra work for women coaches— work that most men coaches relegate to a "team mom." Reminiscent of an employed wife who gets tired of asking her employed husband to pull his share of the housework and finds it easier to simply clean the toilets herself, these women coaches are doing a "second shift" of volunteer work.[10]

An alternative way of setting things up, used by a small number of coaches, involved delegating specific support jobs to families rather than having a team parent. Soccer coach Nikki Lopez, a single mother, spoke of the way she organized support tasks on her girls' soccer team:

> I don't have a team [parent] per se, but I'm really overly organized [*laughs*], so at our team meetings I have sign-ups, and I make sure every parent signs-up for something. So I have parents that volunteer to come help me set up the field, you know, put the nets on the goals, do that stuff. And, you know, it was about half and half . . . I got men volunteering women volunteering, and I don't have a team mom or anything like that, so I don't think any particular job goes to any particular sex. Like the person that was in charge of our banner this year was one of the fathers; [he] coordinated the whole thing.

The very few occasions that a father does volunteer—or is recruited by the coach—to be the team parent are moments of gender "crossing" that hold the potential to radically disrupt the normal operation of the sex-category sorting process. But, ironically, a male team parent can also reinforce common gender stereotypes. Soccer coach Carlos Ruiz told me that the previous season a father had volunteered to be the team parent, but as it turned out,

> he was a disaster [*laughs*]. He didn't do *anything*, you know, and what little he did it was late; it was ineffective assistance. He didn't come, he didn't make phone calls, I mean, he was just like a black hole. And so that—that was an unfortunate disaster. This year, it's a woman again.

This kind of male incompetence at doing "women's work" might be especially familiar to married women whose husbands can't seem to recall how to cook, fold laundry, shop for groceries, or change diapers. The idea that a man volunteered—and then failed miserably to do the team-parent job—may serve ultimately to reinforce the taken-for-granted assumption that women are naturally better suited to do this kind of work. When we asked a homemaker who coaches her daughter's team why she felt it was important for the team parent to be a woman, she explained her reasoning in gender-essentialist terms:

> [Women are] more organized. And because they understand the role, they're more likely to understand the significance of it and the meaning of it and what they need to do. I don't think many dads understand that. That's gender bias, but . . . I think there are very few dads who have that inherent understanding that once they come home from work, or even if they're at work, that their family life is inherent to who they are. Ok, one of the things that my friends who are married to men always complain about . . . is, "He's great, he's helpful, but I have to ask him."

THE DEVALUATION OF WOMEN'S INVISIBLE LABOR

It takes an enormous amount of dedicated volunteer labor to keep a youth sports team, and especially an entire league, running smoothly. In her study of a Little League Baseball league made up of thirty teams, Sherri Grasmuck estimates that the 111 league administrators, head coaches, and assistant coaches contribute a total of 33,330 hours of volunteer labor in a season—an average of about 300 hours per person.[11] Grasmuck's calculations do not take into account the behind-the-scenes supportive labor that team parents (usually moms) do. But a study of Little League Baseball in Texas focused on just that. Janet Saltzman Chafetz and Joseph Kotarba observed that "team mothers" in this "upper middle class, 'Yuppie' Texas community" contribute labor to their sons' teams in ways that result in "the re-creation and strengthening of the community's collective identity as a place where, among other things, women are primarily mothers to their sons." Most all of the team mothers in this community had college degrees, but fifteen of the twenty studied by Chaftez and Kotarba were full-time homemakers whose husbands were employed as "physicians, lawyers, corporate and public administrators." Chaftez and Kotarba conclude that "women, especially mothers, are expected to support Texasville's version of the cult of the child."[12] These Texas "team mothers" are similar to many of the South Pasadena "team moms" in my study, both in terms of their education and social class and in terms of their family structure. The Texasville mothers appear to be doing even more labor than their busy South Pasadena counterparts: they commonly prepare and serve food for the kids and coaches; plan and organize collective eating; and organize arts-and-crafts activities. However, these differences are only a matter of degree. The South Pasadena team moms are doing these same kinds of activities, thereby helping to enhance the social cohesion of the team, the league, and the community.

Despite the importance of the work that team parents are doing, it is not often recognized as anywhere equivalent to the importance of the work done by coaches. Of course, the team parent typically puts in fewer hours of labor than does the head coach. However, in some cases, the team parents put in more time than some assistant coaches (dads, for instance, whose work schedules don't allow them to get to many practices but who can be seen on the field during a Saturday game, coaching third base). Yet the team parent's work remains largely invisible, and, as we have seen, coaches sometimes talk about team parents' contributions as trivial or unimportant. Several coaches, when asked about the team-parent job, kind of pooh-poohed it as "not very hard to do," or "an easy job." But like many behind-the-scenes sorts of jobs, there is more to the team-parent job than meets the eye. Elena Rosas told me that, given her full-time job as an educator and her family obligations, she often found it difficult to do all of what was asked of her as a team parent:

> It demands much more time than most people realize, or that even I did. The team roster, the practice schedule, who's gonna bring the snacks, who's gonna work the snack bar. And the biggest problem for me was when somebody couldn't do the snack bar, then I'd have to find someone to cover, which at times translated to, *I'm* covering to do the snack bar. And it was continuous throughout the entire season, and then I had to figure out the gift for the coach, and some people wanted to contribute *very* little, you know, a dollar or so, and other people were insulted—and so, money

transactions—that also was uncomfortable . . . so I just thought, "It's too much." The rosters, making them on the computer, making copies for everyone—I remember giving it to them and they said, "You know, can you try a different font?" (*She laughs.*) That's when I decided, you know, I don't want to do so much of this.

My observations suggest also that the women serving as team parents are often doing this job as one of many volunteer jobs they do in their community, while nearly all of the men who are coaching are engaged in this and only this volunteer activity (an issue I will explore more in chapter 6). A field note from a boys' baseball game illustrates this:

> It is the second-to-last game of the season. During the first inning, Dora, the "team mom" shows up and immediately starts circulating among the parents in the stands, talking and handing out a flier. The flier announces the "year end party," to be held in a couple of weeks. She announces that she will supply ice cream and other makings for sundaes. Everyone else can just bring some drinks. She also announces (and it's on the flier) that she's collecting $20 from each family to pay for a "thank you gift . . . for all their hard work" for the head coach and for each of the three assistant coaches (all men). People start shelling out money and Dora starts a list of who has donated. By the start of the next inning, she announces that she's got to go, saying, "I have a Webelos [Cub Scouts] parents' meeting." She's obviously multitasking here as a parent volunteer. By the fourth inning, near the end of the game, she is back, collecting more money and informing parents on details concerning the party and the upcoming playoffs schedule. Finally, during the last inning, she sits and watches the end of the game with the rest of us.

As this story shows, team parents like Dora are doing work before, during, and after the game—making fliers, communicating with parents, collecting money, keeping lists and records, organizing parties, making sure everyone knows the schedule of upcoming events. And she's sandwiching this work around other volunteer activities with another youth organization. This kind of labor keeps organizations running, and it helps to create and sustain the kind of vibrant community, "for the kids," that people imagine when they move to a town like South Pasadena. In the words of sociologists Peggy Petrezelka and Susan Mannon, it is women's invisible labor that is "keepin' this little town going."[13]

THE SEX-CATEGORY SORTING PROCESS

In this chapter, I have revealed the workings of what I call the *sex-category sorting process*. Through this process, the vast majority of women volunteers are actively sorted into a team-parent position, and the vast majority of men volunteers are sorted into an assistant coach position, which in turn serves as the key entry point to the pipeline for head coaching positions. To say that people are "sorted" is not to deny their active agency in this process. Rather, it is to underline the fact that what people often think of as "free individual choices" are actually choices that are shaped (both constrained and enabled) by social contexts. In particular, I have shown how women's choices to become "team parents" are constrained by the fact that few, if any, men will volunteer to do this important, but less visible and less honored job. Women's choices are enabled by their being actively recruited—"volunteered"—by head coaches, and sometimes by other parents on the team, to become the "team mom." We have seen how men's choices not to volunteer for team-parent positions and instead to volunteer as assistant coaches, are shaped by the gendered assumptions of head coaches and by informal interactions at the initial team meeting. Moreover, the terms "coach" and "team mom" are saturated with gendered assumptions that are consistent with most people's universe of meanings. These gendered meanings mesh with—and mutually reinforce—the conventional gendered divisions of labor and power in the organization, in ways that make peoples' decisions to "go with the flow" appear "natural." And we have seen how having women do the background support work while men do the visible leadership work on the team is also made to appear natural, to the extent that it reiterates the gender divisions of labor that many parents experience in their families and in their workplaces.[14]

In short, people's gendered sense of identity, their informal gendered interactions and language, the gendered divisions of labor in their organizations, and their commonly held beliefs about gender and families together fuel a tremendous inertia that tends mostly to make this profoundly social sex-category sorting process appear to be natural. As sociologists Maria Charles and David Grusky have astutely asserted, "The insidiousness of essentialism"—the belief in natural, categorical differences between men and women—"is that it clothes segregation in voluntarist terms."[15] It seemed to me at times that, despite the evidence around them of a sex-category sorting process at work, many of the people we interviewed held stubbornly to their belief that every individual was doing precisely what she or he had freely chosen to do. People's adherence to an ideology and language of individual choice, as the words of soccer coach Al Evans illustrate, makes it difficult for them to see and understand the social nature of the sex-category sorting process:

> In most teams, you've got the team manager or your team mom. I hate to use the—to *genderize* that position—but generally that is what happens, is the mom gets picked to do that.
>
> [She's picked, or she volunteers?]
>
> She volunteers.

The sex-segregated context of sport is a key to understanding the power of essentialism in this sorting process. Unlike in most other institutions, the move toward equality (e.g., the passage of Title IX, the explosive increase in youth sports for girls, expanded high school and college sports for girls and women) takes a sex-segregated form, backed not by ideas of integration but by a kind of "separate but equal" ethic, which continues always to make gender salient. Time after time, I hear leaders of leagues, and some women coaches, saying that the league leadership works hard to recruit more women coaches but just can't get them to volunteer. The *formal agency* here is to "get more women," but what sociologist Pat Martin calls the *informal practicing of gender* amounts to a collective and (mostly) non-reflexive sorting system that, at the entry level, puts most women and men on separate paths.[16] We will see in subsequent chapters how this informal practicing of gender also creates a kind of glass ceiling on women coaches, *and* on men coaches who do not display the "proper" masculine style. The mechanisms of this collective practicing of gender are individually embodied and displayed, given voice through informal interactions, made to seem normal through their congruence with family and workplace divisions of labor, and supported by essentialist ideologies. These mechanisms are embedded in youth sports in taken-for-granted ways.

But showing the dominant pattern—the social reproduction that results from this sex-category sorting process—tells only part of the story. Not everybody goes with the flow, not all the time. People sometimes choose to push against the current, occasionally through overt acts of resistance, and more often through quiet, informal, actions that break or skirt the normal rules of operation. I have shown how a few women resist being assigned to the position of "team mom"—by refusing to volunteer, by jokingly supporting each other not to volunteer, or by insisting on acting informally as an assistant coach even when their activity is defined as that of a team mom. And I have also shown how some coaches (usually women, but a few men) have consciously broken with the dominant pattern of recruiting volunteers at the outset of the season—by taking "team-parent" responsibilities themselves, by not creating a team parent but assigning tasks to families instead, or by consciously recruiting women to help as assistant coaches. In addition, some coaches recognize the tensions inherent in the gendered language of "team mom" and consciously— sometimes humorously—bring these tensions into their conversations with others. These kinds of challenges are usually handled and managed in ways that eventually reproduce the dominant pattern (e.g., publicly presenting at the season-ending party a "team-mom" award to a woman who has been informally acting as an assistant coach all season long). But challenges and small acts of resistance also call into question the "naturalness" of the normal categorical division of labor between women and men. They create possibilities for change by demonstrating to other adults—and, crucially, to the kids—that women don't always have to play the background support "mom" roles, while men don't always have to play the leadership, coach roles.

While these mostly informal moments of resistance are important and provocative, by far the most profound challenge to the categorical sex-sorting process in youth sports takes place when a woman formally takes on the role of head coach. In the next chapter, I will examine the experiences of women who have done just that.

THREE "We Don't Like Chick Coaches"

WOMEN AT THE HELM

Amidst the happy chaos preceding South Pasadena's annual AYSO opening day ceremony, Suzel and I are approached on the field by Ellen Lessing, a soccer coach we have recently interviewed and who now seems anxious to speak with us. Ellen, who has served as a head coach for several years, complains to us that she is not wearing her new official white "AYSO Coach" shirt because the league had ordered them this year in sizes too large for most of the women. "If I wear the shirt, it's so baggy on me it hangs below my shorts and I look pregnant. But if I don't wear it, people don't recognize me as the coach!" Later, at the team picture-taking, the guy in charge of posing Ellen's team chooses the tallest dad (an assistant coach, dressed in a white shirt), refers to him as "Coach," and poses him in the middle of the team picture. Ellen has to tell him that in fact she is the head coach. A few minutes later, Joan Ring, another coach whom we'd recently interviewed, approaches us and says, "You've got to interview me again!" so she can tell us about the troubles she's been having with her new assistant coach. "After our first practice last week, he criticized me in front of some parents—he said, 'Inexperienced coaches always run too many drills.' I told him that I'm not inexperienced, that I have several years of coaching experience. And then he pulled out his credentials and said that he's coached soccer for twenty years. I took him aside and told him, 'Look, these girls need strong female role models. And out here, that's me. I'm the coach, so you've got to back off, okay?' "

Barbara Jones, a self-described "full-time mom" currently coaching a boys' under-8 soccer team and serving as a South Pasadena AYSO board member, initially laughed when we asked her why she thinks there aren't more women coaches in the league. "Ha! Yeah, we don't like chick coaches in South Pasadena!" But immediately following her tongue-in-cheek quip, her voice turned more serious, and she listed several possible explanations:

> I think, socialization-wise, probably there are more men who grew up with sports. There are less women. I think women are also busier, you know, I think in a lot of relationships it's hard for the women to just say, "I'm goin' out to coach Suzy's game and you take care of the other two or three kids at home." I think it might be tougher for them just logistically. And I just think they're just more hesitant. They probably aren't as familiar. They don't know the sport. Maybe they're less comfortable with sports generally. But it may be that the league has been not encouraging them or, you know, not kind of reaching out. [Last year] I wasn't chosen to be a girls [age]-10 coach, and I was somewhat surprised by that, especially when I saw my daughter's coach. I was, like, "You picked *that* over *me*? I mean, *come on!*" So, I'm not sure. I think it's probably a combination of a lot of things, and it would be nice to try to change that.

Jones's statement captures many of the themes I will explore in this chapter, concerning the low number of women coaches and the challenges and barriers facing the few women who do coach. She begins with a (half serious?) joke about community opposition to women being coaches. But her tone turns fully serious as she speculates about reasons why individual women would not choose to coach: they are "busier" than men with managing family "logistics"; they are less "comfortable," and thus "hesitant" to coach, due to having less familiarity with sports.

But vying with these individual explanations are questions that suggest that the youth sports context is a less-than-welcoming place for women coaches: perhaps the league isn't "reaching out" to women? And she punctuates this by noting how her own experience of not having been chosen to coach a girls' under-10 team started to feel suspiciously like discrimination, especially once she saw how bad her daughter's male coach turned out to be: "You picked *that* over *me?*"

Time and again, as I listened to women coaches talking about their experiences, these same sorts of tensions emerged: on the one hand, they speculated that perhaps women chose not to coach, or they quit coaching, mostly for individual reasons: not being "comfortable," not having enough sports background or experience, or just simply being too busy. But on the other hand, their statements also point to the constraints, prejudices, and unique problems that women coaches face: maybe, their stories suggest, women coaches just aren't competing on a level playing field with the men.

This chapter will explore the ways that women coaches' experiences are shaped and constrained by the context of youth sports, mostly through subtle interpersonal dynamics rather than through overt discrimination. I will first describe women's paths into youth coaching, and I will demonstrate how the coaches' emphasis on what I call "kids-knowledge" versus "sports-knowledge" relates to how long they will stay in coaching. Next, I will focus on the constraints that women coaches commonly face, including covert exclusionary practices, a double standard that subjects women coaches to critical scrutiny, attempts by some men to challenge women coaches' authority, and men's use of playing-field space and of their own loud voices in ways that intimidate and marginalize women coaches. Women coaches, I will show, develop strategies in response to these constraints. Many quit after one season; some coach for several years but cycle back to coach younger siblings, thus avoiding confrontations with the more "intense" and "serious" coaches who dominate the older kids' age groups. And a few develop individual and group-based strategies that help them to navigate their way successfully into the ranks of coaching in the older age-groups, thus challenging the centrality of men's control of youth sports.

BECOMING A COACH

Women's stories about how they first decided to become head coaches were varied. A few became head coaches for reasons directly related to their kids' self-interests. Two said that they were new to the community and were told that if they signed up to coach, their child would be assured a place on a team. And three mothers said that they volunteered to coach after being disappointed with the low quality of coaching that their children had received the previous season. Isabel Bacad, for example, said that she decided to coach her son's soccer team because, "We had a bad experience last year, where his coach wasn't very good and he didn't really learn any skills at all. So I figured . . . if *he* can coach—I know a little bit more about soccer than he did—so I figured I might as well just go ahead and have my own team and be the head coach."

Most of the mothers we interviewed became head coaches after a year or more serving as assistant coaches. And nearly all of them spoke of having to overcome doubts before taking the leap into head coaching. Several, like Joan Ring, were uncertain of their willingness to take the kind of scrutiny they knew they would be subjected to as head coaches: "Your reputation in the community is on the line. [Everyone talks about] who's a good coach, the nice coaches, the inept coaches—you don't really know where you are, but you don't want to be terrible." And nearly all of the women spoke of having to overcome a lack of confidence about whether they had the ability to be head coaches. Terri Patrick said, "I was very hesitant to be a head coach, thinking I just don't know enough." The women don't see men having this same problem with confidence. Ellen Lessing said, "The men don't lack confidence; they figure 'Oh, I can read a book about soccer.' I can't really speak for the men, but I see some men coaches who have never done anything with soccer. And they don't seem to lack the confidence like the women do." Similarly, Barbara Jones, speaking of the difficulty she has had in recruiting women soccer coaches, says that, "For some reason men, it doesn't bother them that they never played or they don't know [the game]. They *think* they know, [so they] are the ones that are coaching. You know what I'm saying? And so, they're out there yelling, 'Do this, do that, do that.' But the women, they're just like, 'I just am not gonna do it, because I don't know what I'm doing.' "

As Barbara Jones's words suggest, league officials frequently said that they try to recruit women coaches, but that they just can't get them to volunteer. Some of the women coaches that we interviewed, especially those in baseball, were skeptical—even sarcastically so—about this claim. However, several of the women coaches told us that that they had indeed been recruited by a male league official, or by another male coach who encouraged them to coach. In her book on Little League Baseball, Sherri Grasmuck describes what she calls "race sponsorship [that] occurs when an individual or family enters a formerly exclusive space through alignment with, or sponsorship by, an individual with legitimate membership status."[1] Grasmuck used the concept of "sponsorship" to describe how a previously all-white neighborhood Little League Baseball league successfully integrated African American kids, largely through friendly and supportive white "sponsors." A similar concept of "gender sponsorship" is useful in describing the several women coaches who were "sponsored" by supportive men coaches and league officials, who recruited and then, sometimes, continued to support them. Wendy Lytle was mentored and encouraged by a man for whom she had served as assistant soccer coach: "He was a great guidance to begin with—and every time I meet on the field now, he is like, 'You are still doing it! I am so glad I didn't put you off.' " June Park was also serving as an assistant soccer coach when she was recruited by Bill Munson (whom she described as "Mr. AYSO"): "He told me he thought that I should be a coach, and we talked for a while, and so sure enough I went and became a coach. And he kind of showed me, you know, taught the course that I took."

Some of the women coaches said that men league officials, coaches, and sometimes their own husbands were instrumental in helping them to build confidence that they could be head coaches. Shelley Parsons was reluctant at first, even though she'd coached basketball and her daughter had been in soccer for years:

When I signed my son up, they asked if I would coach. And I said, "Well I've never coached before, soccer. I've coached basketball, but to be honest with you, my daughter's been in soccer for years but I've never coached it." And they [said], "Well you don't have to really—you don't have to play it to coach it." They said, "We'll send you to clinics and we'll give you support, but we really want women coaches." They said that they found that a lot of kids do better with females than they do with some of the men. That's what they told me, and they wanted to have more women involved in AYSO. So they kinda talked me into it.

[Who's they?]

The people who are at the sign-ups for soccer. They were men. So they persuaded me to try it. And so I tried it. And I went to all the clinics, and they give you a nice little packet of information and fundamentals.

This formal recruiting and training for new coaches is built in to AYSO but is far less prevalent in LLB/S, where informal networks seem to rule. One of the rare women softball coaches, Jessica Torres, credited a male league official with recruiting and encouraging her to coach: "He was very supportive, and I think he actually came to me with the offer. Because they were kind of really needing some managers this season, and I just jumped on the opportunity. And I was really scared: I would say yes, and then say no, and then say yes, and so he really pushed me along."

Barbara Jones explained how informal support from male coaches can help to build confidence and enjoyment for newer women coaches, but her words also underline how rare this kind of support is: "I have actually had a couple of male coaches come up to me and say, 'Great game. Your team is very well coached.' Which, when a man says that to me, I think, 'You know what? You're an okay guy.' 'Cause there's not a lot of guys who can say that to a woman coach who just beat them. Men do not like to be beaten by women coaches." Indeed, though several of the women we interviewed broke into coaching with the support of individual men, this kind of gender sponsorship seems rare and idiosyncratic; it is certainly not built into the formal operation of the leagues. In fact, one woman (whose first name might also be read as a man's name) laughed as she told us that she was recruited by mistake after checking the box on the sign-up sheet that indicated she was willing to coach. "So when they called the house, my husband answered the phone and they said,

'Oh you said you'd coach,' and my husband says, 'No, I didn't say I'd coach, my wife did.' Ha! He said they were like, 'Oh, ok.' "

DIFFERENT PATHS THROUGH COACHING

Women's assessments of their experiences in coaching range from the extremely positive to the singularly nightmarish. I have identified three patterns that can be seen as distinct paths for women coaches: what I call "Stoppers" are women who coached for one year (occasionally two) and then quit; "Cyclers" are women who coached younger kids' teams for one or two years and then cycled back to coach younger teams again for one or two years, thus coaching three or more years but never breaking into the higher-aged kids' teams; and "Gamers" are women who began coaching the younger kids and then broke through the age-based glass ceiling to coach in the older kids' age brackets.

By far, Stoppers are the most commonly found types among women coaches, especially in LLB/S. There are some Cyclers in AYSO, but not many in LLB/S. Gamers are few and far between, but they are more prevalent in soccer and almost nonexistent in LLB/S. The numbers for South Pasadena LLB/S are especially stark: from 1999 to 2007, only 36 baseball or softball teams had women managers or co-managers.[2] Of the twenty-eight women who served in this capacity, twenty-three were Stoppers (twenty-one of whom managed only one season, and two of whom managed a year of T-ball and a year of Coach-Pitch). There were two Cyclers and three Gamers, all of whom coached girls' softball. Two of the Gamers co-managed with husbands, while one worked with her husband as her assistant coach (a phenomenon that I will examine later in this chapter). Gamers are nonexistent in boys' baseball. From 1999 to 2007, only 6 of 273 boys' baseball teams (2.2 percent) had women coaches, and 3 of these 6 were clustered in 1999. Of these 6 teams headed by women, none were in age-groupings above age 10.

The women interviewed for my study included six Stoppers, seven Cyclers, and nine Gamers. I explored what led so many women to quit coaching, some to cycle back, and a few to continue on. The interviews revealed that women coaches brought two different kinds of knowledge—which I call "kids-knowledge" and "sports-knowledge"—to the experience of coaching. As soccer coach Pam Burke, a Cycler, explained it, "There are two different components of coaching. One is the knowledge of the game. The other is knowledge of kids. And if you are a mom, you've got some experience with that. And dads do too, but they have a different approach—sometimes they do. I think parenting skills or mothering skills can benefit a team, as well as a knowledge and ability to teach soccer." As I will show, the way that an individual coach emphasized, relied upon, or balanced these two kinds of knowledge was correlated with whether she was likely to be a Stopper, a Cycler, or a Gamer.

Kids-Knowledge: "It's Like Being a Mom"

When asked how they initially dealt with their lack of confidence in deciding to become a head coach, many women spoke of the special knowledge and skills they have as mothers and/or as teachers working with young children. Shelley Parsons, a Cycler coaching under-8 boys' soccer, described this kind of knowledge as a valuable resource: "I guess what helps me, I think in my favor, is that I've always worked with kids—kindergarten through high school, I've worked with kids as a counselor and school administrator. I know kids and I know all the things they're going through." Isabel Bacad, a Stopper, was recruited to coach and suffered some initial doubts, due to her lack of experience with soccer, but eventually, "I just said sure, I'm game for anything. I'm an elementary school teacher you know, and so I can do kids. I mean it's not that big of a deal for me. It's not like intimidating or whatever."

Most Stoppers and Cyclers seemed very aware that their kids-knowledge was especially valuable in working with the younger kids but perhaps less so with the older kids. Many of the women coaches described this kids-knowledge as being grounded firmly in their role as mothers. Barbara Jones, a Cycler, suggested that kids-knowledge is a resource that men rarely bring to coaching: "Especially in the younger ages, you have to be super patient with these kids. You have to be super encouraging. It's like being a mom. I mean, you know, it's not a lot about strategy at that level . . . and to me the best coaches are, you know, good with the kids, very positive. . . . Now, there are men who don't do that. They want to win." Another Cycler, Lillian Mohr, coached T-ball for her older son, and then switched back to T-ball for her younger son:

> It was partly for fairness to the boys, but it was also because I prefer working with younger children, where it's more about working with children and less about your sports expertise. It's more about talking to kids, at this age, than it is about knowing high-level soccer stuff. I'm a good teacher, you know. I know how to teach. [It's] my belief that with the little guys, it doesn't matter much what the sport part is, it's more about the kid part. [What matters is] knowing how to talk to kids, knowing how to explain something so they get it, knowing how to keep their attention, how to keep it active, knowing how to be positive, encouraging.

These women invoked mothering skills to build confidence in their ability to coach and also as a way of valorizing the positive things that they bring to children's sports. However, embedded in the comments of many of the Stoppers and Cyclers who leaned on kids-knowledge was usually a recognition that, for coaches in the higher-age-level teams, sports-knowledge becomes more and more important, while kids-knowledge becomes less important, and even gets devalued.

Sports-Knowledge: "I Understand the Game"

Many of the women coaches we interviewed had a great deal of sports experience in their background, while some had less. Ellen Lessing said that she often felt insecure about coaching, due to her lack of team sports background: "As I grew up, I played tennis and no competitive organized team sports. I am pre–Title IX. I am fifty-two. There was no organized sports. So I never played any of these sports—I didn't really know too much about any of the other sports." By contrast, Shelley Parsons is nearly a decade younger than Lessing. Her youth spanned the boom in girls' sports sparked by Title IX, and she amassed a wealth of athletic experience:

> When I was a kid—I'm forty-four—we had a great PE program and there was an intramural program, but competitive sports didn't get off the

ground 'til my junior year in high school. I think that was when they passed that proposition where girls need to have equal rights—Title IX—so when that started, yes, then I played basketball, volleyball. It was a small school—we did everything. I got recruited in a college to play women's rugby.

Most of the women we interviewed were in their mid-thirties through their early forties, so they were young enough to have played a part in the boom in girls' and women's sports. Norma Delgado described herself as a "classic jock," winning four athletic letters in high school. A few of the women had several years of competitive soccer experience, and drew specifically on that knowledge in their youth coaching work. Barbara Jones said she was happy to coach because, "I've played a lot of soccer, and I understand the game. . . . I know the sport." She explained how this kind of experience gives her confidence when she's facing men coaches:

> I'll tell you what's interesting. Like, *you* don't know about soccer? Most of these *men* don't know about soccer either! But, for some reason, they're not intimidated to go out there and scream and yell at the top of their lungs [*laughs*]. You know? And it's really interesting, because I find, having played the game, I mean, I think I know the game pretty well—you know, I can totally see plays developing, I totally know how to position people, you know, I understand the game in my head and I can watch games and kind of rip them apart a little bit, but I don't think men who haven't played [can].

The Gamers my our sample tended to have especially impressive amounts of athletic experiences—usually with both individual and team sports, and often on high school, college, and adult league teams. A few of the Gamers said that they had gained confidence from having played competitive sports with and against boys, a phenomenon that sociologist Barrie Thorne calls "gender crossing."[3] As a youth, June Park was one:

> You name it, I played it: fencing [*laughs*], field hockey. I always thought maybe I could be a football player when I grow up. I'll be the first woman football player. And you know they never made it seem like anything odd, where we grew up. It was never really an issue, like "Oh a girl's joining

Little League" or whatever. I mean a lot of teams that I played on were boys teams.

Nikki Lopez, another Gamer, started playing soccer at age ten on a girls' AYSO team, but when she got into her teens, there were no girls' teams to play on:

> I wanted to play in high school, but there wasn't a girls' team. So I tried out and won a spot on the team. Because I was the only girl and I played a lot, it caused a lot of conflict with whoever was sitting on the bench if I was on the field. They were not happy about it, that there was a girl on the field . . . [*laughs*] so that was a little difficult. I'm not a huge person, I'm a very slight person, and was smaller then, but I was quick and I could play the game and I could kick far. But I also noticed that I got away with a lot of things, because I was the only girl on the field—that the referees would never card me regardless of what I did—so I probably became a little more of a dirty player, an aggressive player, than I would have under other circumstances. A lot of it though is kind of self-preservation when you're out there and you're playing with guys that are fifty to eighty pounds more than you. But yeah, I would often have referees come up and put their arm around me and say "Honey, you know you're not supposed to do that." [*Laughs.*] So nothing really bad, but definitely kind of pushing the limits. I loved playing the game, and there were guys I got along with very well on the team, and had some interesting experience as far as the opponents. There was no kind of in-between—they were either not aggressive or they were overly aggressive. You know, they either left you alone or they were trying to kill you.

Lopez's experiences of competing against the boys taught her not only knowledge of the game of soccer, but also embedded in her an "aggressive" style, a "kind of self-preservation," that allowed her to compete and enjoy herself even in the face of teammates or opponents who might resent her presence or "were trying to kill her" her on the field. This ability to negotiate an otherwise intimidating, male-dominated space benefited her later, as a youth coach. Similarly, Delores Quintero, a Gamer in Little League Softball, had played many years of sports and had worked as an umpire, starting in her early teens. These experiences, she said, gave her the knowledge and confidence to become a coach. She also credited her father and bothers for encouraging her, and for toughening her up in ways that prepared her for becoming a successful athlete, umpire, and coach:

> Dad taught me how to pick up a glove and I handled myself on the field from the time I was a little girl. It was my favorite game. You know, he taught me how to throw a football. He taught me how to play a lot of sports, but softball was my preferred sport and so I've just been playing it pretty much all my life. I had one older, one younger [brother]. It was a challenge. It made me have to be a little tough, a little rugged. And, you know, there were objections here and there by my mother, but she pretty much went along with it. I was very much a "daddy's girl," so, you know, my father was very partial—probably the biggest women's libber around—pre–Title IX—and in a *Hispanic family!* You don't find that a lot either. And he was very, very into having me be just as good as the boys.

Quintero credits her youthful experiences with her father and her brothers as having made her "a little tough, a little rugged," a predisposition that helped her survive and thrive as a softball coach. Other Gamers drew on their experiences as PE teachers and coaches. Tracy Nash combined a huge amount of experience playing sports—from grade school through college—with several years of experience as a high school PE teacher and coach. "[Coaching] was my occupation for ten years—I graduated from college, got this teaching job at a high school, and then spent every afternoon coaching high school kids until I got married, and then when my daughter turned five was when I kind of started muddling in the AYSO, even though I didn't have any soccer background. [But] I figured I had been a coach before so I can maybe be better than anybody out there."

THE GLASS CEILING ON WOMEN COACHES

Together, kids-knowledge and sports-knowledge are resources, or "capital," that women variously combine, mobilize, and display in coaching. Scholars have used the concept of "social capital" to describe skills and abilities (like formal education) that individuals absorb and then utilize to gain access to, or advantages within, various social fields.[4] I have suggested here that women coaches bring both kids-knowledge and sports-knowledge to their coaching, and that those who emphasize the former are more likely to be Stoppers or Cyclers, while those who emphasize (and often have more of) the latter are more likely to be Gamers. This idea is useful in illuminating the personal attributes or liabilities that women bring to the coaching experience, but it also has its limitations.

Taken alone, a focus on individual capital might lead us to conclude that there are so few women coaches who end up being Gamers because they tend too often to rely on the "wrong kind of capital" (i.e., kids-knowledge instead of sports-knowledge). There are two things missing from this perspective. First, a focus on the individual attributes that women coaches bring to sports might fail to examine how other fields—like families or workplaces—are structured by gender in ways that have encouraged women to absorb and deploy kids-knowledge while limiting their access to other kinds of knowledge. Second, a focus on the personality factors that women bring to coaching risks ignoring *what women are up against* when they enter the coaching ranks. Gender is not simply embedded in the bodies and personalities of individuals in the form of skills and knowledge that predispose them to make certain choices and to thrive or fail in certain contexts. Moreover, organizational contexts are themselves gendered in ways that subject women to particular constraints.

When we look at the experiences of women in youth coaching, they look similar to women's experiences in various professions where entrée is constrained (as we saw in chapter 2) and informal dynamics create a kind of "glass ceiling" that prevents most women from moving up. Research has shown that these kinds of constraints are particularly salient for women in the profession of college and elite-level coaching.[5] And just as in other professions, the ceiling on women coaches in youth sports is not fully visible, as it is constructed through informal dynamics that run counter to the formal statements of inclusiveness and equal opportunity in the organization.[6] So an experienced woman coach who wants to be a Gamer but is not chosen to coach teams in the higher age levels is left to wonder: is she is a victim of gender discrimination, or was she denied only after a fair assessment of her abilities in a very competitive field? After all, there are fewer teams in the higher age levels of soccer, baseball, and softball, so there are simply fewer opportunities for all coaches—men and women—at these levels. June Park, a Gamer who had several years of experience coaching boys' and girls' soccer, had had a very successful season and expected to coach her daughter's under-12 All-Star team. She and her male assistant coach conducted the All-Star team selection together, but from there on, it was not smooth sailing:

> It's a really corrupt system. It's a mess. And that year in the beginning I picked the team, and everybody thought I was the coach. *I* thought I was the coach. *Stanley, my assistant coach,* thought I was the coach. It turned out we got the letter, and it said that *Stanley* was the head coach! He said he was [surprised], and I think he was. So yeah, I was pretty upset about that. I wasn't too happy about that. This was last year, and Stanley kind of made some phone calls, and I made some phone calls and said, "You know, this is really odd." So then Stanley said, well, why don't we just be co-coaches or whatever. He volunteered to step down or something, and it just seemed like such a big to-do, you know? I was—at that point, I was embarrassed, even though I had called these people and said, you know, What in the world are you doing?

Her hunch as to what was going on was that there was a local old boys' network operating—the kind of network that is particular to community youth sports—that she had not seen in her experiences in medical school or in the teaching profession:

> The division coach and the regional coach administrator, I think the two of them—they're all friends—I mean they basically all grew up together, they all went to high school together, they're still here, their families are here, and now their kids are here. When I started, I was like some Pollyanna that thought that, you know, men and women, they just do things equally and that's the way it is, and you kind of just go by your own. I went to med school, and I think most of the environments that I've been in people have been very careful to be very fair, and so I just thought that's the way people would be. I mean they have daughters, they have wives, they have spouses—. But when it came to sports it just turned out to be some kind of back room boys club, I guess. You know, their big goal is to beat Arcadia, just like when they were in high school. [*Laughs.*] You know, beat Glendale. That's what I've decided now that I'm sour grapes.

[*Laughs.*] I don't know what they make of women coaches anymore. I mean, they *say* that that is such a great thing and everything, and maybe they mean it. I mean maybe they've convinced themselves that they mean it and they think I'm the most obnoxious person on the planet. I don't know—I mean they seem to think that I'm perfectly fine. I know all these people socially—I mean I see them all the time. And they don't seem to think that I'm a pariah normally. I mean they include me in things, but then they exclude me from these [coaching positions].

Most women coaches' feelings are not so clearly ones of having been excluded. Some have vague suspicions that they have been treated unfairly, but they tend to couch their stories in the language of individual predispositions (a preference for running teams according to kids-knowledge over sports-knowledge) and of an individual's choice to opt out of coaching, or to cycle back and work with younger kids. Norma Delgado, a Stopper who coached T-ball, said that she feels comfortable coaching the little kids because "there's no win or lose. [But] I, for myself, would be reticent to coach in the upper levels because I don't know if I want to deal with all the crap that goes along with coaching the upper levels. Because once you get to the upper levels, you get those horror stories, and I know I can see them coming." Kate Kaplan, a Stopper who coached one year of girls' softball experienced some of the "horror stories" that Norma Delgado feared. Though she came to coaching with plenty of sports participation experience and having worked as a school physical education teacher, Kaplan approached the coaching experience by emphasizing her "kids-knowledge," and she was then stunned by how serious and competitive the other coaches (all men) were. She labored to explain how difficult it was to live out her expectations and values about girls' softball in this "dog-eat-dog, competitive world":

> I just wanted them to have a good time. I also just kinda wanted them to see, you know, a female coach who was interested in the game, liked the game, who wanted to give back to the community. I don't know, I wanted them to have a good time, to play some different positions. I didn't get to do that really. So, um, yeah, it was hard time. I didn't want it to be like this dog-eat-dog, competitive world. I guess I just picked the wrong league, and I learned that on day two.

Wendy Lytle, a Stopper, agrees, saying that at the higher age levels, soccer "gets too serious. I think probably I could just about coach a girls' team, under-10. But I think beyond that, the dads would not respect me as a coach. I would feel that they didn't think that I knew what I was doing. This through the years has predominantly been a male sport, particularly in California. And we [women] don't feel confident. We feel, we feel that it's more of a men's field further up. And all the coaching up the wazoo for ourselves, I don't think would build up my confidence to take it much further than under-10s."

The Cyclers among the women coaches seemed most consciously aware of how their decisions to stay with the younger teams reflected an understanding of how "serious" the game (and the coaches) get at the higher age levels. Barbara Jones said that part of the reason she decided not to coach beyond the under-10 age bracket was "there's a little intimidation factor" at the higher levels. Ellen Lessing's words illustrate how women's stories often oscillate between thinking that they *decided* not to go on and wondering to what extent they actually were *pushed out* of coaching. She was very emotional, even to the point of fighting off tears, as she explained why she had signed up this year to coach her youngest child's team, rather than continuing to coach her older daughter's under-9 team, where she had been told by league officials that there were "too many coaches" and that she was therefore not needed:

We never quite figured what happened. But I wasn't chosen to coach. And I don't know—I don't know what it was. The season that I stopped coaching, that's when a man coach called and said, "We have too many coaches." And I said "Fine," and stepped out. Later, I felt it was because there were so many men. I called him back and I said, "You know, just make sure that you have some women coaches, because there tends not to be [many], by the time you get to U-9, which is not very old." And then it turned out, I think, there weren't very many women. And I thought, "Hmm." That was the only time, particularly, I felt, "Hmm" there, might be, you know, kind of the old boys, choosing their friends.

Her description of how this made her feel, and of how she reacted to it, illustrates nicely the dynamic interplay between women's "lack of confidence" and the (often less than fully visible) informal gender dynamics of the organization:

> I have felt squeezed out. And it very easily plays into my insecurities and so I easily bow out. [*She begins to cry, and there is a short silence.*] So, even this year [*she sobs*], I didn't sign up to coach [her older daughter]. I signed up for [her younger son's team]. [*She struggles to continue speaking as she cries.*] Because it's easier psychologically, you know, to just, not be with all those men.

These stories suggest that women coaches are sometimes pushed out of coaching, while at other times they choose to leave coaching or cycle back. But these choices are by no means fully "free" and unfettered; instead, they are shaped, constrained, and enabled by the gender dynamics of the youth sports organizations. In the next section, I will illuminate some of the common problems and constraints that women coaches face.

WHAT WOMEN COACHES ARE UP AGAINST

When sociologists Lewis Yablonsky and Jonathan Brower published *The Little League Game* in 1979, seven years after the passage of Title IX, their chapter on "The Coaches" devoted three pages to "Helen," who was at that time "the only female coach in her league." Helen made a point of saying that she was "not a women's libber," but she still recognized that "being the only female coach in this league, to some degree, I have something to prove . . . . The men in the league don't respond to me very positively. They all seem to think it's novel and interesting to have a woman coach. I do have to prove something as a woman."[7] Reading Helens' words nearly three decades later, it strikes me that there are now more women coaches in youth sports, but not *that* many more. And the experience of women coaches in youth sports has changed, but not entirely. Unlike Helen, few women today have the experience of being the single, token woman coach in an entire league. And some of today's women coaches, as we have seen, benefit from the encouragement and mentoring of experienced men coaches. However, today's women coaches too often feel, as Helen did thirty years ago, that they still "have something to prove as a woman," due to their experiences with men coaches and with the fathers of team players, who "don't respond to me very positively." These informal interactions that women coaches experience—mostly with men—are the building blocks of the glass ceiling that limits the numbers of women coaches, especially in the older kids' teams. In what follows, I will discuss four kinds of barriers that emerged from the interviews: overt instances of sexism directed toward women coaches; men's high levels of surveillance over, and challenges to, the authority of women coaches; men's domination of playing-fields spaces with their bodies and their voices; and the existence of "good ol' boys' networks" of men coaches that informally monopolize information and control of teams and leagues.

Overt Instances of Sexism

Women coaches reported very few incidences of overtly sexist behavior toward them. In particular, they felt that the kids nearly always treated them with respect, and they often felt accepted and supported by parents, league officials, and other coaches. But sometimes men coaches' behaviors or comments communicated sexist attitudes about women coaches. For instance, Ellen Lessing related that while she was coaching a soccer game, her daughter told her that she "heard the opposing coach, a man, say to his male assistant coach, 'I have to talk to that chick coach.' I laughed, and she said, 'Mom [groan], he did not mean hot chick, he meant dumb chick!'" A male coach's look, a snub, or an overheard comment about a "chick coach" might lead a woman to question whether she is being treated with respect. But it seems that the "family-oriented" context of youth sports largely insulated many of the women coaches—most of whom are married and nearly all of whom are mothers—from being targets of sexual harassment. However, one of the few younger and single women coaches whom we interviewed experienced what felt like a sexual come-on from a father on the team, as well as some "touchy feely" behavior from a male coach that felt creepy to her:

> I had a dad totally flirting with me—a married man, totally hitting on me. I'd be coaching, and I'd be in the dugout and his daughter would be in

the outfield and he'd come up and like start, "Oh, Su-e." He would come up—he was just very [*imitating a man's lower voice*]: "How you doin'?" You know? "God, you look u-h-h"—you know, just like the whole leering in the eyes. I hated that. And then there was another coach, he was just too touchy feely. I don't know if it was just me or if he was like [that with] other people. But, you know, I didn't—I'm not showing up to softball in like full makeup and a mini-skirt, you know!

These kinds of behaviors by men—while probably technically not "illegal" and certainly open to interpretation—are similar to the subtle forms of sexual harassment commonly faced by women pioneers into previously all-male realms. Some men don't know how (or don't want) to treat women as peers or as leaders, so they revert to familiar and comfortable modes of talking about and relating to them—as "dumb chicks," or as sexual objects. These words and behaviors, in turn, have the effect of making women feel unwelcome, not taken seriously, and even humiliated.

Men Challenging Women Coaches' Authority

One of the most common problems reported by women coaches is a general feeling of being unfairly scrutinized by men (fathers of kids on the team, other coaches, referees, and umpires), and of being subjected to subtle, and sometimes overt, challenges to their knowledge of the game and thus to their authority. All youth coaches know that other adults are scrutinizing their actions, but women coaches understand that they are under a particular kind of gendered surveillance. Barbara Jones said that fathers on her son's under-10 team were questioning her ability to coach but that she didn't know about it until one of the mothers confided in her:

One of the moms came up to me about four games into the season and she said, "I just want you to know [*laughs*] that I overheard some of the men at the very first meeting kind of like a little nervous about what this season was going to be like." She goes, "But you have definitely gained their respect." You know, I think when you're a man coach, particularly of boys, I think there's less questioning; for a man coach, there's a presumption that he knows what he's doing and there's no question. Even when they're complete blithering idiots as coaches, 'cause I've seen that too. And when you're a woman, even if you're confident . . . you don't get that same presumption. You kind of have to prove yourself.

As Jones's words suggest, while people might assume that men coaches know what they are doing, women coaches are often assumed *not* to know what they are doing. Instead, they have to prove themselves as knowledgeable and capable. A myriad of experiences reinforce this feeling. Joan Ring said, with an incredulous tone, that when she first started coaching her six-year-old son's soccer team,

> I remember I called up this one family—you have to call them first and contact them—and the dad says, "So, what are your qualifications?" *You know?* "Oh! Um, I played one year in college." I didn't have any [coaching] qualifications, but I actually have played. It turns out he really wasn't a factor—just sort of an aggressive attorney [*laughs*]. Actually, in the three years I coached [my son], [there was] another aggressive attorney, and he would question things I would do even though I don't think he knew anything about soccer. Like, if I ran a drill, he'd say, "Are you sure that's in the drill book?" or "Is that a real drill?"

Some women coaches have their authority questioned and challenged by their male assistant coaches, sometimes right in front of the kids. Wendy Lytle said bluntly of her assistant, "I think he would like to take over." Kate Kaplan said that, despite her efforts, her assistant coach basically did take over:

> It is just like I was never doing enough. I got just kinda pushed around a lot. I mean, the assistant coach really [would say] "Oh, let's do this," and then we'd do that and he would change the positions around and it would just totally mess everything up. And then I was constantly like battling, to get in my feedback, or my opinion. Part of me thinks that [it's] really because I am a woman, or because I am young and don't have a kid. You know? I don't know. *And* he was a really nice guy. Don't get me wrong. But he had a really strong personality.

Pam Burke, coaching an under-10 boys' soccer team, had the opposite problem:

I have no assistant coach, not because there aren't men who could help. But a man doesn't want to be an assistant coach to a woman. They don't. I mean, there's one of two kinds of men that would do it: one that is secure enough in who they are and they see this as a fun activity, coaching their son and other kids. Or someone who wants to take over. He says, "Well, my boy's got a woman coach, I'd better get in there and, you know, do this right." So I don't have either of those.

Umpires and referees sometimes treat women coaches or managers differently than they'd treat a man. More than once I have observed a male umpire in a baseball or softball game who between innings will approach a woman manager, put his arm around her shoulders, and offer unsolicited advice about game strategy. Delores Quintero, who co-managed girls' softball with her husband, told me that she experienced some of this sort of condescension, and that she also had been treated unfairly by umpires:

> I was thrown out of two games for questioning umpires. I was completely valid in my questions. I did it appropriately without foul language, without losing control, and yet I was ejected from games. They never ejected my husband from a game, and I really believe that these umpires— always men—were somehow insulted by a woman questioning them, because the difference in how they would treat me and how they treated my husband was completely—really obvious, very obvious.

At times, umpires or referees try to help women coaches, whom they suspect are being harassed by men. "Here's how bad it got," Joan Ring told me. "The ref came up to me and said, 'Is this guy annoying you?' I laughed and said, 'Yeah, he is, but there's nothing we can do about it. He's my assistant coach.'"

Much of the negativity that women reported getting from men coaches was subtle and is better described as "bad vibes" rather than as direct hostility or as a challenge to the woman coach's authority. Soccer coach Carol Morris said, "I think there are a couple of coaches that don't want to lose to me. I think they feel that that if they lose to our team, it's not their girls losing a game to our girls, it's like they're losing to me, and I'm a girl, and the last thing they wanna do is lose to a girl. And I get that strong feeling from two coaches." When asked "And how do they give you those feelings?" she replied, "You can just tell. You can just tell." Shelley Parsons said a similar thing about her male coach opponents in soccer: "My team won a lot of games this season, [and] some of the male coaches have a hard time losing to a female. I just sense it—I don't know—because they're not friendly at the end of the game, you know? You can just sense it."

Body Politics on the Field

As I showed in the previous chapter, the masculine space of the playing field sometimes make women feel like intruders, and thus less likely to be willing to take on a coaching position. I got a glimpse into this while watching one of my son's baseball games, and I recorded the following field note:

I'm sitting in the stands at a boys' Little League Baseball game next to Dorothy Watson, a popular local grade-school teacher who has come to see some of the boys in her current fifth-grade class play (she will leave in the third inning to catch a girl's softball game, in which another of her students is playing). At one point, the boys on one team miss a ground ball, kick it all around the field, and throw it away wildly, as two runs score and the batter ends up on third base. Michael, the assistant coach, is sitting in the dugout as the play progresses (regresses?) and he goes ballistic: he leaps to his feet, his hands like claws gripping the top of the metal screen in front of him, his arms yanking his whole body up and down as he hops on his toes and yells and screams throughout the play: [*First, to his son, the second baseman*] "Catch it!" [*Then to the center fielder, who proceeds to the let the ball get by him*] "Get in front of it! Stop it!" [*Then immediately to his son again*] "You're the cut-off man—GET IN POSITION!" [*His son, who is not in position, misses the throw, and the ball is picked up by the shortstop, who turns to throw to third base. Michael yells again*] "No! NO!! DON'T THROW IT! HOLD THE BALL! HOLD IT!! THROW TO THE PITCHER!" [*Now, as he sits down and his son gives him a brief sidelong glance, he yells again to the kid*] "Don't give ME a dirty look. YOU missed the ball. You gotta WANT to catch the ball." [*And then, broadcasting to the entire team*] "Guys, you gotta WANT to catch the ball!" Dorothy Watson turns to me and says with a chuckle, "Gee, somebody ought to offer that guy a glass of water or something. He needs to calm down." I laugh, and add that Michael is often very intense. Dorothy nods toward the field and replies, "That's why I refused to coach Little League." I mentioned my research on coaches and asked her to tell me more about her comment. "Several times, over the years, I've been asked to manage a girls' softball team. I always refuse. I know it would be awful. I come out here and watch games. The guys—when they get out here—they transform themselves. One guy who's coaching now was my student years ago. You couldn't find a nicer, gentler guy. But when he gets out here, he starts yelling and screaming like a crazy man. I just couldn't handle that." I asked her if she had played baseball or softball and she said, "Sure! I played right on these fields as a kid. My dad coached Little League on these fields. This is my town. I know these kids. And I love baseball. But I just couldn't handle that."

This woman had all of the "capital" one might expect she would need in order to have the confidence to take on a youth coaching role: experience playing baseball and softball, lifelong roots in the community, years of experience working with kids, and a deep knowledge and love for the game of baseball (as an example, the next week she would distribute baseball scorecards to her students and teach them how to keep score while watching a baseball game on television). So it was not her lack of experience, lack of ability, or lack of knowledge of the game that kept her from volunteering. It was her perception of how otherwise nice and gentle men "transform themselves" on the field, "yelling and screaming like a crazy man." She told me twice: "I just couldn't handle that."

Still, some women do decide that they can handle it and do volunteer to be head coaches. And they are often very aware of having to contend with the ways that some men use space and their loud voices in intimidating ways. Two women described having to contend for space with opposing men coaches on the soccer field as "intimidating." Pam Burke described how the coaches' box, ostensibly a shared space for coaches during the game, is actually a space that some men dominate with their bodies and their voices: "There was one of me and there were three of them. And you are only allowed to have one coach in the coaching box. And they had three—three men. . . . They [yelled over me], physically pushed me out of the way. You know they would run right through me, just basically. My kids couldn't hear me trying to, you know, *coach* them. And that was a horrible experience."

Many of the women coaches talked about the ways that men's loud voices dominated the practice and game fields. Norma Delgado described men baseball coaches' yelling as "horrific . . . sort of a primitive approach to coaching." Kate Kaplan said that her assistant coach in effect used his voice to wrest control of her girls' softball team: "He would, *'Come on girls, come on.'* He would get that real, deep-like, *guy* voice and just kinda, *yell.* And they'd kinda snap to it. When he did that, I was like, "This is *my team!* Why aren't they listening to me?" Joan Ring said that often

the men are just extremely loud, and I've noticed there tends to be one aggressive male coach and for some reason they pull in another aggressive male [assistant coach]. There was this guy [and his assistant coach] and from the very beginning it was two intense screamers, so, of course, I started screaming. I have heard parents say that a coach [that] doesn't talk much during a game, they don't think they're very good. They perceive that as disinterest. They want to hear some talking, but of course they only want it to be positive. But I guess I just felt I was at a disadvantage—they were screaming and their voices are so penetrating. You do feel you're at a little disadvantage if they are screaming so loudly to all their players. And your voice is just [*she makes a high whining sound*]. You know? You get drowned out.

Women coaches who try to contend with men by yelling too, like Joan Ring, may find that their voices are drowned out by men's deeper, louder yelling. Or worse, they may be subjected to a double standard, through which they are judged negatively for being pushy or "shrill." Lillian Morh says that she yelled a bit on the baseball field—and after one game she was taken aside by the division coach and told that she was "being too serious. . . . I was so in shock because I always felt I was not that kind of a coach . . . . I'm encouraging. I do get on the field and as a teacher—I'm not a person that just kind of stands there, you know: *'Go, run after the ball! Come on! You can do it.'* You know? And in a *positive* way. But I suppose to somebody it could look overly serious."

The Secret Language of the Boys' Inner Circle

Rather than reflecting their individual shortcomings, the low confidence levels of some women coaches can be seen as a heightened sense of awareness concerning the high levels of scrutiny, challenges to their authority, overt moments of sexism, and often oppressive body politics that they face, not just as "coaches," but specifically as *women* coaches. Formal training for women coaches helps a bit. AYSO, as we have seen, offers more formal training for new and continuing coaches than does LLB/S. This benefits all coaches but is especially beneficial to women, who face particular challenges. However, as anyone who has started a new job knows, formal training only provides a new worker with one layer of knowledge. Just as important—sometimes *more* important—is the informally gathered knowledge of how things "really" work. This kind of knowledge is passed on through individual mentoring and through group networks. We have seen how some women are ushered into coaching by helpful male mentors. However, others reported in the interviews that they felt locked out of informal networks of coaches and thus prevented from learning much of the knowledge that is crucial to survive (or even thrive) as a youth coach. Nina Ramos said that when she started as a softball manager, she had a good handle on the rules of the game but was surprised to find that there was an unwritten list of rules that she had not been informed of: "During a game, the other coach [was] arguing a play, and he's like 'That's a supplemental rule.' [I said], 'A *what?*' 'Oh, that's a supplemental rule.' 'What is a supplemental rule? You know, if it's not in the rulebook, it's not a rule.' 'Oh no, we made up our own little rules on the side and we got 'em officiated, so now they're actual rules.' 'Well, were you gonna give me a list of those, 'cause I don't know what they are?' "

Kate Kaplan's experience of breaking into head coaching girls' softball as an "outsider"—new to the league, younger, not a mother—is especially helpful in illuminating the importance of informal knowledge. Though she had plenty of kids-knowledge and sports-knowledge going in, she had no idea how little she actually knew about how to operate in this specific context. It is worth telling Kaplan's story in her own words and at length:

I had a really difficult time. It was so difficult that I didn't want to do it again this year. I was the youngest person, I was a *woman,* and I didn't have any kids in the league. [But] I *know* the basics of softball. I *know* how to teach the girls all the rules and how to play and game strategy and all that stuff. But I just felt like I never had enough information. Like, I felt the other coaches were speaking a *secret language,* I mean, to each other, and they were always trying to win. I had trouble with that. I had trouble knowing basic stuff. Like the dads tended to take care of the field stuff—raking the dirt, chalking the field. I didn't even do stuff like that. Like, I guess you should know if you're going to be a coach, but I always felt embarrassed to ask. I don't know how to run the chalker, I don't know how to rack it properly. They just say, "Here are the keys to the shed." And they have an automatic pitching machine and they don't teach you how to use that. So I'm stupid and I lug that 120-pound thing in the back of my truck, go over to the middle school, get it out, and I can't get it to work. There's no, like, you know, "This is how you do this, this, and this." None of that, 'cause everybody already knows how to do it. I mean, in a way, there's no opportunity or chance for somebody like me to break into something like this. I mean, there isn't just room for that. It is like this language that you don't know. It's weird, it's hard to explain, I mean, it's like, [*she takes a deep breath*], like walking into a room and these people already all know each other. And you don't know anybody, and they're, they're *nice* to you, but they don't tell you the kind of things that will help you become a better coach. I don't know, it just felt like I constantly never knew what they were talking about. Like, you know, field etiquette. I guess this is like an example of the secret language: nobody ever told me that you can't walk out to the mound, out to the rubber, in softball. And the only way I ever learned that was watching the other coaches. Like, you know, etiquette, or the unwritten rules, I guess. Does that make sense? I don't know—I felt like I was constantly having to, like, *survey* all of the other coaches and *watch* their every move and make sure that I replicate that, exactly that way. Yeah, that's pretty much what it is.

[How did that feel to you?]

I was very frustrated. I was very stressed. I felt extremely, um, I just felt *this big* [*holding her thumb and forefinger barely apart*]. *Small,* like I could never measure up, I could never be, *the coach.* I never felt good; I felt like I sucked. Like, everyone's looking at me [saying], "*Kate Kaplan* is the worst coach ever!"

Kaplan's lack of access to the "unwritten rules" and the "secret language" of the insiders made her feel incompetent, "small," and negatively judged. Ultimately, these kinds of feelings made it difficult for her to see herself legitimately as being able to "measure up" as *the coach.* She turned out to be a Stopper—one year in, and then out—and suspected that others saw her as "the worst coach ever."

Though their stories were not as extreme as Kate Kaplan's, other women coaches talked of how they struggled with feeling like an outsider with limited access to informal information. Several of the women coaches described the workings of AYSO and LLB/S as "an old boys' club," as "male dominated," or as a "good ol' boys' network." These terms invoke images of backroom politics, of entrenched control by a few men. Joan Ring laughed as she described the meeting where the soccer coaches chose the All-Star team: "You have this really long meeting where you all talk about every single player—it takes hours—and then you vote. And there was like three female coaches, and we were laughing because it's basically like twelve other [men] coaches, and it's like Boy Scouts, where it's like, 'Oh, your daughter was so good. I think everyone's in agreement here that Joe Schmoe's daughter is just a fabulous player.' So, it's just like we've got like this good ol' boys' network." Ellen Lessing repeated an "old boys' network" rumor that I heard several times (sometimes about Little League, other times about AYSO) but was never able to verify:

> There are a group of men, in softball and AYSO, who grew up together in South Pasadena and who are reliving their youth by organizing the sports, and they have fun at it. I heard that they like to sit at the same table at Gus's B-B-Q, because it is the table that the old head of AYSO used to sit at, you know, in high school, with his buddies. So there's a deeper history to it, that somebody [new] who is coming to a meeting saying "Can we make a girls' team?" doesn't know about. It is not necessarily malicious. But, uh, it's just . . .

Whether the story about the inner-circle of men meeting regularly at a local restaurant and bar is true or not, the fact that this story was repeated speaks to the women coaches' sense of being excluded from the

informal circles of power. Like backroom corporate executives or politicians, these informal networks of men coaches *rule* youth sports organizations. And one of the major ways that they rule is by circulating stories
and information that become like the "secret language" that so befuddled Kate Kaplan and Nina Ramos, along with the other women coaches
who broke into coaching assuming that their formal knowledge of the
game and their experience in working with kids would be enough. For
these two Stoppers, it was not enough.

WOMEN COACHES' GENDER STRATEGIES

I have argued above that women coaches within youth sports bump up
against gendered barriers that are created through everyday, informal
interactions, rather than through conscious discrimination or overt sexism. The fact that these barriers are informal makes them less visible,
and thus very powerful in shaping women's choices and experiences. If
the issue were simply the presence of a few overtly sexist men, it would
be clear what was causing women's troubles. To the contrary, as we have
seen, many women coaches punctuated their stories about their problems in coaching by emphasizing that the men coaches are really "good
guys." Lacking evil sexist men to blame, and lacking an analysis of gender as a dynamic of organizations, many women coaches are left to wonder about their own "lack of confidence" and to tell stories of personal
"decisions" to quit coaching, or to cycle back, rather than talking about
being squeezed out of coaching.

On the other hand, some women coaches manage to survive, and a
few actually thrive. How do they do it? Sociologist James Messerschmidt
argues that there are "situationally dominant gender practices in particular settings."[8] Women and men tend to mobilize different resources,
and they are held accountable for "doing gender" in ways that are consistent with the expectations within a setting. Youth coaches are "accountable" for certain practices in the context of coaching. As we have
seen, women coaching the youngest kids' teams can negotiate these
expectations by importing conventionally "feminine" practices (what I

have called kids-knowledge). But as they move up the age groupings, the context changes, and coaches are increasingly accountable to have and display sports-knowledge. Women with lots of sports background have a harder time than men in achieving legitimacy as coaches when they mobilize their sports-knowledge. This dilemma creates for women coaches what Messerschmidt calls "gender challenges," which are "contextually embodied interactions that result in gender degradation."[9] Coaches lack a language of gender (for the most part) to talk about these challenges, so they emerge in the interviews couched in an individualized language of women's "lacking confidence," which then leads women to conclude that the men just "have more confidence" to rise above the challenges and fears of degradation. As we will see in the next chapter, this unitary view of the confident man is extremely oversimplified. For now, I want to focus on how women deploy certain strategies to confront gender challenges and to avoid degradation.

Women coaches' gender strategies are similar to those described by social scientists who have studied the experiences of women pioneers in previously all-male professions. In her classic study of women in corporations, sociologist Rosabeth Moss Kanter argued that the proportion of women in an organization shapes how women are viewed and treated, and also sets parameters that limit the ways that women can maneuver in the organization.[10] Kanter described organizations where the proportion of women was 15 percent or less as "skewed"; organizations where the proportion of women was between 16 percent and 35 percent she described as "tilted." Women in a "skewed" organization tend to suffer from numerous disadvantages attached to tokenism, including lack of access to informal networks of support and advancement. Drawing from Kanter, in her study of women coaches in elite Canadian sports Nancy Theberge argued that, as tokens, these women experienced "heightened visibility and performance pressures."[11]

The proportion of women in South Pasadena LLB/S averaged 5.9 percent during the course of my study, which placed them firmly and consistently within the "skewed" range and put women coaches in the position of being "tokens." Theberge argues that in highly skewed organizations women's strategies are severely constrained by their high visibility as tokens. Those who survive tend to deploy two strategies: "fitting in" by appearing to be "one of the boys," albeit one who is exceptional compared with other women; and "demonstrating ability" and thus proving that you can play with the boys. Through these strategies, the token woman who succeeds in the skewed organization does so by setting herself off from other women, becoming a kind of "fictive," or "honorary," man (albeit one who is always still subject to a double standard in proving herself as a legitimate coach).[12] As I will show, some of the Gamers in my study—especially in LLB/S—deploy this sort of individualistic strategy.

By contrast, in South Pasadena AYSO, the proportion of women coaches averaged 13 percent during my study, and nudged up to 14 percent in 2005, 16 percent in 2006, and 19 percent in 2007, bringing the proportions to the threshold of what Kanter called a "tilted" organization. Women in "tilted" organizations also often suffer disadvantages, but they at least have access to small networks of women coworkers who potentially can offer support and become sources of informal mentoring. This higher proportion of women in soccer clearly helps to open up some of this kind of elbow room for women coaches. I argued in chapter 1 that the differently gendered history of soccer in the United States, compared with baseball, has contributed to a different gender regime and a different set of gendered meanings about these sports. To reiterate briefly, men tend to feel that they "own" baseball (and often, by extension, softball), but most U.S.-born men did not grow up playing soccer and thus don't feel as much emotional connection, knowledge, or "ownership" of soccer. This different gendered history and the higher numbers of women coaches in soccer work together to create some space within which women maneuver, as participants and as coaches.

Context matters. Several women soccer coaches said that they would never consider coaching in baseball. As Ellen Lessing put it, for a mom to be a coach "is more accepted in soccer, I think, than in basketball or softball, because, you know, the Anglo population did not play it. A lot of the dads in soccer are going, 'Well, I didn't play it, I don't know anything about it.' Whereas in softball or in basketball, they're kinda like, 'Hey, this is our arena.' So it is a little easier [for women] at that entry level in soccer." And Nancy Morris said bluntly of coaching baseball, "I don't think there's a woman out there who has the guts to just go out there and do it. I'd be surprised if I ever saw a woman coach a baseball team other than like T-ball. In baseball it's still a man's world, so I don't believe that there's any encouraging of mothers to step up and get up there and coach."

Several women who had coached both AYSO and LLB/S said that the formal training they got in AYSO contributed enormously to building their knowledge and confidence. By contrast, this kind of training was mostly unavailable in LLB/S. On the other hand, as I have argued thus far, many of the barriers facing women coaches are informal. Organizational structures, like formal training sessions for coaches, do matter, but the people who are *running* these trainings matter too. Kathi Ralston attended a regional AYSO training for coaches and one for referees, and was appalled at how sexist the guys who taught the classes were. She and the woman coach she attended the classes with were made to feel invisible, or like unwelcome outsiders:

> I went to the referee class and it was all men—very few women. And the man who ran it was an older guy—he'd reffed for like thirty years. And he talked about refs *as* men, which looking around the room [*chuckles*] seemed to be a fair representation. But it did bother me. And he talked about the kids as boys. He definitely talked about the coaches as men. And then the one example he had as a woman ref—he had these scenarios, where he would say, 'What would you do as a ref?'—and the scenario where he had a woman ref, she was making a *mistake* in the scenario! (*Laughs.*) So I was sort of struck by that. At the coaches class, the one head coach would talk very quickly about some things, and a woman coach near the front raised her hand and said, "I'm sorry, I don't understand." And he went very quickly through it again, and *then, on purpose,* he jumped way up to some sort of college level, and I could tell everybody was confused, and [the woman coach] next to me whispered, "This guy's a bit of a jerk." And then he pointed back at the woman and he said, "And if you understand *that . . .*"—and he kind of belittled her. And I doubted that he would have done that to a male coach. I just felt that he felt free to do that.

How do women coaches survive within such a context? In this section, I will discuss three strategies—looking and acting the part; being competitive; co-coaching with men—that some women coaches use to navigate their way around the informal barriers that they routinely face.

Looking and Acting the Part

When many people think "coach," they automatically (and unconsciously) assume "man." Therefore, like women in professional fields of employment, women coaches are often very conscious of the importance of looking the part of a coach. The vignette that opened this chapter described women soccer coaches' dismay when, at the beginning of the season, they found that the league had not ordered coaches' shirts that fit them. They were faced with a challenge: don't wear the shirt and risk reinforcing the perception that they weren't really coaches; or wear the shirt and look ridiculous (or, as Ellen Lessing said, like you're "pregnant") in a shirt that hangs to your knees. An ill-fitting shirt would not likely be as huge a problem for men coaches, but women coaches are aware that that they are being scrutinized—that they have to prove that they are "really coaches." The first time I saw Lillian Morh coaching on a soccer field, I noticed that she wore a whistle around her neck but she never seemed to use it. A few weeks later, when I interviewed her, I asked her about the whistle, and she affirmed that she never uses it, wearing it only for effect: "It makes me look like the coach." And that led her to talk about how she had dealt with the too-large coaches' shirts:

> I don't wear my coach's shirt. The league ordered a bunch of mediums, larges, and extra larges. There's never any smalls ordered. And I said, "Do you think you could send me one small shirt so it actually fits me?" And then [the league head] said, "Why don't you send me three smalls?" So they sent me three smalls—this is hilarious because they're still sittin' over there: they don't have "coach" on 'em! Even Board of Directors' shirts: we order men's sizes and the mediums. I mean, I'm tiny, but the mediums never fit me. I've never worn my coach's shirt, and I've said, "Why don't we order these in women's sizes?" And, in fact, for opening day I said, "I am buying my own shirt that says 'Board of Directors' 'cause my other one is ugly and doesn't fit me." And I ordered a women's small and had my own shirts made.

Mohr's strategies—to wear a whistle, to pay to have her own small-sized shirt made—can be seen as responses to the gender challenge she faced as a woman coach. Others reported that they strategized to look and act the part of being a coach by consciously displaying sports-knowledge and attitudes that they hoped would win them respect. Delores Quintero, a softball coach who is a Gamer, has specific gender strategies that she deploys to get respect on the field. About her strategy for dealing with a new umpire, she said:

> It's like you need to prove yourself because [an umpire's] assumption is that you probably lack knowledge and ability and you probably need help. Well, I'm a very take-charge, leadership kind of person. So I come off as a very strong personality, particularly on the field. You know, you talk about "game face." I smile and I conduct myself appropriately, but at the same time, I think my manner has somehow made the officials maybe take note that, "Okay, I think this one maybe knows what she's doing or what she's saying here." For example, we're meeting [with the umpires] for ground rules on the field and I'll be very specific about certain things I'm asking, and right there they're starting to pick up that oh, okay, they have to answer questions that maybe they hadn't thought about. So I put them in a position where they have to show *me* what *they* know. I'll ask about equipment: "Have you taken a look at those bats? I was looking at a bat over there and I'm not sure if it's legal. What kind of ball are we using?" I'll ask them some questions that will make them think and a lot people may not be asking, and when that happens then they become a little bit defensive almost—and I don't do it to attack, I just do it to let them know I'm very thorough and I want to make sure everything is just right.

On the softball field, Quintero strategically and consciously displays an assertive and confident demeanor—a "game face"—to gain the respect of the men. And she purposely uses her deep knowledge of the game to put a new umpire on the defensive: "they have to show *me* what *they* know." She imagines that this strategy leads the umpire to see her as a kind of exception: while other women "probably lack knowledge and ability . . . this one maybe knows what she's doing." Similarly, Rosa Ramirez, another Gamer in girls' softball, attributes her successes to the fact that she is not like most of the other women:

I tend to think I'm different from a lot of the moms out here.

[In which way?]

In the respect that I—I'm very vocal. I speak my mind, and sometimes these dads come out and sometimes try to make you feel like, oh you don't really know, and I don't put up with that. I just don't. There's no reason why I should, so I don't. You have a lot of moms out here who have this, "Oh, I don't know anything," you know—*timid*—and that just blows me away, because I'm sure that when it comes to your business or whatever career you are in, you're not like that. You know, it's the same type of thing. I mean, why should you feel inferior to a man? There's no reason for it. And I [am] well known: even the umpires, they tease and [say], "Oh no, here she comes." But I speak my mind.

Ramirez uses verbal assertiveness to demand respect as a coach: "I speak my mind." And like Delores Quintero, her gender strategy positions her as an exception, as different from most of the other moms, whom she disparages as "timid" in the sports context. It was striking to me that the women we interviewed who were most likely to adopt the most assertive stance in this regard tended to be women of color—three Latinas, an Asian-Pacific Islander, a Filipina, and a woman of mixed racial/ethnic background. Though I will develop more analysis of race in chapter 6, I want simply to note here that Latina and Asian American women are often stereotyped as less assertive and tending toward quiet subservience to men. This is certainly not true of the women of color in my study.

Being Competitive

The official ethic underlying the AYSO and LLB/S is to downplay competition. At the lower age-levels of soccer and T-ball, no official score is even kept in games, but parents will joke, often with a wink, that coaches (and some of the parents) actually do keep track of the scores and always know who "won" the game. In the higher age-groups, it becomes more and more competitive, and this is one of the main factors that leads women coaches who emphasize kids-knowledge and a participation ethic to quit coaching or to cycle back to stay with young kids. But those who do move up, the Gamers, have to adjust their philosophies and strategies in order to survive in the more competitive age groupings. Joan Ring is a Gamer in soccer and is well known by parents and other coaches as a model of "positive" coaching: she emphasizes participation and fun, and feels that it's important to rotate kids around so that they can learn and experience different positions on the soccer field. But this strategy, she found, put her teams at a disadvantage when playing against coaches who placed greater value on winning.

> My feeling is they stress winning too much. I mean, I do not believe it should be that way, because you start making decisions just to win and you're not making decisions to coach out of a want to teach girls better skills. I mean, maybe a girl you have on the defense, they just scored ten goals on her, but actually in the long run that will be good for that girl and maybe for your team. If you're just thinking about winning, you don't have any time to spend on that. You just have to go for the win. Like last year—always before, I rotated all the girls to every position. I thought that was right. And then later on I thought, why don't [the other coaches] rotate them? Well, we'd get slaughtered, because then the other team immediately got their defense set and that's how they [won]. So that's what I'm gonna do this year. So, yeah, but I think if there weren't winning, it would be so much better. They just emphasize it way too much. Even though AYSO does not mention winning in any of their materials—you know, balanced teams, everybody plays, have fun. There's nothing about winning. But it's *all* about winning.

Ring's words register her disapproval of the ways that coaches' strategies undermine the officially stated AYSO values (which she shares) of balance, participation, and fun. But she also reports that holding to these values led her teams to get "slaughtered," so this year, she had decided to stop rotating her kids around so much and to follow suit and develop more competitively successful strategies. All youth coaches face the challenge of navigating this tension between being competitive enough and not being overly competitive ("too serious"), and the range within which women coaches can carve out a strategy is especially narrow. Softball coach Jessica Torres described the tension between the competition and her own values as creating agonizing decisions for her:

> I really wanted to make a point of not coming to win. I really wanted to teach the girls to play well and learn to love this game and want to come

back next season. I really wanted to try to not make it just about winning—wanted to play, to learn to get along and be a team. And part of that was having the girls play more than one position, so that they could feel comfortable out in the field and not think that, "Oh, I'm just the first baseman. I can play other positions." Some parents were not happy with that, and I tried to explain it to them, how my philosophy wasn't about winning, [and] not to feel discouraged [*slight laugh*] because we hadn't won a game, [but] I see a lot of improvement and I see the girls having fun. Towards the end of the season, Ella was pitching really well, and that's when another parent wanted me to put in her daughter. And I said, "Um, we're really getting to the end of the season here, we have like five or six games left. And although we haven't won a game, and I've said it many times that it's not just about winning, I'm beginning to think that maybe it would really do something for these girls to win one game, so unless Ella's pitching really really bad, I don't expect to pull her out of the game." Even my other coaches were saying, "Jessica, you can't do it; if we're close to winning a game, you have to let the girls try to be able to win a game." I didn't wanna be not liked, I guess, and I was really trying to please everyone. And some coaches told me that I made a mistake by doing that as well. And I think, you know, it's true: you just can't please everyone. And not that you have to be mean to people, but, um, I don't know, I still haven't really figured out how I'm gonna play that one next time around [*laughs*].

[You are still planning to manage next year?]

Yes, I think so. I think at the end of the season, I was like, "Ugh, I can't do this again!" But now that I've had a break from the stares and the looks and the complaints—I feel I love this game, so I think I still want to be involved at this level.

Torres mostly held fast to her noncompetitive ethic, but she did make the decision to stay with her best pitcher, rather than to give other girls an opportunity to pitch, on the chance that they might win a game. She knew that either way, "You just can't please everybody." And though she said in the interview that she thought she'd continue coaching the next year, she didn't. She was a one-year Stopper, and it's likely that this tension between her values and the competitive ethic in the higher-aged teams was part of her decision not to coach again. A few women coaches seem fully to embrace the competitive ethic. Delores Quintero, who prides herself in her competitiveness, described herself as a "survivor" who was known to be a very successful coach of championship teams.

> [In] South Pasadena, it's generally very men-controlled, and I've found some opposition there to my competitive nature. A couple other coaches accused [me] of having a chip on my shoulder because they didn't agree with some of my strategies. They didn't like what was happening. I don't put winning above everything else, but let's face it: you join something, you wanna win. I'm an open book. I don't hold back. It's obvious I'm competitive. And for me to bring it as a woman, I think there were a few men that were threatened.

> [So, how did they respond to you then?]

> Somewhat negative. They liked those championships that came to the program. So I found there were some men that wanted to take credit for a program, because they'd been in it for a while. And I let it be. I don't need to be the center of attention. My purpose is there with the children. I wanna win, and I teach kids how to win gracefully, without talkin'. I don't like big mouths, I don't like a lot of talk. And so you show me on the field and then, that's it. And like I said, I just found that there were men that opposed my style. I saw them throw the ball! *Ha!* I could see 'em throwing the ball around and analyze that they haven't had a lot of experience themselves! They told me that I had a chip on my shoulder. I've been used to getting put down by men and even women all my way up the ladder. When you start reaching a higher level, I'm hearing them say stuff. I think some of them had a chip on *their* shoulder because maybe I brought something to the table that they didn't have—and I don't even want to go into that I'm Hispanic, okay? I don't even wanna play that card, 'kay? But I'll play the woman card plenty. Yup.

What Quintero, Ring, and Torres described is a gendered double standard: if women are not competitive as coaches, their teams will get "slaughtered" and they are unlikely to be taken seriously as coaches; if they are very competitive—even successfully so—then they are open to criticism for being *too* competitive, for "having a chip on my shoulder."

Men as Buffers

Women coaches' gender strategies—trying to look and act the part; being competitive but not too competitive—often leave them very little space within which to maneuver. One strategy that seems to create more maneuvering room for women coaches is co-managing with a man, often one's husband. Delores Quintero has teamed with her husband for fourteen years: "Baseball, he was the manager, I was the coach. Softball, I was the manager, he was the coach. My husband and I were quite a duo." As we have seen, Quintero sees herself as a highly competitive and successful coach. However, her words also suggest that her husband serves at times as a kind of buffer for her: "I did find times when adult parents would really observe closely to verify whether or not I really knew what I was doing or what was going on. When I worked with my husband, I would always let him kind of take the lead, particularly in the early stages of the T-ball/Baseball years. And so I was more of his assistant, so it wasn't a big factor."

Nancy Morris co-coaches soccer with her husband. Her words suggest that perhaps his presence opens space for her to mobilize her kids-knowledge in ways that insulate her from criticism that otherwise might come to a woman coach who deemphasizes competition. When we asked if she felt respected as a coach, she responded with the plural, "we": "Yes—we feel very respected out there. . . . It's just the whole relationships—[my husband] and I as managers. I think it might be easier for us because one of our goals in coaching or managing is having fun. And having fun with the girls, and teaching like team spirit, and not being as competitive as many other coaches are being competitive."

As a gender strategy, co-coaching with a man appears to broaden the space within which a woman coach can maneuver. This appears especially to be true in LLB/S; two of the four women Gamers that we interviewed in softball co-managed with their husband, and one had her husband as an assistant coach. However, the following field note from a girls' softball game raises questions about whether this strategy might also prevent women coaches from being seen fully as leaders:

> I sit down next to Beth, a mom I know. Her ten-year-old daughter's softball team is in the field. I ask her who the manager is. "Oh, we've got the greatest manager, Willy. He's so good with the girls. We are so lucky to have him." Another mother, sitting behind us, concurs: "Yeah, Willy is so terrific." I tell them that I'm doing a study on youth coaches, comparing

the experiences of women and men coaches, and say that it's hard to find women baseball or softball coaches to interview, since there are so few. Beth says, "Oh, we've got a woman co-manager on our team, Rosa! It's a husband-wife team." It turns out it's Rosa Ramirez, whom we have interviewed, but as I scan the field looking for Rosa, I don't see her immediately. Indeed, while their team was in the field, Willy was visibly out on the field, standing, squatting, verbally positioning the girls; Rosa was in the dugout. When the team came to bat, Rosa coached third base. It strikes me as funny that, initially, Beth and the other mother in the stands had spoken of Willy as the manager, and didn't seem to think of Rosa until I mentioned my research.

I found it interesting, in reflecting on this field observation, to recall Rosa's response to our interview question about whether she feels that parents fully respect her as a coach. "Yes, I'm fortunate enough that I have that support. I mean, it's known that my husband is signed up as manager, but it's my team and they know it." But when I glimpsed Rosa and her husband during that game, through the eyes of two parents in the stands, it led me to wonder: *Do these mothers actually see Rosa as her husband's "assistant"?*

Co-managing with a man, as a gender strategy, clearly helps some women survive and thrive in a male-dominated context. This, and the other individual strategies I have discussed above, are useful in helping a few women "tokens" to fit in. However, these strategies rarely if ever seem to challenge the gendered barriers in the organization in ways that might lead to change. To the contrary, most of these women seem to be "doing gender" in ways that simultaneously give them enough elbow room to work in a "men's world," while not challenging the dominant values or the gender dynamics of this world. However, there are other dynamics, and other signs of challenge and possible change.

CHALLENGING THE CENTRALITY OF MEN

I have argued thus far that much of women coaches' agency can be defined as "reproductive"—that is, their actions for the most part reproduce, rather than challenge, the structures of AYSO and LLB/S. However, it is overly simplistic to conclude that women coaches are always "doing gender" in ways that keep these organizations in stasis. There is plenty of evidence that the very fact of the women's presence as leaders on the kids' athletics fields is disrupting a long-standing gender binary that places men in positions of public authority and control and women in positions of domestic support. Women coaches are out there on the playing fields, demonstrating to themselves, to other women, to men, and to the kids that women can be leaders in sports. This in and of itself is a radical statement, especially given sport's historic role as an institution through which ideas of men's "natural superiority" over women are constructed and naturalized. To adapt a term from Francine Deutsch, the very existence of women coaches may contribute to "undoing gender."[13] For example, even in the midst of a horrific season during which her team was losing nearly every game and she felt she was a failure, Kate Kaplan's presence as the only woman softball coach in the girls' majors league made a difference:

> It actually caused some moms to start rumbling about the fact that aren't any female coaches in the league and that this was the first time that they had seen [one]. I had one mom pull me aside. "Come here for a second." I said, "Okay." And I went over there and stood next to her and she was like, "You know"—she kinda whispers—"I just want to let you know that you are just great and there are a lot of moms that are talking about you and it is about time. You know, these dads have been running this league for as long as I can remember, and we just need to get more women in there."

Women coaches disrupt the gender regime and contribute to change in ways that go beyond their mere presence. Some see themselves as pioneers who are blazing a trail for other women. Carol Morris said that she feared she would fail and be publicly exposed as a bad coach, but her words expressed a stubborn toughness in the face of men's skepticism: "I made it very clear to these dads, I'm going out there and I'm going to do my best, and if I fail, well I failed, but I know that I've tried. And if I succeed, great, maybe there'll more moms will come out."

Some of the longer-term women coaches—especially in soccer—are active in recruiting, inspiring and mentoring other women to coach.

Several women we interviewed talked about Joan Ring as an inspiration for women AYSO coaches. Wendy Lytle says she was inspired to become a coach by watching Ring coach her daughter. Veronica Leonard learned from watching Ring how to coach in a way that foregrounds kids-knowledge and positive values, even in the context of a highly competitive atmosphere. "Joan is so patient and she's so positive. And at the end of every practice and after every game she gives each girl like a positive reinforcement comment—a detailed thing about what they did that was so great. And on the way home in the car my daughter remembers it and she says it back to me. She's like, 'She told me I was a tough player.' I mean, that to me is what I want the experience to be—positive like that." Ring is also an advocate. After she had been nosed out of coaching, Ellen Lessing says Joan Ring (then serving also as a league official) said to her " 'How come you're not coaching? We should have women.' I said, 'Well I *did* sign up.' And she was shocked and she said, 'Next year, for every woman who signs up, I'm going to make sure that they get chosen, because there aren't many women who even sign up.' " This kind of feminist advocacy by women for women is far more apparent in AYSO than in LLB/S.

Several women said that they felt supported by being able to talk with other women coaches. Ellen Lessing said, "I just think, you know, when I coach against [she names three other women coaches], there's just a feeling of, we know each other, we're friends, you know, we have a different connection. You know it is just the camaraderie. [When] I meet another female coach, I have this, 'Oh, I don't know you, tell me about yourself.' That isn't there with the male coaches." Similarly, Shelley Parsons said she felt very isolated as one of the very few women coaches, but felt buoyed that there were two other women coaches in her girls' under-8 soccer league. A conversation with a fellow woman coach gave them both the opportunity to valorize approaches to coaching that differed from those of the men: "It was nice to see another female coaching. And one of them came up to me and said, 'I like the way you coach. All you said was nice things to your kids.' She goes, 'Some of these guys are real jerks, aren't they?' I say, 'Yeah, they are, because some of the guys yell and scream *'Go for it, go for it!'*' " These comments from soccer coaches hint at the fact that numbers do matter. Kanter said that corporate culture was not changed by the simple existence of a few token women; however, she hypothesized that there might be a "tipping point," when the proportion of women in an organization reaches a critical mass where women might begin to change the culture and values of the organization. AYSO is far from reaching this "tipping point," but women's comments about the value of seeing, talking with, and learning from other women coaches suggest that this kind of change is possible.[14] It appears that within AYSO—by 2006–7 a "tilted" organization, in terms of its proportion of women coaches—there is a growing space for women to move beyond the individualist gender strategies typical of isolated tokens in "skewed" organizations like LLB/S.

In fact, some of the women coaches who had complained about the dominance of the "old boys' network" in AYSO seemed consciously to be building a new network of women. Terri Patrick said that she sees herself as "an active recruiter of other female coaches." Several women we interviewed mentioned Joan Ring and Barbara Jones as being at the center of an effort to build a supportive network of women soccer coaches. Jones confirmed this:

> I actually have suggested to some of the women—Joan and Pam—that we ought to have a woman coach's night, just like a pizza and beer, or pizza and Diet Coke, or whatever you want to call it, where we just get together and we can grouse about the guys on the sideline that are out of control, and just kind of talk about what's goin' on in the season—just have fun. Not that I wouldn't want to have guys there, but I think at some point when you don't have a critical mass—you know, I don't want to say it's affirmative action—but we don't have a critical mass of a certain kind of people, maybe you want to outreach and try to bring them in.

In addition to recruiting and supporting other women, some of the women coaches spoke of women's presence as a positive example for girls to emulate. Rosa Ramirez was taken aback when she saw that a girl she was trying to help on the field took her less seriously than she did the male coach. "She actually looked at me like, 'Are you serious? You don't know what you're talking about.' And then her [male] coach came over and told her the exact same thing and her reaction was very different. And then I realized that there's a problem with a girl's sport being managed and coached by just men to the point where if a woman tells a girl something, they don't believe that you really know what you're doing. So it was last year that I decided I was going to take a team this year. And I try to encourage other mothers to do it." A few women, like Delores Quintero, said that they consciously strive to encourage their own daughters to become involved as coaches:

> It's been tough working in a man's world. In fact, I'll share with you the advice that I gave to my daughters and sometimes I'll tell others: in the game of softball, baseball, whatever—it's all about strikes, right? I tell them, "Look, girls: strike one, okay, you're a woman. Strike two: you're a Hispanic woman. Don't strike out girls. I'm sending you out the door with two strikes. You've gotta be tough." That's what I tell my girls.

For Quintero, this toughening up of her daughters extends to learning to be coaches themselves in the future:

> My kids—I get 'em out there and help. As I started coaching my two youngest girls in softball, I had my two oldest kids come and show up sometimes to assist with certain drills or to just offer help with throwing techniques, catching, maybe. I bring my daughter who was a shortstop for years and say, "You know what? I'd like you to work with my shortstop this afternoon, so why don't ya come to practice?" So my kids have been raised to share their knowledge, and I've noticed that they're all pretty good at it, so it's nice. I'm looking forward to coaching again and have my daughters assist me.

Similarly, Jessica Torres, who worked many years as an assistant coach and had recently started managing her own team, says of her daughter:

> My daughter's not going to be one of those softball players that goes to college, but she loves the game, you know. I said, "Well, you can still coach, you can be an umpire." I wanted her to help me as well, so she would come out on occasion and work with our catchers, 'cause she is a catcher. I wanted her to get that aspect of it too, [so] that maybe she'll start coaching someday. You know, again: getting more women to do this kind of work.

Like Torres, Delores Quintero saw herself as more than a "role model" for girls to emulate. She actively encouraged the girls on her team to stay in the game as coaches:

> It's one of those speeches that I always have for my teams: Girls, please. We need you in this game. Come back and give your time to other girls. If you love this game then teach it to somebody younger than you, officiate the game, become a student of the game, and really pass that along. Someday, most of you girls are going to be moms. You don't want to just let Dad do all that stuff. Not when you've got this kind of experience. You want to do it too.

In contrast to women coaches' individualized strategies for survival as tokens, these *collective* strategies by women coaches can lead to structural changes in youth sports organizations. When women actively recruit other women, build supportive networks for women coaches, and consciously socialize girls in ways that encourage them to become future coaches, their efforts promise to increase the numbers of women, creating more space for a wider range of approaches to coaching and thus the possibility that men will be decentered from their positions of domination and control in the organizations (and, as we will see in the next chapter, opening space for the participation of different kinds of men). For now though, these women are still very much a minority, operating at the margins of organizations that are still dominated by men. What is the experience of these men? The next chapter will focus on this question.

FOUR

"You Don't Have to be
a Drill Sergeant"

MEN AT THE HELM

I am enjoying dinner on a warm July evening in the yard of Will Solomon, the coach of my son Sasha's 11–12-year-old summer baseball team. Will had volunteered to coach during this "lower-key," summer season, he said, because the spring Major League season had been "a very bad experience" for his son, who "was really bummed about baseball at that point, and I thought that was a shame." "It gets so serious at that level," Will explained, and he hoped that by coaching summer league, he'd give his son a "positive experience" with baseball. Will did turn out to be a fun and supportive coach, very low-key and good with all the kids. I especially appreciated his style, because Sasha too had had a less than successful spring season. After a couple of summer games, I noticed—even though in this league there were more talented players than in the spring league—that Sasha was swinging the bat better and making good, consistent contact, sometimes ripping solid line-drive hits. It seemed to me that Sasha was just more relaxed, looser, and I attributed that to the lower pressure, the fun context that Will had created on the team. I asked Will if he intended to volunteer to coach next spring, during the regular season, and his response was unequivocal: "*Ha!* There's *no way* I'll coach in the Majors next spring. Anyway, I doubt they'd have me." A few weeks later, when I interviewed Will, I asked why he doubted he'd be accepted as a Majors manager, and he said, "I figure I'd be considered not serious enough." "I don't get it," I said. "You are a great coach, and I'm not sure too many people in town have more sports experience than you." "I guess it's a couple of things," he explained. "One, I don't think they'd want me to because I'm not as focused on the baseball side of it as I am on the sort of kids side of it, and I think [in the Majors] they start to get real serious about the baseball side. And the other thing is that there does form sort of a club among these coaches at the Major League level which I didn't see at the American and National level. These guys, they're coming out [to games] when their teams aren't playing, to watch the other teams and scout 'em, you know, and [to] understand how different hitters hit and how different pitchers are pitching and stuff—I'm just not interested enough to do that. So I think probably they wouldn't want me, you know. I mean the *kids* would. But the coaches, the powers-that-be wouldn't."

Women coaches tend to contrast their own struggles with a view of men coaches as almost uniformly "confident," even when the men lack coaching and/or athletic playing experience. While there is some truth to this perception, my observations and interviews reveal a wider range of experiences among the men coaches. We will see in this chapter that some men coaches, in fact, struggle to muster the self-confidence needed to become a coach. And as the composite field note and interview segment with Will Solomon that opens this chapter suggests, some men, like many of the women coaches, have to grapple with managing the tension between an emphasis on kids-knowledge and one on sports-knowledge.

Will Solomon's words introduce another important theme of this chapter: although the vast majority of coaches are men, they don't share equally in the power and public status of coaching. In fact, among the men who coach youth sports there is a hierarchy that is expressed in two dimensions. First, certain types of men are selected out of coaching by what I call the "gender-sorting system." I will describe how men coaches' on-field displays of masculinity (including especially the use of their bodies and voices in the gendered space of the playing field) become increasingly narrow as they move from the younger age-levels of sports to the older age-levels. We saw in chapter 3 how the same process resulted in the selecting-out of women coaches who emphasized kids-knowledge in the approach to coaching. In this chapter, I will show how this gender-sorting system also selects out the men who are less "serious" about sports, and how in this community the most honored form of masculine display for men coaches ultimately becomes one of quiet control, characteristic of hegemonic masculinity in professional-class work and family settings. Second, we will see how this gender-sorting process reflects and re-creates an "inner-circle" of men who set the tone, run the show, and make other men, like Will Solomon, feel either like outsiders or like marginal participants who doubt that they'd be "accepted" as coaches by the "powers-that-be."

BECOMING A COACH

Some men saw their initial decision to coach their kids as the expected, normal thing for a dad to do. Mark Daly said that when it came time for his child to start youth sports, he just jumped right into coaching. "I don't think it was really a question—I think it just happened. I mean, I think it was assumed. I don't know if I made a conscious decision one way or the other." Similarly, Tony Barnett said, "Oh, I think it becomes the thing to do. You know these organizations all need parents to coach, I mean, there's lots of kids, and if you're not coaching, you know, the question is how else are you going to contribute? And coaching seemed more fun. So, I think it's just one of the things you do."

Most of the men, though, were not uniformly confident in their abilities to be head coaches, and a few spoke of fears, of a lack of "comfort" and of doubts that they could or should take on the more high-profile position of head coach. More than the women coaches, a major source of many of the men's initial doubts was a perceived lack of *time.* Nearly all of these men are holding down full-time, often highly demanding jobs and professional positions. Many said that they wondered, at first, whether they could commit themselves to the hours it would take to practice, prepare, and play games. I will discuss this issue of gender relations and time in the context of work, family, and community volunteerism more extensively in chapter 6. For now, I want simply to note that many of the men coaches feared—at least initially—that there would be a tension between their careers and their ability to commit to the head coaching job. The men we interviewed found ways to negotiate this tension during Little League or soccer seasons. And most of them eased into coaching through a year or two of assistant coaching.

The assistant coach position, as we saw in chapter 2, is the most common point of entrée into the coaching pipeline, and men tend to be ushered directly into this position, while many women are diverted away from it, toward the "team-parent" position. Indeed, the men rarely spoke of becoming an assistant coach as anything but a simple personal decision on their part. And once in the coaching pipeline, most of the men found that the doubts or fears they had had about coaching were alleviated. Soccer coach Tony Barnett said that his time as an assistant coach taught him both the technical knowledge about soccer and some important interpersonal skills. As he watched the other men coaches, he realized that one of the key skills he needed to develop concerned projecting a level of self-confidence that he didn't necessarily feel: "I think I've learned from Dale and some of the other coaches that I've watched that you have to have a certain amount of, uh—whether you're feeling it or not, you have to project a kinda self-confidence—like I say, even if it's there or not."

Many of the men were actively recruited from the assistant to the head coaching ranks. Doug Berger was helping out as an assistant softball coach, and before he knew it, it seemed, he found himself "volunteered" to manage a team.

> I think I was volunteered—Yeah, it was my daughter and, they were putting a team together and I got volunteered to that, come to think of it. Didn't ask me much about experience, but thankfully, I knew what I was doing. I don't remember any kind of interview, asking me "Ok, well what do you know?" Yeah, I was volunteered.

George Starr also found himself recruited out of the assistant coaches' ranks. At first, he was "just a helpful parent, so they asked if I wanted to be a manager for the minor program." And after some reluctance, he said, "Okay, I'll do it." As assistant coaches, Berger and Starr had become members of the coaching network and were now fair game for recruitment into head coaching. Other men, though, spoke of having volunteered after watching others coach their kids and concluding that they could do better. Most of these men were drawing on enormous wells of athletic experience, in organized high school, college, and, in a couple of cases, professional sports. Albert Riley, who played baseball for a local university and then a few years of professional ball, said that the reason why he got into coaching was "because I saw the way that they were coaching and I preferred doing the coaching myself. And really I have much more background, as far as participation, than the majority of these people, so I felt that that I had a expertise in these areas so I could do it. I felt that I could do a better job of doing it." Most of the men we interviewed had not played professional sports. More typical was the response of Don Clark, who, when asked what sports he had played in the past, laughed and said:

> The list would probably be shorter if I tell you what I *didn't* do. Almost every sport: I played Little League Baseball, soccer starting at nine years of age, played flag and tackle football, basketball, regular baseball, what else? . . . Swam competitively, surf, ski. . . . The soccer and Little League baseball were non–school related, the swimming was non–school related . . . the basketball, some of the baseball, and the football were all school-related.

As we saw in the previous chapter, some of the women coaches too had a great deal of athletic experience to draw from. But the men's stories speak generally to a lifelong immersion in sports that is both deeper and broader than that of most of the women coaches. Given the generation that most of these adults grew up in, this is not surprising, because even in the 1970s and early 1980s, the number of opportunities, as well as the social and familial support for girls' and women's sports, was still at the takeoff point. A 2008 national survey of parents in the United States illustrates this disparity. The study found that 80 percent of fathers had participated in at least one team sport in high school, while only 50 percent of mothers had done so. Not surprisingly, the study found that parents who had participated in high school team sports were more likely to get involved supporting their children's athletic activities.[1]

Which sports men had previously played mattered. Since many of today's adult men in the United States grew up playing baseball, and rarely soccer, this had an impact on their feelings about coaching these sports. Ted Miller coached some soccer, but was more confident coaching softball, due to his baseball background. He said he had "maxed out" on soccer at under age-12 and would not coach at the older age-level because, "I think my technical soccer skills aren't necessarily strong enough, or I don't feel like they're strong enough to coach the girls at that level . . . although I could coach anywhere in softball. I played baseball growing up, a lot of it, so I'm very familiar with the sport and feel like my skills in that sport are much better." On the other hand, some men thought it was easier to coach soccer than baseball or softball because, as Jon Gaines put it, soccer is "really a relatively simple game and can be learned quickly . . . . Baseball, I think you do need to have some experience. You have to. There are a lot of skills that are really hard to teach. You have to know how to throw a ball, I think, to be a baseball coach."

Some coaches said that their motivation in getting into head coaching was, at least in part, based in a self-interested advocacy for their own child. John Gaines said that his son gets more playing time than other kids because his dad coaches the soccer team: "We play seven a side and nine kids on a team, so with every kid having to play three quarters, there's one child on every team that can play the entire four quarters. Um, and I clearly have favored my own son for most of those games— but I don't think anybody'd argue that he's not the best player there." Other coaches, like Michael Ortiz, spoke of "politics" as a reason for getting into coaching. As an assistant, Ortiz was dismayed that his son, a "talented player," did not get chosen for the All-Star team. He expressed his concern to another coach, and ended up concluding that he needed to become a manager, to ensure his son a chance at the All-Star team next season:

I said, "This isn't right. I mean he's a better player." And basically what I was told was, "Well, you don't coach." And, you know, essentially that was the response I got. "It would have been really nice if you had been there to be able to vote." And the only people who can vote are coaches. And, you know, that was told to me in various ways . . . so, that bothered me. The reason that those players were on that team was because every one of them had a dad who was a coach or their dad was a best friend of one of the coaches. It's just, you know, to see my son have to sit down and [see the All-Star teams] play with [those other] players really frustrated him, because they weren't as good as he was and, you know, I want him to be challenged and stretched in his ability and he just wasn't getting that, so—so that's why I coach.

In girls' softball, pitching is the most central, high-status, and arguably the most highly skilled position on the field. And several coaches said that it's not a coincidence that many of the girls who do most of the pitching are the daughters of managers. Alan Lindgren said that if you have a daughter who can pitch, she may not get the opportunity unless her dad is the manager:

> You'll probably see this especially in softball, that in the major leagues, [age]-10 and [age]-12, there're five teams and there're basically five pitchers, and the father [of the pitcher] is the manager. . . . I wouldn't say it's mandatory, [but] if somebody else has a daughter [who can pitch], you know, you're second on the team—you don't necessarily get the opportunities. So there is that dynamic, but it's not so self-serving in that they say, "Oh, my daughter's gonna do it," you know? I mean there're not that many people who are wildly unrealistic about their daughter's ability. I haven't really seen that. But they just tend to gravitate toward it because, oh hey, you know, it's fun, she can do it, and, you know, you just sort of get involved and can nurture that.

Both of Albert Riley's daughters are good pitchers, but neither of them pitched until their father started coaching their teams. He says that, "I can see, though, if a coach has a daughter and they want that daughter to pitch and get innings in, then I would encourage them to manage a team. I would definitely do that, because there's a lot of girls who want to pitch, but the manager has a daughter who pitches, so they don't get really any pitching in."

Clearly, entrée into the head coaching job was not as difficult for men as it was for the women coaches we interviewed. The major strains and tensions that I found with the men concerned their movement beyond the youngest kids' teams into the higher age categories, where there are fewer teams and the game gets more "serious." As the coaching pipeline narrows, so too does the range of acceptable coaching styles. Coaches feel the squeeze; some opt out, while others adapt themselves to the shifting context. As I will describe in the next section, at the heart of men coaches' decisions to opt out or to adapt and stay to coach the older kids are different (and at times conflicting) styles and displays of masculinity.

COACHES' MASCULINE DISPLAYS

In recent years, several stories appeared in the mass media about abhorrent misbehaviors, including overt acts of violence, committed by parents and coaches in youth sports. In addition to these high-profile cases, the public has become increasingly intolerant of authoritarian youth coaches who treat kids like Marine Corps recruits; what used to be considered normal coaching behavior is now commonly seen as abusive behavior toward children. In response, national sports organizations now focus attention on coach training and on the public dissemination of "positive coaching" philosophies. On February 24, 2006, the Little League Baseball and Softball national organization announced their new partnership with the Positive Coaching Alliance (PCA), which was already affiliated with AYSO.[2] On their Web site, LLB/S wrote, "Mirroring the basic values of Little League, the goals of PCA seek to replace the 'win-at-all-cost' model of coaching with the Double-Goal Coach model, where goal No. 1 is striving to win and (the more important goal) No. 2 is teaching athletes positive and enduring life lessons."[3]

The two aspects of the Double-Goal model reflect the two kinds of knowledge that adults bring to coaching. As we saw in the chapter 3, every coach has to negotiate the tension between employing kids-knowledge (which emphasized healthy fun, providing each child with positive encouragement, and equal opportunity) and employing sports-knowledge (which emphasizes the acquisition of the technical skills and strategies that further the goal of winning). While individual coaches attempt to strike their own balance between these "double goals," it is clear that as kids and coaches move up in the age-ranks of youth sports, the institutional expectations of how these dual goals should be balanced tip and teeter on a seesaw-like balance. At the entry level, with 5–7-year-olds, the weight of the balance is tipped far toward PCA's goal no. 2, what I call "kids-knowledge." As coaches move into working with intermediate-age groups of kids (8–10-year-olds), the seesaw tips toward the other direction and levels out (resulting in more obvious tensions than existed in the younger age-levels). When coaches reach the higher age groups, 11–14-year-olds, the balance tips dramatically toward goal no. 1, what I call "sports-knowledge," with an emphasis on skills, performance, winning, and an individual star system that nudges less-skilled kids toward less playing time and affords them fewer opportunities to try out new positions.

The kids feel this change, of course. Some quit playing after a couple of years, while others adjust to the increasingly competitive atmosphere. Parents are aware of the transition too, and describe it (often with mixed feelings) as having the effect of making the game more "serious" and "intense." This transition is reflected in the personalities of coaches who move through the ranks. I will argue that the shifting angle of the dual-goals seesaw is a contextual factor that evokes different strategies from the coaches and calls forth, at each level, a dominant kind of masculine display from them.

In her study of Little League Baseball in a gentrifying Philadelphia neighborhood, sociologist Sherri Grasmuck points to strains and tensions between coaches' different masculine styles. Many parents, she observed, stereotyped the coaches as either "Yellers" (men who coached like drill sergeants) or "Fuzzies" (men who had a soft and nurturing style with the kids). This dichotomy is a familiar one. In fact, in a 1979 study of Little League Baseball, Lewis Yablonsky and Jonathan Brower observed "two extreme types of coaches . . . the *humanistic* coach cared about children . . . and endowed most of the baseball activity, both games and practice, with an aura of fun, [and the] *macho* coach was egocentric, focused on winning at any cost . . . super-critical and caustic in his demeanor toward his players."[4] Yablonsky and Brower noted that most coaches fell somewhere between these two extremes, and Grasmuck too found considerable individual variation among the coaches. Still, the men Grasmuck studied tended to fall into two general groups: "Fairmounters" were working-class white men who were born and raised in the neighborhood, and they tended to have high levels of baseball expertise, to emphasize competition, and to utilize negative reinforcement with the kids; "Newcomers" were racially diverse professional-class men, first-generation neighborhood residents, and they tended to have less baseball knowledge and to emphasize instruction, using mostly positive reinforcement. The "tough masculinity" of the Fairmounters often clashed with the "tender masculinity" of the Newcomers.[5]

Grasmuck deftly shows how different styles of masculinity vie for dominance within a single Little League Baseball league. In my study of coaches in South Pasadena, I also found tensions between different styles of masculinity, but these tensions did not so much lie along a working class vs. professional class axis, or a "native" vs. "newcomer" axis. Instead, the tensions I observed were related to the styles of men who were coaching different age-groups of kids. In short, I observed that the context of youth sports calls forth, rewards, and punishes different forms of masculinity for those coaching different age-groups of kids. Some coaches successfully shift their styles as they move up, while others don't (or won't). The progressive narrowing of acceptable displays of masculinity results in a particular, honored form of masculinity becoming "situationally hegemonic."

Next, I will describe four age-based contexts (summarized in table 1), and I will show how each context encourages a particular balance on the "kids-knowledge" vs. "sports-knowledge" seesaw, and thus tends to reward a particular kind of coaching style. I begin my descriptions of each of the four types of coaching masculinity by drawing from my field observations. On several separate evenings, I walked around the South Pasadena Arroyo, stopping for a few minutes or more at each of the four or five baseball games that were being played. At one end of the Arroyo, the littlest kids (5–6-year-old girls and boys) would be playing T-ball, and the next-higher age-group (6–7-year-old boys, with a few girls) would be playing Coach-Pitch. At the opposite end of the Arroyo were two standard-sized Little League Baseball fields on which I would find Machine-Pitch (7–8-year-old boys), American League (8–9-year-old boys), National League (mostly 10–11-year-old boys), and/or Major League

Table 1 Male Coaches' Masculinity Displays in Different Age-based Contexts

	Kids-knowledge vs. sports-knowledge balance	Coaches' voices	Coaches' bodily postures	Situationally dominant form of masculinity
Ages 6–7	80%/20%	Encouraging; softer tones; taglines, like "Okay?"; emphasis on positive messages; endearing forms of address ("Baby")	Kneeling, bending over to talk with kids; hands on shoulders of kids; nonthreatening demeanor; coach on field with kids in soccer and T-ball	Teddy Bear: warm, nurturing, fun
Ages 8–10	60%/40%	Encouraging, but more yelling out of directions; criticisms muted or given privately	Conflicted in how to negotiate space; coach on field at times (Coach-Pitch), but less so	Crossing Guard: there to help, protect, and direct; friendly and fun but clearly in charge
Ages 11–12	30%/70% (This is the biggest leap, according to coaches, where it gets "serious.")	Loud; more yelling; deep, commanding voices; more public criticism and expressions of disappoint-ment; occa-sional whining and sarcasm	Hyperkinetic; fidgety, often tortured; bossy; introduction of hand signals to players on offense and defense; coach stays in coaches' box	Drill Sergeant: let there be no mistake; he's the boss who attempts to control everything toward the goal of winning

Table 1 (continued)

	Kids-knowledge vs. sports-knowledge balance	Coaches' voices	Coaches' bodily postures	Situationally dominant form of masculinity
Ages 13–14	20%/80%	Less yelling; quiet control; emphasis on internalization of rules, strategy, and knowledge of game; longer postgame speeches	Alert but mostly quiet communication; signals more prevalent; calm, restrained demeanor punctuated by occasional outbursts; arms crossed, clipboard, talking strategy with assistant coaches	The CEO: wants a smoothly running machine out there, and expects everyone to be prepared, knowledgeable, and "on the same page"

(mostly 11–12-year-old boys) games being played. And in the very center of the Arroyo, on a full-sized baseball field I would watch a Junior League (13–14-year-old boys) game.[6] As I made the rounds from field to field, I would occasionally stop and talk with a parent or a coach whom I had previously interviewed, but mostly I would watch the coaches, listen to their voices, and take notes on what I saw.[7] In each age-based context, I concluded, there was an expected form of leadership, which I will describe as the four "ideal types" of coaching style.[8] While not every coach conformed neatly to this standard—in fact, there was a good deal of variation—it nevertheless became apparent to me that, in each context, individual coaches had to negotiate their own way through the tensions that were built in to the dominant form of masculinity. In terms of social theory, these are examples of "situationally hegemonic" masculinities.[9]

The "Teddy Bear" Coach

As I approach the T-ball field, there's a game in progress, and I count six coaches, all men, scattered among the children on the playing field. The batter hits a sharp grounder up the middle past four defenders into center field. The coach at home plate says, "Great hit, Tina—run! Run to first!" Meanwhile, two infielders and three outfielders are racing after the ball. A coach, with a big smile on his face, is in hot pursuit, telling the infielders, "Stay on second base, guys," and then telling the outfielder who picks the ball up, "Throw it to second base." Meanwhile, the first-base coach is clapping, then he puts his hand gently on Tina's shoulder and nudges her toward second base, saying "Take second. Go to second base, Tina!" The outfielder throws the ball toward second, but there's nobody there to catch it, so it rolls right up on to the pitchers mound. The third-base coach has raced onto the field nearly to second base, holding two hands over his head as a stop sign: "Stop there, Tina, stay at second. Beautiful hit!" A coach who's standing in the infield area says, "Great throw, Tommy!" and then to the infielders who had been out of position, "Good hustle, guys! Next time the ball goes to the outfield, you guys need to cover second base, okay?" Another coach retrieves the ball, walks with it to home plate, and positions himself on one knee, briefly placing his hands on the next batter's ankles, showing him how to position his feet in the batter's box. The coach stands up, places the ball on the tee, and yells out, "Okay, be ready, fielders!" The batter swings too low, hits the tee, and the ball plops to the ground. "Good cut!" says the coach, "This time, try to keep your swing level, okay?"

For the youngest kids' entry-level teams—ages 5–7—coaches are expected to be fun, encouraging, nonjudgmental, and nurturing. They are supposed to give each of the kids equal playing time, let them play a variety of positions, and they are expected to downplay or ignore competition and winning. For the youngest teams in AYSO and LLB/S, no official score is kept, so supposedly there are no winners and losers. But parents frequently joke about how coaches, and some parents, actually do keep track. Tony Barnett says that even with his under-6 and under-8 soccer teams, "Coaches know you get the glory if you win, and then everybody says it doesn't matter if you lose, but you know we all keep track [*laughs*]." Still, at this level, the dominant ethic is to downplay the competitive aspect of the game, in favor of fun and personal growth.

What results is a mostly unspoken consensus that coaches' emphasis should be about 80 percent focused on kids-knowledge and only 20 percent focused on sports-knowledge.[10] That is, coaches are expected to teach young kids some of the fundamental skills and rules of the game, but they are expected during practices and games to mostly adopt a nurturing and caretaking style that deploys more of what people commonly define as "feminine" interpersonal skills.

These kinds of expectations at the entry level, as I showed in chapter 3, create an opening for women coaches to use the considerable amount of kids-knowledge that many of them have from their experiences as mothers and teachers. The men who coach at this level display what I call the "Teddy Bear" style of coaching. The coaches are right out there on the playing field alongside the kids, where they are delivering close-up instruction, positioning the kids, orchestrating their actions, often bending over or even kneeling down to their level. This bending over sometimes is helpful in delivering mechanical instruction, as demonstrated in the field note reproduced above. However, it's also a way of closing the size gap between much-taller coaches and their tiny charges, thus creating a less threatening demeanor. Teddy Bear coaches also make themselves nonthreatening to little kids by softening their own voices. It's not simply that they seem consciously to deliver consistently positive and encouraging messages to the kids; the men coaches at this level also frequently mute the power of their voices, using less volume and somewhat higher-pitched voice intonations. They also frequent employ taglines at end of a shouted-out command that might otherwise be taken as a criticism: *"Next time the ball goes to the outfield, you guys need to cover second base, okay?"* When my son was six years old, his soccer coach frequently ended an instruction to one of the kids on the team with the tender, upward-lilting phrase, "Okay, baby?" Studies of gender and language have long shown that these are common linguistic conventions adopted by subordinate groups of people. The male Teddy Bear coach is, in effect, publicly projecting a bodily demeanor and vocal style more common to a feminine habitus.[11]

Many men seem to be very comfortable adopting this nurturing posture with little kids; indeed, they are clearly enjoying themselves on the field. Some men, though, have a hard time picturing themselves as Teddy Bear coaches, and prefer to wait until their kids are a bit older and the game becomes more serious before they start to coach. Doug Berger coached both his daughter's soccer teams and his son's baseball teams for several years. However, as he explained: "[My daughter] probably started when she was six. So she went through one year, possibly two years where somebody else coached her. Um, I'm not as patient with the real little ones [*laughs*] as I am as when they get bigger. So I know she had at least one, probably two coaches before then—I started coaching her when she got a little bit bigger." Berger's sense that he lacked the "patience" to coach the 5- and 6-year-old kids is perhaps an expression of discomfort with the way that the context calls for coaches to interact with kids in ways that are conventionally defined as feminine.[12] This reluctance on the part of some men likely helps to create some space for women, and for more-nurturant men, to coach at the entry level of youth sports. Soccer coach Mark Daly sees himself as inept at working with very young kids, but he deals with this by bringing in high school girls to serve as his assistants; these teen girls supply the kids-knowledge that balances out his own emphasis on sports-knowledge. Daly explained:

> I don't ever feel like I am good with kids. It's much easier to coach the high school girls than it is to coach the little kids. I am not a get-on-the-ground, roll-around-and-play type of coach or dad, you know. But you know how some people are great with kids—I am not one of those guys. But what I do is I get two of the high school girls to help me coach, and they get service hours from their school. And the ones who have helped me are very get-on-the-ground, play-with-the-kids, have-a-good-time. [They] run around, get them all pumped up, high fives, the whole thing, you know. The kids love it, and they come to practice, they run and jump on her, and they cuddle, you know what I mean, all that kind of stuff. Ah, whereas, uh, I can't do that, because I am just not that kind of guy, um. And so, I think the parents last year were appreciative of the two girls who helped me.

Whereas Berger and Daly each might see himself as "not that kind of guy," there are some other men who prefer not to move out of the comfort zone of working with the youngest kids. Like many of the women coaches, these men either opt out of coaching older kids or they cycle back to work with a younger sibling. Tony Barnett explained why he cycled back twice, so that he could coach all three of his kids' soccer teams, never moving beyond the under-8 group:

> I mean under-6, under-8—Who cares? I mean, that's just bumblebee soccer. You try to make sure the kids have a good time, you try to teach them a little bit of skills. But I took my two oldest and I stopped at under-8, in part because I had more kids to teach, as they were younger—but you know, probably in the back of my mind I said, "Look, you move up to under-10, you start to actually have to pay attention"—so I was probably a little hesitant to move up to that level. It's the first time they keep track of standings, and there's playoffs, and so the intensity ratchets—it ratchets up a little bit.

Eric Caldwell is another Cycler who coached both of his kids' under-6 soccer teams but preferred not to move to the higher age-groups. He embraces the kids-knowledge that he brings to the activity and values most the idea that the kids on his team are going to have such a good time, that they will all want to continue to play next year: "If there's gonna be one coach who is going to put an end to your kid's progress in that sport, its not gonna be me. I'm going to encourage them to have so much fun, and praise them so much that they're going to look forward to it from the time they stop playing their last game until the start of the next season. They are going to say, 'Gosh, I'm really looking forward to playing soccer.' That's my entire goal."

The "Crossing Guard" Coach

> Tonight, as I walked from field to field to watch snippets of different age-groups playing baseball, I paused to watch an inning of a playoff game for 8- and 9-year-old boys. This game had a high intensity that I could hear and feel as I approached. It was the third inning, a 4–3 score. I stood behind the third-base dugout to watch and listen to the coaches and the kids. All three coaches on this team were extremely verbal men, two of whom were hyperkinetic. One of them paced back and forth in front of a fifteen-foot-long space in front of the dugout, keeping up a consistent verbal chatter; to me, he looked like he had to pee or something, with his

constant stop-and-go pacing. With his team in the field and a runner on base, the inning ended with a short pop-up toward the pitcher's mound; the pitcher ran to it, dropped to his knees, and barely snagged the ball before it hit the ground. A second later, the ball popped loose, but the umpire had signaled "out." Nevertheless, the coach leapt into the air and sprinted a few steps toward the field, yelling, "He caught it! He had control! He had it long enough! He had control!" He finally realized that the ump had in fact called an out, but still he couldn't contain himself; standing on the playing field itself, he clapped his hands and repeated, now in a more celebratory way, "He had control! Yes!" I strolled to the first-base dugout side and struck up a conversation with Ellen Lessing, who had just walked off the field, where she was working as the third-base coach for the other team. Parents and coaches on her side of the field were worked up too, but they were not nearly as loud as the other team. Ellen explained, "This is the championship game and we especially want to beat these guys because they are so loud." In fact, she tells me that their team's parents were (jokingly?) accused by a parent on the other team of "not caring enough," because they weren't very vocal in cheering their kids on, so she said with wry laugh, "Against these guys, we make a real effort to whoop it up." I told her of my observation that usually the coaches in this league tend to be very vocal, very loud, but very positive, and she said that they are not always positive, and that in fact her team had had to complain earlier in the season about the coaches on today's opposing team for "non-positive" yelling during a game.

Unlike entry-level coaches, who are free to move all over the field with the kids, those who coach at the intermediate age-levels are confined to coaches' boxes (for soccer and baseball/softball) or to the space immediately around the dugout (in baseball/softball). As a result, as soccer coach Eric Caldwell explained, at the older levels, "you are off one side and you can't really be on top of a player, so you've really got to broadcast your voice to get people to do things." And unlike coaches at the entry level, who can play fast and loose with formal rules of the game, coaches at this intermediate level are expected to conform more closely to the formal rules of the game. Coaches are still expected at this level to downplay the importance of winning and losing; however, scores are now formally kept, and people cheer madly for their team's successes, and take notice of their losses. While coaches at this level are expected increasingly to be instructional with the kids, they are still expected to couch their instruction in entirely encouraging and positive comments. What results is a ratcheting up of the emphasis on winning and performance. Negotiating this rapidly tipping seesaw (60 percent kids-knowledge versus 40 percent sports-knowledge) creates noticeable strains for coaches.

The dominant mode for men who coach at this level is what I call the "Crossing Guard" coach. Like a school crossing guard, this coach is confined to a particular physical space, within which he can move around but from which he must direct traffic and ensure the kids' safety. The school crossing guard is your friend. He is there to help and protect you; he'll joke around and engage in friendly banter with you. But in the final analysis, he is clearly in charge, and he knows that he will be held accountable for outcomes.

Coaches at this level feel the increased scrutiny from parents and other coaches. They are not supposed to be "too serious," they know. But they are also supposed to know the game, and to impart skills and game strategies to the kids. Ted Miller coaches his daughter's under-10 soccer team and says that sometimes other coaches have said to him, "Ted, you're not intense enough, you're not competitive enough." In his view, the level of competition is sometimes "quite intense. I think it's over the top." Balancing his less competitive values with the increasingly competitive context in which he finds himself has led to some conflicts, like the time he successfully asserted himself with his more "intense" assistant coach:

> I got into it with my assistant coach because we were in a playoff game and we were winning, I think, by a couple of goals, and there was a player in a particular position that gave up a couple of late goals, and so the score became tied all of a sudden right at the end of the game and he was telling me, "You need to move that player to another position and get somebody back there." And I elected not to do it because I didn't want to hurt the kid's feelings, didn't want the kid to know. The kid was doing the best that she could, and I didn't want the parents to feel like the kid was being moved, and it just wasn't to me that important, and so I left the kid and the coach was very upset. Ultimately, we won the game in overtime, so it worked out, but I got into it visibly on the sideline with the coach and, you know, he was one of these coaches— opposite coaching style, intense, versus my more relaxed style—and he

just didn't approve of what I was doing. I told him, "Look, I'm not going to move her."

Will Solomon, as we have seen, was comfortable coaching baseball in
the more "relaxed" context of the summer league but said that there was
no way he'd consider managing in the Majors. The intensity, he said,
"steps up at each level—American to National is a step up—the skill
level, the intensity of the coaches definitely changes. The skill level of the
kids go ups 'cause a lot of the kids are just frustrated, drop out at that
point, but the intensity level of the managers is what goes up the most,
and particularly from Nationals to Majors—yeah, I can really see it."

Michael Ortiz felt the ratcheting up of the emphasis on competition
when he moved up to coach under-10 soccer. The kids want to win more
at that age, he says, and, "I think so the parents kind of ratchet up a little
bit of the pressure there, too, on the coach." Carlos Ruiz agrees. A soccer
coach for several years, Ruiz observes that a lot of the pressures that
coaches start to feel at this level come from parents: "AYSO talks about
sportsmanship and everybody plays and balanced teams, and I think
that's all accepted at some level by everybody, [but] winning is still really important. And I think it's *very* important to parents; I think it's
somewhat less important to players. But winning is still very very important, and I think that the higher you go in terms of the age groups, it
becomes less acceptable to have a coach who's not gonna win."

Parents sometimes create strains for coaches, because they often have
different views of how "serious" the coach should be. A summer baseball team of 9–11-year-old kids that my son played on was, to me, com-
fortably low-key, and Coach Rick seemed to me to be doing a great job of
keeping it fun, while rotating kids around to give them a chance to try
different positions, including letting a few kids pitch for the first time.
But as I describe in the following story, taken from my field notes, one father made it difficult for Rick to run the team in this way:

> A dad with two boys on the team paces nervously back and forth from
> the stands to the dugout. He tells me that he coaches in another league, in
> a town adjacent to South Pasadena. I comment that our pitcher is throw-
> ing hard, and he launches into a critique of the boy's pitching mechanics.

It turns out that this becomes a recurring theme. No pitcher takes the mound over the next three weeks without this guy coming to the dugout, offering unsolicited analysis and advice to Rick, and to dads of pitchers, on the flaws in the kid's pitching mechanics, and what should be done about them. He does seem knowledgeable, and Rick once tells him somewhat defensively, "You know a lot more about pitching and baseball than I do. I mostly coach high school football and AYSO, but I don't know as much about baseball." This dynamic strikes me, in terms of the kinds of pressures that managers can face from parents—pressures that question directly or indirectly the manager's knowledge base, competence, etc. After all, Rick is a highly experienced coach, is himself very athletic, but is still put a bit on the defensive by this guy's assertiveness and his knowledge of baseball.

In addition to negotiating contradictory expectations from the parents—to ratchet things up but to not be *too* intense—coaches at this age-level have to deal with another contradiction: their own physical containment during games, combined with the fact that kids at this level still have not developed and incorporated the full range of physical skills and knowledge of the game, make it difficult for these coaches sometimes to impart instruction in ways other than yelling. Their criticisms are often muted or given privately as kids come off the field. Still, coaches at this level tend to yell a great deal, although they still try—very consciously, it seems—to yell at the kids in "positive" ways that are encouraging.

A good number of coaches opt out of moving up to the next level of coaching. At the age-10 level, as we saw in the previous chapter, there is a kind of ceiling on women coaches moving up to coach older age-levels of kids. And this is more the case in baseball/softball than it is in soccer, a sport in which there are a few women coaching the higher age-level teams. That soccer has a more permeable ceiling is due, in large part, to perceptions by many coaches that it's "easier" to coach soccer, that baseball or softball coaching requires a deep, experiential knowledge of the game—knowledge that few women have, and some men don't have either. Lenn Molina liked coaching his young son's baseball teams for a couple of years, but as his son got older, Lenn decided to focus on soccer: "I sort of decided baseball, as you move up, you really have to know the game, because baseball's very competitive in our area [*laughs*], and you got a lot of dads, and it's mainly dads in baseball—in soccer it's more mixed—who played the game and know the game, and I didn't feel competent to, you know, move up." It was striking to me that Molina noted three factors—experience-based technical competence, the "very competitive" baseball atmosphere in South Pasadena, and the fact that Little League is dominated by "mostly dads"—as factors that led him to opt out of coaching baseball. That he could feel more comfortable in the more "mixed" context of coaching soccer echoes what some men have said about the gender composition of workplaces: all-male work environments tend to create more narrowly policed definitions of masculinity with which many men are uncomfortable, while substantially sex-integrated workplaces tend to broaden the range of acceptable masculinities, making it possible for men of different types to feel comfortable. Sex integration can benefit many men.

The "Drill Sergeant" Coach

Noise. I decide to sit for an inning and just listen, not watching too closely. I hear a cacophony of men's voices—barking orders, positioning corrections—to the mostly 11- and 12-year-old boys in the field. It's the two teams' head managers mostly that I hear, but also base coaches and an occasional father in the stands or behind the backstop. In a stretch of about thirty seconds, I hear this: One team's manager, Donald, yells to the center fielder, "Eddie! Eddie!—Move a couple steps to your right!" The opposing manager yells to the kid at the plate to "swing at the good ones." Simultaneously, their voices on top of each other, Donald barks to the shortstop, "Andrew—Get in the ready position," as the third-base coach yells to the kid on second to "Be ready to run on a passed ball." An assistant coach echoes Donald: "Ready positions—Everybody!—The ball might be coming to YOU!" The kid at the plate takes a strike, and his manager yells out, "You gotta swing at 'em if they're close, Jimmy!" A dad in the stands exclaims, "Good pitch," and Donald yells to our third-baseman, "If he runs, you gotta cover third!" "And Tommy," he yells to the left fielder, "you gotta back up any throws to third!"

Ages 11 and 12—especially Little League Baseball's Major Leagues—is where everybody seems to agree things get "really serious." While managers are still expected to watch out for the kids' physical and emotional safety, the coaches, the kids, and many of the parents at this level expect to win. Here is where everybody experiences the steepest ratcheting up of competition, resulting in what I estimate to be a 30 percent kids-knowledge versus 70 percent sports-knowledge tip of the seesaw. This set of expectations creates the conditions for the emergence of what I call the "Drill Sergeant" coach.

At this level, most of the women coaches and most of the "less-intense" men coaches have opted out, cycled back, or been pushed out. The men who remain tend to be seen as "serious" coaches who adopt a commanding style. The Drill Sergeant coach is the undisputed boss on the field. During games, these coaches are spatially confined by the rules, so they attempt to establish control of what happens on the playing field through the use of their voices and bodies. Drill Sergeant coaches yell loudly at kids, employing deep, commanding voices. Gone are the apologetic-sounding, lilting taglines of the Teddy Bear (and sometimes the Crossing Guard) coaches. Drill Sergeant coaches are more likely to publicly criticize their players for a miscue or for a mental error during a game. At this age level in baseball, managers deploy increasingly complicated hand signals that they flash to their kids throughout the game. Kids are taught to look at the coaches between every pitch for signals: for the batter, whether to bunt, swing, or take a pitch; for the base runner, whether to steal; on defense, whether to try a trick play to pick off a runner. Some managers signal the catcher or pitcher in order to call every kind of pitch he would like the pitcher to throw. What results is a systematic attempt by managers to fully orchestrate what happens on the field. When kids miss a sign, or do not follow their coach's instructions, they hear about it immediately, as the following field note from a 10–12-year-old boys' baseball game illustrates:

> Coach Gordon's level of intensity has risen in recent weeks as the playoffs approach. The team is tied for first (partly because Gordon successfully protested a game in which his team did not play—the manager of the team with whom we are tied did something illegal, so a win was reversed to a loss). In today's game, this occurred: Jonathan is a young (ten-year-old) rising star on the team. A big kid, his arm is a gun, and he hits hard

line drives. He also plays on the town's traveling club team, so he's really a prospect. Coach Gordon rides him harder than other kids, I think because Jonathan's got talent and promise, but also because he plays with a casual approach and sometimes makes careless errors (the errors appear thoughtless, like an errant throw from his catcher position back to pitcher, but may just be the result of the fact that he really is young and doesn't yet have full control of his very strong arm). It's the top of the first inning, with Clayton pitching and Jonathan catching. Clayton is wild, and walks the first two batters. Gordon begins to get visibly agitated, moving about in front of the dugout and yelling instructions to Clayton to "Just throw strikes; keep your pitches down!" With runners on first and third, and no outs, the runner on first attempts a steal to second. Gordon immediately yells to Jonathan, "No throw! No throw!" But Jonathan guns it to second anyway. It's a good throw, but too late to get the runner. Worse, the runner at third scampers home. "Time!" Coach Gordon barks very loudly at the ump. "Billy! Get on the [catcher's] gear! Jonathan! Sit down! Eddie! Take over for Billy at first!" As Billy runs in to put on the gear, Jonathan trudges back to the dugout with his head down. As he arrives, Gordon barks at him, "What were you thinking? Didn't you hear me say 'No throw'? You've got to be thinking out there!" After no more than a dozen pitches, and no outs recorded in the first inning, Gordon has pulled his starting catcher, publicly chastised him, and sat him down in the dugout.

The goal of this kind of orchestration and managerial control is winning. While some parents are uncomfortable with this level of coaching "intensity," others fully approve. The next night, at practice, I asked Jonathan's father how he felt about his ten-year-old son being publicly chastised, perhaps humiliated, by the coach. He chuckled and told me that his wife "won't come to any of the games anymore. She's fed up with having to listen to Gordon yell at Jonathan." I asked him how he felt about it. "I think it's great. I'm glad: [with a laugh] I come out here with Jonathan, and when I yell at him, he just shrugs it off, so I'm glad someone else is doing it!"

Some coaches, though, are seen by other coaches as too competitive. Albert Riley was described by several of the coaches that we interviewed as "over-the-top" in his competitiveness and emphasis on winning championships with his girls' softball teams. Riley sees himself as competitive too. When asked how he balances the league's emphasis on giving all kids a chance to play and try new positions, with the value placed on winning, he labored a bit to explain why he would not jeopardize his team's chances to win by removing his daughter from the pitcher's mound simply to give another girl a chance to try her hand at pitching:

> I'm a real competitive person, I love to win, you know, but it's not a win at all costs. I mean there's a balance between winning, teaching, and having fun, but girls that want to pitch, they need to be on another team, and at the lower levels. I would not—I would not jeopardize, if we were winning, you know, eight to nothing—I wouldn't want to jeopardize our team, because it's unfair to the rest of the girls, if I take my daughter out, say, and I put another girl in and the other team rallies and we lose nine to eight. It's not fair to the other girls who have worked hard to get that lead, and then all of the sudden it's almost like we're throwing it away.

Coaches like Albert Riley understand that even for the older girls in Little League softball, a 100 percent emphasis on winning is not fully accepted by many parents and coaches, so Riley negotiates the tension between having fun and winning by redefining fun *as* winning:

> You know, the Little League really tries to emphasize it's all about the girls and having fun and all that. Well, you know what? I agree with that to an extent, but I can tell you unequivocally that a team that is one [win] and fifteen [losses], they're not having fun. You know if you're winning, you're gonna have fun. That's the bottom line. I think all the coaches respect me—there's a couple that I've had, uh, you know, had some issues with. It's hard being on the top. It is. I think that, um, you know, we win the championship every year.

The Drill Sergeant coach, in the South Pasadena context, is an inherently unstable form of masculine display. We saw in the previous chapter that a few women attempt to embody this hypercompetitive form of leadership and are held to a kind of gender double standard that is very difficult to navigate. But men coaches, too, get the clear message that the Drill Sergeant coach can go too far, can be "too serious," "too intense," "too over-the-top." Coaches know they have to self-censor their more extreme tendencies in this direction, and most do. Campbell Weber told me that when he was coaching the 11- and 12-year-old kids, "I find myself [yelling at the kids] and I'm not sure I have the right temperament to do this, but I'm doing it. I'm very aware of this, so I really try to keep it in control. These *are* kids."

Other coaches never fully embody the "yeller" approach that's so visible at this level of competition. Instead, their voices are less than fully commanding, their public criticisms taking on a tone of whiny disappointment at the kids' lack of focus or their mistakes. And if coaches won't self-censor or mute their more extreme Drill Sergeant coach tendencies, the league will do it for them. More than once I heard coaches—usually college-educated, professional-class men—talking about two white working-class fathers who had been "weeded out" of coaching Little League because they were "over-the-top," "way too serious" coaches who "always had something [negative] to say to the umpires." One of these men who was weeded out was viewed by one of the coaches that we interviewed as "a negative coach.... [He] knows a lot about baseball—he played. But [he's] really a negative coach. Kids are gonna do more wrong than right. I can sit there and find a flaw with my son in every at-bat, in virtually any situation. His foot was wrong, react quicker, whatever it is, I can find the flaw. To what end? [*He laughs.*] This is *Little League*. It's *fun*. [But] there is an increase in negativity, in response to failure, as you move up in years."

Similar criticisms of negativity were frequently made by South Pasadena coaches and parents about the mostly Latino coaches from surrounding towns like Alhambra, Temple City, or El Sereno, whom our kids would play against in regional playoff games. (I will discuss this social class and race dynamic more in chapter 6.) In fact, in its extreme stereotypical form, the Drill Sergeant coach is not an acceptable form of masculinity in South Pasadena. To move on to the next level of coaching, men have to define themselves *against* this masculine style, by showing an ability to impart sophisticated sports knowledge to the kids, while simultaneously showing a high level of *self-restraint* and projecting a coaching style of quiet control that emphasizes the internal, mental aspects of the game.

The "CEO" Coach

As I walk up to the Juniors field, I see that there is a runner on first base, and I hear some chatter from the 13–14-year-old boys in the dugout cheering on their team's batter. Just outside the dugout door, the team's manager stands, writing something on a clipboard. The batter takes a long look at the third-base coach, who claps once, brushes his left hand across his chest, touches the brim of his cap with his right hand, brushes his chest a second time, claps his hands twice, then puts his hands on his hips. The boy steps into the batter's box and takes a practice swing or two. Meanwhile, the manager of the team on defense stands just outside his team's dugout quietly talking with his two coaches, one of whom holds a pencil and scorebook with which he's tracking the pitcher's pitch count. One of the coaches says "Time, Blue" to the umpire, and walks slowly out to the pitcher's mound to talk with the pitcher and the catcher. The conference over, the coach returns to the dugout and mutters something to the manager; the batter steps back into the box and the pitcher delivers a pitch. Before it even reaches the plate, the defensive manager yells out, "Nice pitch!"—but the umpire calls it a ball. On the next pitch, the batter pops it up to the shortstop, ending the inning. As the boys run off the field, they gather around their manager, who says a few words to them. They all clasp hands, a boy yells out "One–two–three," and they all yell "HITS" as they move into the dugout.

At the 13–14-year-old level, the kids have several years of playing experience under their belts and are now playing on a full-sized field. One of my surprises in doing this research was in discovering how consistently *quiet and restrained* the managers and coaches are at this level. My observations through age-12 baseball had brought me to a tentative conclusion that the ratcheting up of competition led the coaches to become progressively louder and more aggressive as they moved up. In fact, before I spent two seasons watching Juniors baseball, I imagined that I might give my chapter on men coaches the title "Going (Gradually) Berzerk," to reflect this ratcheting up of verbal and physical intensity. So I was surprised to find that the ideal-typical coach at the end of the youth sports pipeline—at the 13–14-year-old age-level—was not what I came to call the "Drill Sergeant" coach. Instead, the dominant coaching style was one of quiet control, what I came to think of as the "CEO" coach.

At this level, coaches are alert, focused, and contemplative. During games and practices, they project a calm and restrained demeanor, punctuated only by the rare verbal outburst that stands out as atypical. The CEO coach rarely moves about in an agitated manner; instead, during games, he stands, or he sits on a five-gallon paint can used to hold baseballs, and when he moves onto the field to talk to a player or to the umpire, he strolls with a calm, self-assured gait. CEO coaches rarely get into open confrontations with umpires; mostly, they try informally and indirectly to influence the umps, by quietly suggesting between innings that the opposing pitcher might be balking, or by yelling (supposedly to their own pitcher, but as much to the umpire) "Nice pitch!" as a ball is still on its way to the plate. The CEO coach occasionally yells out the name of a fielder, then gives him hand signals instructing him to position himself differently. The kids know that they must continually look to the coaches for signals, which at this level become more sophisticated: before each game, the coaches will go through the signals with the kids, often changing them each game.

There is far less yelling from coaches at this level, but that does not mean that the coaches are any less into controlling what happens on the field. The CEO coach assumes that the kids have internalized the rules of the game and have embodied basic skills and strategies that should now come "naturally." During one game—an ugly loss marked by numerous uncharacteristically sloppy plays in the field and on the bases—a usually stoic manager had barked loudly at the kids several times. Afterward, he sat them all in a circle on the grass, and in a very calm and rational voice, criticized them for their "lack of focus" and their "mental errors." "Guys," he concluded, "I shouldn't have to be yelling at you out there." His main point of emphasis was that the boys should by that point in their baseball careers understand the fundamentals, and should know when and how to execute them. He, as the manager, should be the one who quietly and efficiently orchestrates the team's strategies. The CEO coach wants a smoothly running machine out on the field, and he expects everybody to be prepared, knowledgeable, and "on the same page" with respect to the group goal of winning. He also expects the less-skilled players to understand that it's their job to subordinate their playing time to the more-skilled players, for the good of the team. Campbell Weber was managing a Juniors team of 13–14-year-old boys when I interviewed him. His description of how he shifts his style and emphasis when coaching older kids illustrates the CEO coach's philosophy:

> At the lowest levels, everything the kid does is good. The fact that they did *something* is just thrilling . . . . I certainly treat them differently. When you have a team of eight- or nine-year-olds [*laughs*], the attention spans are much less, the expectations are much less, the concerns for making sure it's fun are much higher.
>
> By the time they are twelve or thirteen, the fun of practice *is* practice . . . . I think I expect more as they get older. If you want to play baseball at this level, you better learn how to field! That ball's coming at you! You become more demanding that players play at their top level. Baseball is as much a mental game as it is physical, and as kids get older, I expect more of them to know what to do. It's a lot like running an office.

The CEO coach emerges over the years as the hegemonic form of masculinity in the South Pasadena youth sports context. As in other social contexts, there certainly are other, competing forms of masculinity. But the CEO coach, in this context, is an example of what sociologist James Messerschmidt calls "situationally dominant gender practices in particular settings."[13] Many of these men are in the professional/managerial class—they are attorneys, medical doctors, college professors and administrators, real estate or sales managers, architects, and professionals in the entertainment industry. Indeed, Annelies Knoppers and Anton Anthonissen, who study sports, have argued that there is currently a historical congruence between dominant "managerial masculinities" in large organizations and emergent styles of male leadership in sport.[14] The sociologist Peter Levin, in his study of commodities-exchange workers, argues that ideals of competence are at the heart of dominant forms of masculinity in this work context, and that competence is defined largely by one's ability to keep cool under stressful conditions and to successfully deploy a kind of controlled aggression. Levin said that the men he interviewed often credit their past sports experience in helping them to remain cool under workplace stress.[15]

In my study, I have seen that the ability to keep cool works in the other direction as well. These professional-class men transport their styles of leadership from their workplaces to the coaching of the older kids: "It's a lot like running an office." And they collectively police the acceptable form of masculine leadership by weeding out the "over-the-top" Drill Sergeant coaches, some of whom are working-class men. The CEO coach is no less competitive than the Drill Sergeant coach; to the contrary, he clearly wants to win games and championships. For two seasons, I served as the scorekeeper on my son Sasha's Juniors baseball team. Very rarely did I see a manager fly off the handle at an ump or publicly yell at or criticize a player in ways that seemed routinely to occur at the previous level. Below the surface, though, there was considerable cerebral jousting between managers, who were wary of each other's tricks. For instance, each time our team would play a particular team, our manager would ask me to pay careful attention to any changes in the other team's lineup, because, he said, their manager "may seem to be a nice guy, but he's notorious for trying stuff, to get the upper hand." As the sociologist Jennifer Pierce's study of litigators revealed, lawyers make use of what she calls "strategic friendliness," the goal of which "is to *win over* or *dominate* another." This masculine domination, according to Pierce, takes on a particularly class-based form that differentiates itself from working-class styles of competition and domination:

> In a middle class job such as the legal profession . . . intimidation depends not on physical ability but on mental quickness and a highly developed set of social skills. Thus, masculinizing practices, such as aggression and humiliation, take on an emotional and intellectual tone specific to middle-class occupations and professions.[16]

This masculine leadership style links also with the dominant values of professional-class families. As Annette Lareau has argued, the middle-class "concerted cultivation" of children is based on the idea that children need to become self-motivated through internalization of rules and knowledge that give them the tools to navigate their way through social institutions. The resulting "sense of entitlement" helps middle-class youth learn "how to make rules work in their favor" and is thus a key element of the generational passing-on of class privilege.[17] In sum, together, the three contexts of professional-class workplaces, families, and youth sports form a nexus for the creation and validation of a particularly class-based hegemonic masculinity: the CEO coach.

HOW THE GENDER-SORTING SYSTEM WORKS: TWO CASE STUDIES

The four age-based coaching styles I have described above can be thought of as situations that are systematically structured both by the formal rules of the youth-sports organizations and by the informal expectations and values of parents, kids, and coaches. Just as the sex-category sorting system that I described in chapter 2 channels men volunteers toward coaching and most women volunteers toward being team parents, this gender-sorting system systematically routes coaches toward adopting particular forms of masculine leadership and display that become more narrowly defined as the coaches move toward working with older kids. The social structure of youth sports, however, does not force individuals to act in particular ways; it shapes possibilities by encouraging or discouraging certain styles, by constraining or enabling certain actions. I will now outline two case studies of men who navigated this gender-sorting system in very different ways. Over the course of several years, George Starr coached T-ball through Juniors baseball by adjusting his style in conformity with the dominant standards at each level. Harold Zing, by contrast, was abhorred to find himself over-conforming to an over-the-top, Drill Sergeant style, and opted out of coaching, to spare himself and his son.

Mr. Little League: A Case Study of George Starr

I'm watching Sasha's National League (mostly 10–11-year-old boys) game, and things are falling apart. The team has not scored many runs today, and the boys are making lots of error in the field. George Starr, the head coach, seems increasingly agitated and has started yelling at the kids and questioning the umpire's calls. At one point, when our catcher makes an ill-advised wild throw that allows two more runs to score, Starr yells the kid's name out—and then a second time, with a drawn-out, somewhat pleading tone: "*Robert!* Roooberrrt . . . What are you doing? C'mon guys, you gotta *pay attention* out there!" One of the moms behind me in the stands says to the other parents, "Jeez. What's with George?" Another mother chuckles and replies, "Yeah, he was such a teddy bear a couple years ago." She's right. I've watched George Starr for several years now—twice when he was Sasha's coach and other seasons when he coached opposing teams. As a T-ball coach, George was warm and fuzzy. A big, hulking guy, he was kind of a gentle giant on the field—as the mom said, a "teddy bear" with the little kids. He ran fun practices, made a point to let kids try out lots of different positions, and in games, he never challenged or criticized umpires. He was encouraging to the kids, even when they made mistakes. In short, the kids were comfortable, and the parents loved his style. A couple of years later, near the end of the season, I spoke with a father whose nine-year-old son had been playing on George's National League team. When I said that I'd liked George's tender and supportive style with the kids, this dad said that he wasn't entirely happy with George's coaching style this year. "You know, George is a nice guy, but maybe he's too low-key sometimes. I don't think [my son] is learning enough about baseball as he would if he was playing for a more serious coach." This year, by contrast, in National League there's been more conflict on the field, and unhappiness among parents, some of whom think George has become *too* serious. We are now six games into the season as I write this, and I've noticed that George yells at the kids more this year—most commonly by blurting out a boy's name in an accusatory style when a kid makes a mistake in the field. He gripes about the umpires and has gotten into a couple of scrapes with them. He doesn't rotate the kids in their positions as much. (And there have been some bruised feelings, with a couple of parents griping about how George "favors" his son as a pitcher when in fact his son's not among the most skilled pitchers.) George is louder during games than he used to be; and, indeed, I notice this is generally true of all managers and coaches this year. Scores, win-loss records, and standings are frequently discussed during games, practices, and in George's after-game talks with the kids and their parents. To be sure, he is still generally encouraging and positive in his approach with the kids—there are other teams we have played against this year whose coaches yell a lot more than George does—but there's no doubt that his style has shifted pretty radically as he's moved up the ranks.

When I interviewed George Starr after that season ended, he reflected on his move up from the younger teams to coaching the older kids. In fact, this was Starr's second time coaching Little League Baseball teams.

One of the few working-class men coaching in South Pasadena, Starr had previously coached an older son and was now moving up through the ranks for a second time, this time with his younger son. He seemed to me to be such a seasoned and confident veteran coach—I actually had come to think of him as "Mr. Little League," after I'd heard a parent call him that a couple of years ago—so I was surprised to hear him say that when he'd coached his first son's teams, he'd been reluctant to move up and work with the older kids:

> I was kinda of coerced to go up there. They kept asking me, and I said, "No, I like staying in the 8–9-year-olds." It's really nice down there, and I didn't think I was really ready for older kids. And it was a different style of baseball, a little bit more intense, more, uh, more coaching philosophy up there. When you get to the 10–11–12's, they are stealing [bases], you play with less players on the field. You have to have a little more strategy—pitching comes more into effect, where you have to think a little bit ahead, as far as innings ahead: who do you want to pitch, what type of situations you are going to get into. So I stayed with the 10–11–12's for two more years. And then I took the step up to the next level, which is the Major League. It is the same age group, but they are just a little bit, you know, more quality of players—more intense, and you play with more strict rules . . . . And then you have, you know, confrontations and, you know, coaches do get more intense: "Oh, you missed that call," you know. "If you had two umpires" . . . blah, blah, blah . . . . And then it gets worse—I never coached the 13-, 14-, and 15-year-olds. And I'm sure that I'll do that with [my son]. You know, in about four more years. But I heard it is a lot worse up there, too, because it's real baseball. Everything like you see in Major Leagues, that's what they do. And the field is bigger and the coaches just always, you know, want that extra edge, and they will do whatever they can to get it, so . . . You know, I've seen a few games but not, not many so, uhh . . . I don't know about looking forward to going up there, but I am sure I will with [my son].

And he did. Four years later, with a new season of Juniors baseball beginning for the 13–14-year-old boys, I spotted George Starr on the field with his new team. I recorded our conversation in my field notes:

> As George walks off the field I call out to him, so he comes over to say hi. Standing with the screen between us, he's elevated maybe three feet

above me on the playing field as I stand in front of the grandstands, and I tell him that we are having our beginning-of-the-season parents' team meeting today. He laughs—kind of scoffs, really—and says, "I don't need a parents' meeting. At this level, I yell and they do what I say!"

Despite his joke, I noticed, as the season progressed, that George Starr, like the other men who were coaching the Juniors, didn't yell very much at all. Long gone was the Teddy Bear style he'd so successfully deployed with the littlest kids. There were no bodily or verbal gestures that seemed intended to make him seem nonthreatening. But gone, too, for the most part, were his Drill Sergeant outbursts of criticism and disapproval to his boys on the field. In fact, as I watched him manage probably eight or ten games over the next two seasons, I never saw him yell in anger or frustration at any of his players. Though other working-class men seemed to have been weeded out of coaching at the previous level, George Starr had successfully adopted the style of quiet control that is so common among coaches at this level. He had shifted his personality and style over the years; I'd watched him transform himself, settling finally into the CEO style of masculinity that is hegemonic among South Pasadena coaches.

Opting Out: A Case Study of Harold Zing

Our team eventually loses this 10–12-year-old boys' baseball game 18–6 (and, as the sports cliché goes, "it wasn't that close": five of our team's runs came in the final inning, when the other team put a pitcher on the mound who seems never to have pitched before). Our coaches are beside themselves with what they see as the kids' lack of focus and their poor execution throughout the game. More than once they yell at the kids after a bonehead play in the field. In the first inning of this game, we go down 1–2–3. In the bottom half of the inning, the opposing team bats around, scoring several runs; our pitcher walks a few, but mainly it's our team's poor fielding that's the story. Harold Zing, our assistant coach is especially upset. He first positions himself standing in front of the dugout. As the kids take the field to start the second inning, he yells, "You've all got to WANT the ball; let NOTHING get by you; STOP EVERY BALL!!" Before nearly every pitch, he exhorts the infielders, "DOWN AND READY!" Often, he gets more specific: "BEND YOUR KNEES! DODGERS! EVERYBODY—BEND YOUR KNEES! DOWN AND READY! WANT THE BALL!!" Sometimes, he will point out one kid who appears not to be ready: "Danny! Down and ready!" Or he will move someone: "Sasha! Move in a step! No! Toward the grass! There!" The tension level is high, and it gets worse as our kids start missing balls, and throwing balls away. A batted ball gets by Alan, the shortstop, and then right through the left fielder, as three runs score. Harold yells: "Alan! You gotta stop that ball!" The manager chimes in, with more of a pleading voice, "C'mon, guys, you gotta stop the ball. Get in front of it!" After about five batters and more of the same, Harold moves into the dugout, sits, puts his head in his hands, and starts muttering to himself. One more error and he leaves the dugout, walks up the right field line a ways, and sits on the grass, leaning against the chain-link fence, and says nothing more until the end of the inning. It seems to me like a kind of self-banishment. In the stands, the parents sit in what seems to be a stunned silence. One of the moms breaks a silence by yelling some encouragement to the fielders: "Come on, Dodgers, you can do it! Down and ready!" Another mom takes up the chant: "Yeah, Dodgers! You can do it! Come on, guys!" In the third inning, with our team losing 10–1, we have the bases loaded. Hope springs eternal, as Alan stings a hard drive to right, but the outfielder leaps and snags it, making a beautiful catch to end the inning. The kids on our team moan, and one says, "That's no fair!" Coach Harold nearly explodes, wheels around to face the dugout and yells at our kids as they pick up their gloves: "THEY make the plays! THEY don't run away from the ball! They make the plays, is all it is! You guys gotta want the ball like their guys want the ball!"

Two years later, I was at one of Sasha's games and went to the snack bar to buy some sunflower seeds, Harold Zing was working behind the counter. As we struck up a friendly conversation, some havoc broke out on the playing field of 10–12-year-old boys. The manager was in the process of going slightly berserk, chastising a boy for making a throw that the manager had explicitly told him not to make. Harold chuckled and quipped, "That's the way *I* would be if I'd stayed in coaching! It would have been ugly! I prefer working the snack bar."

CREATING AN INNER CIRCLE

It may seem to be purely an individual decision that leads some men to opt in and others to opt out of this gender-sorting system in youth sports.

However, the creation of a situational hegemonic masculinity, like the CEO coach, is fundamentally a *collective* project, based in group values and interactions. There is an inner circle of men (joined in AYSO by a small number of women) who run these youth sports organizations, including creating and enforcing the dominant values as to what constitutes acceptable or unacceptable forms of leadership. How is the inner circle understood and experienced by youth coaches? When we asked coaches whether there was an inner circle, most said that there certainly was, but almost nobody claimed to be part of it. Most of the women coaches, as we saw in the previous chapter, see the inner circle as being made up of men. But most of the men coaches do not feel themselves to be part of the inner circle. Some men feel like real outsiders; others feel themselves to be at the margins of the inner circle but not fully a part of it.

The inner circle is a real group that wields a great deal of control over what happens in the leagues: they decide who to allow to be a head coach, how teams will be constituted, and which kids will be on the All-Star team. However, the inner circle is also a *symbolic* site, where the central ideals of situational hegemonic masculinity are constructed. Hegemonic masculinity serves as a symbolic exemplar that anchors men's privilege; however, few men actually conform fully to this narrowly defined expression of masculine power and status. Hegemonic masculinity is created generally along two gender axes: first, it is defined in opposition to women—and to anything that is considered "feminine"; and second, it is defined against other forms and styles of masculinity that are marginalized or subordinated.[18] In the following sections, I will discuss these two aspects of hegemonic masculinity in constructing the inner circle in youth coaching.

Men Coaches' Attitudes toward Women Coaches

Many of the men coaches we interviewed had not thought very much about the question of why there are so few women coaches. Alan Lindgren said that now that he thought about it, there were no women coaches in the girls' softball league that he was coaching in, and he was not sure why that was so. "I think people would be very open and would encourage a woman to do it, but for some reason, and despite the growth of softball, you know, maybe it's just, you know, a few years behind it's maturation, because there are not very many women involved." Albert Riley too said that he was not sure why there were so few women involved in softball coaching. When asked if he'd try to recruit a woman assistant coach, he first said, "If there's a gung-ho woman who wants to be involved, I would take 'em in a second." But he followed that statement by suggesting that most women just might not have the right stuff: "But I think most of them don't have confidence in their ability as a player, you know, so they don't want to get involved. You know they can't even, they can't catch a ball, or they can't throw it right, or whatever, so they won't do—they won't be involved."

Several of the men coaches recognized that from a woman's point of view it might be hard to break into coaching, because, in the words of soccer coach Doug Berger, women might see coaching as a "male domain." Paul Leung said that there are few women coaches because: "I think, very similar to my wife, she's just—they're not interested. It's like 'Whoa, maybe I shouldn't do this—maybe this is a man's thing.'" Similarly, Tony Barnett said that women may hesitate to volunteer to coach because they are a bit "cautious . . . I think they get nervous. Probably rightly so, [because] there's a little bit of an old boys' network among the coaches. And it's hard, hard to break in, particularly as you move up." Alex Riley was talking about how difficult it is for a new man to break in to the inner circle of softball coaches, and Suzel asked him, "How do you think it would be to break in if you're a woman coach?" Riley responded:

Um, well, it's hard to say, because we don't have any women. I've seen at other levels where there are more women coaches. Typically, as the kids get older—particularly the boys—the women coaches drop off . . . . In terms of a woman breaking into the circle, though, and what I've observed in the past, there tends not to be a problem in the U-10 area. I think it's more as they get older—I think it would be very difficult for a woman to break into the circle, for example. There's one woman in particular I think could do it in our region, but she's a very aggressive woman who played pro football in the professional women's league. So I think she would have no trouble with it.

Riley's statement illustrates two points that I have made previously. First, men's assumptions about women's low levels of sports competence helps to construct the glass ceiling that keeps most women from moving into coaching kids over the age of ten. And second, if a woman is going to have a chance to coach, and especially to break into the inner circle of coaches at the higher age levels, she had better be able to muster an impressive amount of sports capital, like having played professional football. In fact, there were no men whom we interviewed who expressed any opposition to the idea of women being head coaches; however, many of them believed that most women just simply didn't have the sports knowledge, aggressiveness, competitiveness, or desire to be a head coach, especially at the higher age-levels.

A small number of men coaches, though, did not see women's inability to advance to coaching older kids as entirely a function of something that the women lacked. Instead, they seemed to empathize with what women coaches might have to go through in a male-dominated context. Don Clark says that, at the lower age-levels, he has appreciated "a number of women who are really good coaches." But he believes that most of them don't continue on to coach in the higher age-levels because, "Some of them . . . just don't wanna have to deal with a bunch of testosterone-driven men that sometimes lose focus." Carlos Ruiz recognized that women coaches have to deal with a level of critical scrutiny from parents that most men coaches do not have to endure:

> I think that there would be an automatic question if you showed up with your kids to the first practice and you recognized that the coach was this woman, maybe even, God forbid, a *young* woman, standing there getting ready to direct a practice—that in the minds of most parents, I think, would have a question: "Who is she, how can we know she's gonna be an effective coach for our kids?" I think that that's a question that would probably be present for most people most of the time that wouldn't ever cross their minds if it's a male coach: "Oh well he's here 'cause he knows what he's doing."

As we saw in the chapter 3, the few women coaches who succeed in moving up to the higher-age-level teams do so by deploying certain gender strategies, including, in some cases, embodying and displaying aggressive, hypercompetitive styles. But what happens when a woman coach deploys these situationally hegemonic forms of masculinity? Don Clark seems to recognize the difficulty that women coaches have in a very competitive male environment, but his statement also shows that competitive women are sometimes viewed through the prism of a kind of double standard, and he speculates that while some of the extra burden that women coaches feel is real, some of it might be simply the perception of women coaches who have chips on their shoulders:

> I think a lot of women who could coach are probably intimidated by the environment they'd have to work in. I think it does take a unique kind of woman to hold her own without having to demand that she be respected, but to actually have a presence and a control. I mean, there are certain situations where I've had to be very confrontational with a coach, and, you know, I don't handle it in a way that's demeaning to the other coach or the other person I'm dealing with, but there's just a . . . boom! And a lot women are not comfortable in that head-to-head. Like, last year in girls under-10, I think there were four or five female coaches and I'm sure that they've had to deal with more than I'm aware of, but a couple of them [are] pretty chippy on the shoulder . . . . But, for the most part, I think the vast majority of coaches, male coaches, were real thrilled that they were there. So I think there's some perceived and some reality to the fact that it's a little tougher environment [for women].

Men on the Outskirts of the Inner Circle

Most men recognized that there is an inner circle of men who run youth sports, but almost none described themselves as being a part of it. Ted Miller said that he'd made "a lot of friends through the soccer program," and went on: "I think all the coaches—there's kind of a, you know, a brotherhood so to speak. You know, everybody feels camaraderie towards each other, and they're very supportive." However, Miller does not feel himself to be part of any inner circle of coaches who run things, nor does he really want to be:

> I'm really not part of the, what I would call the in-crowd in terms of the coaching network. And there is a group of them that I think I would

consider that, and I'm kind of outside of that. I think there's a group that's a little more passionate about it, and frankly a little more controlling about it. I think there's many of these individuals who need something to control, and you need those kind of people—otherwise the program doesn't exist—but I'm not one of those. And so I will help out. I like to give my time on the coaching side.

Though he had coached or managed his son's teams for several years and was at that time one of only four men who were managing South Pasadena's Juniors baseball teams, Campbell Weber still felt marginal to the "baseball dads group," saying that he had been "kind of surprised when they asked me to do Juniors." When I asked why he was surprised, he replied:

> Because there are a lot of dads out there with a lot of experience managing and with lots of knowledge, who are part of the baseball dads group. I'm not one of them. There's this sort of cool-dads cluster in Little League, and I'm not part of that group. So I was kind of surprised when they asked me. I think they were having real trouble getting managers. I had volunteered, so I'm on their list. It's not a matter of being disliked or disregarded. It's just that I'm not one of the cool dads.
>
> [What is it that makes one a cool dad?]
>
> Uh, what is it that makes kids popular in high school? It's the same thing. I basically don't socialize a lot. I take a more cerebral approach to life than a lot of them do. We don't come from the same backgrounds; I'm not that sociable.

Albert Riley, as we have seen, is viewed as a highly competitive and successful girls' softball manager, but while he feels himself to be accepted by the inner circle, he does not feel himself fully to be a part of it:

> Well, there's definitely a club of all the coaches who've been doing it for longer than I have. You know, they've been through a lot more of the meetings and the things and sort of know each other. And now that I'm one of them, you know, the guys, as I said, they all know me because, ah, for various reasons . . . . So there's that opportunity to know the people, but there's still kind of this circle of, you know, the guys will all kind of— you know. when people get together to talk about things and they'll kind of get together in a circle? They don't necessarily seek to include the new

guys yet, and I'm not alone in that. I can tell you that yesterday we were doin' a tryout for tournament teams and there was another coach there. This is his first year. And, you know, it's the same thing with him. I've noticed these guys who've kind of been [coaching] for a long time will kind of gather in a little group and start chatting about something, you know, and leave the two new guys to kind of deal with the kids.

Some coaches mentioned that one was more likely to be treated as a full member of the inner circle if one was also part of other powerful local networks, like being a member of the city council or the city planning commission. Carlos Ruiz considered himself to be on the "outskirts" of the AYSO "good old boys' network," which he described as "longtime people": "They would be people whose children participated in All-Star teams year after year, successful tournament teams, who have, uh, extensive personal networks within the city and the community of South Pasadena—political power in South Pasadena, [like] on the School Board."

"It's Not Rocket Science": A View from the Center

How does youth sports in South Pasadena look from the vantage point of the inner circle? Though most coaches we interviewed did not feel themselves to be part of an inner circle, they did mention names of those who they believe are. Bill Munson was one of those named by many women and men coaches as being a member of the inner circle of AYSO.

Indeed, Bill Munson is the quintessential insider. When I interviewed him in the living room of his plush Craftsman-style home, he was in his tenth straight year as a coach for an AYSO team and was serving as a league official. Munson grew up in South Pasadena, attended the public schools, played Little League Baseball and high school football there. After college and med school, he married, returned to South Pasadena, began a medical practice, purchased a home, and began with his wife to raise a family. Despite his wide-ranging athletic experience, and a bit of coaching experience from his college years, when his first daughter began AYSO, he was reluctant to coach, reasoning that he really didn't know that much about the sport of soccer:

My daughter, when she was five, she joined an AYSO team, and her coach was a high school student. And this young lady took these five-year-olds and played with 'em and worked with 'em. And they just loved her, and they had a great time that season. And for me as a parent watching it, on the one hand I really appreciated and admired what she was doing, and on the other hand I thought to myself, "It's not that hard." I mean, *obviously*— coaching soccer—if a high school student can do it, almost anyone can. I didn't know the first thing about the sport, but the next season I told my daughter, I said, "You know what, I'll coach you this year." And I think part of why I did that was in response to the experience she had that spring in Little League, for T-ball. We were disappointed with the coaching, because we felt like the players who didn't have parents who were coaching were really neglected and didn't develop very much, and didn't get much practice and didn't get much of an opportunity. So we were unhappy with the coaching, and so I thought to myself, "You know, gosh, a high school student can do this, and I sure would approach it differently if I were doing it than those guys did." And so in the fall I signed up for the coaching clinic and volunteered to coach. And, you know, I was just amazed at how much they taught me. I mean I didn't know the first thing about soccer other than you have to play with your feet and try and score goals and things like that . . . . But that was really the motivation for me was, I think, the combination of realizing, you know, this isn't rocket science. So that took away some of the fear side. And at the same time, that I think I can do better—I think I can do better for my child.

Bill Munson credits his own revelation that coaching youth soccer—a sport he'd previously had no experience with—was "not that hard," that "this isn't rocket science," to the good job that the AYSO organization does in educating new coaches in the fundamentals of the game. But Munson seemed less aware of how his own considerable capital—lots of athletic experience, insider status as a native South Pasadena guy who'd played community and school sports there, the fact that he is a tall, athletic-looking professional-class white male—also facilitated his ability to quickly move beyond the "fear side." As a league official, he says he works hard to recruit new women soccer coaches, and indeed, two of the women soccer coaches we interviewed credited Munson with encouraging them to coach. But based on his own experience of quickly overcoming his fears of coaching soccer, he remains puzzled and "really frustrated" with his failure to find "ways to beg, cajole, wheedle women to become coaches." He concludes that most of the women in this generation just lack the "confidence" to coach.

What Munson perhaps does not see as clearly is that it's not merely the kinds of knowledge one can learn in a coaching clinic—the formal rules of soccer and a few kicking and passing drills to teach five- and six-year-olds—that new coaches need. As we saw in the previous chapter, for women coaches the "rocket science" lies in gaining access to the "secret knowledge" of the inner circle of established men coaches; it lies in creating strategies to deal with the critical scrutiny of parents, coaches, and officials who assume that you don't know what you are doing until you prove otherwise. Men—especially professional-class, heterosexual men with athletic backgrounds—are assumed by others to know what they are doing, until they prove otherwise. So starting with a minimal amount of knowledge of the sport and how to teach it, a new man coach is off and running, gaining confidence quickly.

A friendly and well-meaning man who by most accounts puts some effort into trying to recruit women coaches, Bill Munson is baffled by what's holding most of the women back. In his experience, AYSO makes it easy for new coaches to learn the game of soccer, and thus to quickly gain confidence, so it must just be that there's some inner quality that a whole generation of women lack. Munson's words and his story offer a good illustration of how privilege operates. He empathizes with women, but his position within the center gives him a particular standpoint on knowledge. For instance, when I told him that many of the coaches we had interviewed spoke of an "inner circle" or an "old boys' network" that controlled youth soccer, baseball, and softball, he replied:

> You know, it's funny, when I first came in, I always felt there was an inner circle that I wasn't part of, and then, you know, becoming involved in the board and the leadership and then becoming a member of that circle, I suppose, you know, I realize that a lot of the kind of conspiracy theories that I had formed were just wrong, you know? I mean that, frankly, you know, from what I could see, there's no organized kind of, um . . .

It seemed to me that the closer Munson got to the center, the less clearly he could see it. By contrast, most women coaches (as well as marginalized men coaches) have different experiential standpoints, positions from which they see different aspects of reality, including usually something that they call an "inner circle" that operates mostly on an informal basis, rather than as some organized "conspiracy." It is important to study the experience and point of view of insiders like Bill Munson, but I find that their point of view is not as useful in understanding how marginalization happens and how inequalities are produced and contested. In fact, studies of members of superordinate groups—heterosexuals, whites, the rich, men—consistently conclude that the workings of power that create and sustain privilege are usually invisible to the members of these groups.[19] That's also true of researchers, such as me. As a white, heterosexual, professional-class man with a good deal of sports experience, I carry with me a considerable amount of privilege. Despite my sociological education and my grounding in feminist theory, and despite a lifelong immersion in sports, including several years of observing youth sports, I did not notice some of the most important informal processes through which women (and some men) coaches are marginalized, until I learned about them by listening to the women coaches' stories. For instance, I never noticed the ways that men coaches so often use their bodies and voices in the gendered space of the playing field, until women coaches told me about it. Sensitized to this issue, I returned to the playing fields and paid close attention to the men's voices, and this yielded rich insights, which I then drew on to create my analysis in this chapter and in chapter 3. In short, my strategy in this study has been to consciously begin with the insights of women coaches, as well as, to a certain extent, those of men who are conscious of their marginal status in coaching— men like Will Solomon, whose story opened this chapter. The standpoints of those on the margins have helped me to ask different questions about the center, and they have sensitized me to see different kinds of things in my field work. My views of men coaches in this chapter were shaped by this kind of feminist standpoint.[20] In the next chapter, I will turn to the question of how the construction of gender in youth sports by adults might impact the kids.

FIVE "They're Different—and They're *Born* Different"

ENGENDERING THE KIDS

The fields are wet on this cool, sunny day in late-January. Suzel and I cut back and forth from the Arroyo, where the boys' baseball tryouts are taking place, to the Orange Grove softball field, the site of the girls' tryouts. Both events are structured similarly, but they differ in some striking ways. The boys' tryout has a serious and formal feel to it. Milling around behind the backstop, the parents joke with each other and talk about how their sons (and they) are nervous about the tryout. Everybody knows that each boy's performance today is being scrutinized and is consequential. One of the parents tells me that he took his son to the batting cages early this morning to get him warmed up for this event; I realize—too late—that I should have done this for Sasha too, to give him an edge. Near the edge of the infield, in short right field, roughly a dozen managers, all men, sit in folding lawn chairs, holding clipboards, chatting with each other. Each boy wears a large number on his chest so that the managers can identify him. When it's his turn, the boy's name and number are announced over the P.A. system, after which the boy steps to the plate and swings at three or four pitches from a pitching machine. Before the final pitch, the coach who is running the machine yells to the boy, "Okay, run the bases on this next one." Whether the kid hits the ball or not, he runs the bases. Next, the boy fields three grounders from the shortstop position and throws to first; he then runs to the outfield and fields three fly balls hit by a machine, and then he's done. The managers in the chairs say nothing to the kids before, during, or after the tryout. But the notes they are taking on how well or poorly each boy hit, ran, fielded, and threw are the data they will use to place the boys in different leagues and teams in the upcoming draft.

At Orange Grove, there is a similar scene. People stand around talking and waiting as individual girls take their turn at the plate, then field and throw a few balls. As at the Arroyo, the managers (mostly men, but I see two women among them) are sitting, and a few are standing, as they write notes on clipboards. One difference here is that the pitching is being delivered "live," not by a machine. The man who is pitching is running a fairly constant monologue, giving tips and encouragement to each girl who steps to the plate. "Okay, Sweetie, watch the ball and hit it." In fact, he seems to call each girl who steps to the plate "Sweetie." There's another man standing near the plate who is giving lots of one-on-one instruction to each girl on her batting stance and swinging mechanics. The girls we are watching here are roughly the same age as the boys we had watched earlier at the Arroyo; however, the tone of the event is very different. The boys' tryout seemed impersonal, very formal. The coaches seemed to assume that the boys knew exactly what to do, and they just sat back and judged the boys' performances. The girls' tryout has a more informal feel to it, and the coaches' interactions with the girls are more directly warm, helpful, and sometimes (from my point of view) condescending in their tone.

Underlying the "everyone plays" philosophy at the heart of AYSO and Little League Baseball/Softball is the assumption that there are benefits for kids—healthy exercise, social development, building self-confidence, and having fun—that every kid has a right to. Every single coach we interviewed said that there was value in sports participation for kids. Doug Berger was happy that his daughter had played many years of soccer: "As my daughter gets older, I appreciate more and more the physical health it's given her. I mean, she's in great shape—she does cross country, she does track—you know, she does all these other things that she probably wouldn't have done if she hadn't have played soccer, because I don't think she was a natural athlete, and it gave her confidence." Pam Burke saw these kinds of benefits as her son's birthright and had decided to coach his soccer team after her son experienced a "horrible" coach: "I said, I am not going to have him turned away from competing in community soccer because he is not the star of the team. There is a place for everyone in AYSO. You don't have to be the star. And everyone should be able to play and have fun, and enjoy it and get better, and learn something, make a friend, and so for that reason I coached his team."

The enthusiasm that volunteer coaches have for the benefits of sports should not surprise us. A 2008 national survey indicated that 95 percent of parents in the United States agree that participation in youth sports raises kids' self-esteem, and a vast majority of adults expect educational, social, and health benefits to accrue to their athletic children.[1] And this parental support for kids playing sports is no longer reserved just for boys. Parents today overwhelmingly agree that sports participation is good for their daughters, too. But my research reveals some striking differences in how boys and girls are viewed and treated by adult volunteer coaches. As the vignette that opens this chapter illustrates, boys and girls can be engaged in a similar activity—in this case, a beginning-of-the-season tryout—on the very same day and yet have very different experiences. Here, as is usually the case in organized youth sports, the kids were sex-segregated, and in this case they had been tracked into playing different sports—boys displaying their baseball skills on one field, girls their softball skills on another. And though the content of the activity was very similar, the adults in charge shaped the informal dynamics of the activity quite differently. After watching these sorts of scenes, and especially after analyzing the coaches' responses to interview questions that got them directly talking about kids, coaches, and gender, I came to see tensions and contradictions between the commitment to equal access to sports for all kids that most adults espouse, on the one hand, and the fact that many adults think about, talk about, and treat boys and girls in quite different ways, on the other hand.

Parents today understand that in the not-too-distant past sports was considered to be just for boys.[2] As such, the institution of sport created categorical differences between women and men that helped to buttress ideologies of male superiority and power and female inferiority and submission. This belief in naturally occurring categorical difference between the sexes—what I call "hard essentialism"—provided the ideological foundation for the ideal post–World War II middle-class family, with a male breadwinner and female homemaker/mother. Today, youth sports can no longer support people's simplistic beliefs in categorical sex difference. In fact, it seems to have become common sense that sports are for boys *and* for girls. The adults in my study uniformly applauded girls' participation in sports, and many spoke of the advantages they think will accrue to girls who play. Soccer coach Al Evans, for instance, saw sports participation for his daughter as a kind of inoculation against sexist dangers that girls and young women face in daily life: "I'm like the original Title IX dad. I so believe, you know, whether my girls are good at it or not, I want her to play, because it's, like, all the things you're fighting against— young women, you know, the billboards, the this, the that, the sexuality of everything, I mean *all* of that. Sports is our like anti-drug program, ultimately." Whether such expectations about the wide-ranging benefits of sports for girls are fully realistic or not, parents' support for girls playing sports makes it far more difficult today for them to hold to simplistic, categorical views of natural sex difference. Girls' and women's massive movement into sport over the past thirty years has made sport a realm of contested gender relations.[3] Participants within such a contested terrain are forced to deal with built-in contradictions. This was reflected in my interviews with youth coaches.

When asked to reflect on whether or how it mattered for boys to be coached by men or by women, and girls to be coached by men or by women, most coaches meandered and often struggled to weave a coherent narrative. I found it fascinating that these thoughtful and articulate people could be so clear-thinking and plainspoken about nearly everything, but when it came to questions about kids, coaches, and gender, there was a great deal of confusion, hemming and hawing, and contradiction in their statements. It often seemed to me that I was hearing them struggling on the spot to weave together a coherent narrative on gender, using threads of thought that clashed with one another. In disentangling these complicated narratives, I have identified three threads that coaches variously wove into their talk about coaches, kids, and gender:

Equality. This view sees social equality between boys and girls, and between women and men, as desirable. The more moderate version of this thread expresses support for girls' participation in sports. The more consciously feminist purveyors of this view see sport as a way for girls to become empowered in a sexist society, and they advocate for more women coaches to help empower girls and to challenge boys' sexist assumptions about women. On its own, the Equality Thread has trouble supporting adults' narratives of children and sport, because sex-segregated sports, divisions of labor in families and workplaces, and essentialist beliefs continue to undercut a full-on commitment to the ideal of social equality.

Natural Difference. Adults who use this thread narrate boys and girls, men and women, as naturally "hard-wired" to be different. In its extreme form, this view sees two binary, categorically different sexes (men are from Mars, women are from Venus) who have traits that (ideally) complement each other—like Yin and Yang, instrumental and expressive, breadwinner and homemaker. By itself, the categorical "hard essentialism" of the Natural Difference Thread can no longer hold up to form a coherent narrative on kids and gender, as it has been challenged by feminist ideals of equality and by empirical evidence that shows that when girls and women play sports, many of them are stronger, faster, and more skilled than many boys and men.[4]

Equity-with-Difference. This thread, a narrative attempt to negotiate the tensions between feminist beliefs in social equality and essentialist beliefs in natural difference, posits girls and boys as separate and different but favors equal opportunities for all kids. I will spend the majority of this chapter discussing the nuances of this thread, and I will show that there are common asymmetries in the ways that adults negotiate the tensions between these two principles when talking about boys or talking about girls. The result is an ascendant gender ideology that I call "soft essentialism."

Though most of the coaches draw on elements of each of these three threads, they don't use them equally. A few use far more of the Equality Thread to weave their narrative of coaches, kids, and gender. A few draw more on the Natural Difference Thread. Most coaches use a bit of each of these first two threads, woven together with a large spool of the Equity-with-Difference Thread, to create the narrative fabric of soft essentialism. In this chapter, I will draw mostly from interviews to illustrate how the tensions within and between coaches' narratives about kids and gender reveal emergent contradictions and tensions in contemporary gender relations, both inside and outside organized sports.

"YOU CAN DO ANYTHING A GUY CAN DO": THE EQUALITY THREAD

It is an accomplishment of feminism that, in roughly three decades, we have changed the ways we think about, talk about, and organize youth sports. A moderate form of the Equality Thread of coaches' narratives about gender was expressed by many coaches as support for girls' opportunities to play sports, and by some as a desire for more "balance" in the number of women and men coaches. A few coaches, more often women than men, spoke of gender and youth sports in more overtly feminist terms. I would define a "feminist" sensibility, in the most general sense, as incorporating three beliefs: first, that sex-segregated institutional arrangements, buttressed by sexist beliefs (and sometimes violence), have systematically harmed and disadvantaged girls and women, while privileging men; second, that the narrow definitions of masculinity that boys are encouraged to adopt in order to compete for a share of patriarchal privilege tend to harm boys and men, narrowing their range of emotional expressivity and damaging their health and relationships; and third, that we should commit ourselves to individual and collective actions that change these arrangements, to move toward social equality that empowers girls and women and more fully humanizes boys and men. Coaches who wove strong strands of the Equality Thread into their narratives tended to invoke one or more of the following three themes: the importance of adult female role-modeling for girls; women coaches as better able to understand and meet the particular needs of girls; and women coaches as helping to generate respect for women from both girls and boys.

Role-Modeling for Girls

Isabel Bacad saw her work as a soccer coach as part of a mission to empower girls to play sports, and to become coaches later in life: "I think it tells them that I can coach—*women* can coach—it's not just the men that can coach sports, and it may push them to continue with the sport or maybe coaching later on too. If they see that other women are coaching, yeah, they can do it too." Joan Ring says that she gets support from other mothers for being a strong female role model for girls: "The mothers—they all say, 'I'm so glad my daughter got you 'cause she needs a role model like you.' And people in the community come up to me: 'Well, maybe my daughter can be on your team, with a woman coach; we've never had one of those.'"

For Pam Burke, being a role model for girls hits close to home. Burke had been a "tomboy" as a young girl, and had experienced the enjoyment of athletic participation but also the pain of being "ostracized and shunned" by both boys and girls during adolescence:

> I think that it is very important for girls to have female role models in athletics, and there aren't many. I remember when I was growing up, I was a tomboy. And for many years I was accepted by the boys, because I could compete—you know, out in the streets, in the playground, in school. Um, but not by the girls; they didn't want the rough-and-tumble girl in their group. But at some point the boys couldn't be seen with the girls—we couldn't be playing together. And so—that was kind of a tough place to be, as a girl who wants to play sports—when the boys start turning away and saying, "Uhhh, this is just for boys." 'Cause you are kind of ostracized—at least when I was a kid, I was, you know, *shunned*, by both groups for a while.

Now, as a mother and a girls' soccer coach, Pam Burke is motivated in part by a desire to create a positive, affirming space where athletically oriented girls feel fully accepted:

> I had [a] little girl on my All-Star team, and she—she reminded me of me. She was a tomboy: she wore boys' clothes, she had a boys' haircut, and her mom told me that year, she had a horrible, horrible year at school. Because that was the year that the boys started rejecting her. And the girls

didn't want her. And she didn't want to be with the girls anyway. She wanted to play sports; she didn't want to, you know, sit and talk about going to mall and braiding your hair and whatever. And she was thankful—her mom was coming to me, to thank me for—showing that it was okay, to be in sports, even as a women, a mother. You know, you don't have to be a *man* to be in sports. You can be a woman, you can be a girl, and still be in sports and still be accepted. And she said her daughter really benefited from having a woman coach, so that was part of my motivation for coaching my daughter's team.

Doug Berger, too, thinks it would be beneficial to have more women coaches as role models, not just to empower girls in sports, but in other aspects of life, too: "My daughter, from a very early age, we kind of instilled in her that you can do anything a guy can do, and she was a cheerleader in junior high school, but she also played soccer and she was good in academics, and it was very important to us that she did all of it, and not just, you know, just get one side or the other. And her coaches in cross-country are female, her coach in soccer is female, and I think it's good for her to have that role model." Berger saw female adult role models in sports as important to his daughter's understanding that she "can do anything a guy can do," and his words invoke an image of a gender-divided social world, to which he wanted his daughter to have full access: having his daughter play sports was part of a hope that she not "just get one side or the other." This idea, that women coaches in sports can help girls to broaden their outlook and their possibilities in life, is a common aspect of the Equality Thread in parents' narratives about their daughters.

Men Coaches Can't or Don't Give Girls What They Need

Some coaches said that they favor having more women coaches for girls because women better understand the particular kinds of problems and constraints that girls face in a sexist society. Pam Burke said, "I think there is a quality or characteristic about women that men often lack or fail to demonstrate, and that is the emotional aspect of supporting their players. I often see men not doing that, and I don't think they do it to be malicious and I'm not saying they are mean to their players, but sometimes they fail to support them emotionally . . . . I don't know if as a rule men are willing to do that, and I think women are." Some of the men coaches spoke of an "awkwardness" in talking about "certain topics" with the girls on their teams. Soccer coach Lenn Molina said he sometimes uses his team mom to talk to the girls:

> I know with men it's kinda hard for [the girls] to relate, and it's hard for *me* to relate to the girls sometimes, and that's why I have a team mom. I go, "Uh, could you?" and she's like, "Sure, I'll help you with this situation." Sometimes it's emotional, sometimes it's—it's physical, sometimes it's, "Well, I don't wanna talk to the coach; coach is a guy"—where they don't wanna tell me, because it's something personal, and they'll go to their own peers first, they always do that, but if they had a female coach, they might open up more.

Molina's description of the girls' needs to talk about "personal" matters, and his acknowledgement that "Sometimes it's emotional, sometimes it's—it's physical" speaks to the awkwardness that some male coaches feel in teaching or counseling girl players, beyond the technicalities of the game. Part of this awkwardness that some men feel with girls has to do with a particular form of gendered surveillance that men commonly experience.

We spoke with soccer coaches about the Safe Haven Certification course that AYSO requires all coaches to take in order to ensure the kids' emotional and physical health and safety. Much of this course focuses on things that coaches should know to avoid any possible hint of inappropriate sexual contact or relations with the kids. Some coaches saw the course as "mostly common sense," and a few saw it as a "total waste of time." Most of the coaches we spoke with recognized the need to be cognizant of this danger when adults work with kids. As soccer coach Al Evans said, "I think that it's a legitimate concern, you know—I've done a lot of research on, like, child molestation and stuff like that—it's bad. I mean, it's like half the women in the United States don't even make it to eighteen without being molested or raped, I mean, it's, like, atrocious, right? So, I mean, all this stuff's very real to me. It's just, it's just living in the modern world."

However, most men coaches recognized how the general climate of distrust of men who work with kids has led them to limit their interactions with the kids in ways that make them "safe" from suspicion but that also severely constrain their ability to interact in an emotionally supportive way. Ironically, it seems to be that the men coaches who are most aware of the emotional needs of the kids are the ones who feel most constrained by the context. Soccer coach Dave Chadwick said that his male cousin one time had a formal complaint filed against him by a parent, who accused him of "inappropriately touching" a boy on his team. The boy had been lying down on the field injured and crying, and the coach had knelt next to him, "in front of probably fifty parents and thirty kids," and was "kind of holding the ankle and just kind of touching down by the shoe, and then he went by the knee and kind of was touching to see if everything was okay. Basically, kind of checking and seeing where did it hurt and was this child going to be able to continue." Chadwick said that this incident, and the general feeling of scrutiny, has led him to be very careful and limited in his emotional and physical interactions with the girls on his team:

> In Safe Haven, it's almost like you have to build a concrete fortress around ya and just—and I understand the liability issues, but there comes a point to where—there was a girl who was five or six years old and it was the morning of the opening day, where they walk around the track and the teams introduce and they wave to the parents in the stands, and this little girl, this little Jenny, she came running up and just grabbed my legs so tight. I mean, she wouldn't let go. It was like, "I need you right now. I need to be hugged." And it's like, I'm sorry, I'm a hugger and— you know, times like that, I mean, *I can't.* When my girls would come up to me and sometimes they get hurt, sometimes they get—all different emotions . . . . I think it's a connection. It's kind of an emotional connection. It's at times a physical connection.

Especially when the situation calls for "a physical connection," Chadwick and other male coaches said that they deploy conscious strategies:

> You know, I'll high-five, or I'll, you know, touch girls on the top or give them a little headlock around the head. I'm very careful . . . . It's an issue, and it scares the hell out of all of the coaches. I mean, we're all living in fear. It is a problem. In terms of being with girls, my general policy has

been that if I'm dealing with kids that are eight and under, I'm gonna hug 'em. They come up to me, they've hurt themselves, they fell and got a little booboo on their knee and they come runnin' over to me and they hug me, I'm not gonna turn 'em away. I make it open in front of the whole field, protect myself as much as I can. As the kids get older, I'm more careful. It's head, sometimes hand on the shoulder, on the side of the head, high five, top of the head—very, very, very careful. It sucks.

This practice of patting kids on the tops of their heads (mentioned by several of the men coaches) as a substitute for hugging, is reminiscent of the strategies used by male elementary school teachers studied by the sociologist Paul Sargent. Male teachers, Sargent said, may be privileged in some ways, compared with their female counterparts who far outnumber them, but they are aware of being under constant suspicion and scrutiny as potential child molesters, and they respond by never allowing a child to sit on their laps, giving head pats instead of hugs, and never being alone with a child.[5]

Though suspicion and scrutiny of men may explain some of the male coaches' emotional distance from their players, and some of their awkwardness in talking with girls about "personal" issues, it is likely also grounded in men's having been raised as emotionally stunted, "normal" boys who have had their capacity for empathy systematically suppressed.[6] Some men coaches' lack of emotional support for their players can extend to sexist (albeit unintended) damage inflicted on girls. A woman soccer coach e-mailed me a few months after I had interviewed her, appalled by the following story about her daughter Meryl's male coach's incompetence and insensitivity to girls' common body issues:

Meryl has a male coach in GU10. At the first mini-practice, she is the oldest and twice as tall as the others in this two-year grouping. She is muscular and bigger. The coach has coached his sons in the past, 12 yr. old and 15. He tells the little girls, "Do a toe kick." This is something that from day one, you try to school out of kids. That is not how you kick in soccer. When I comment, in shock, he has this, "these are little girls" reply—"this is all they can do." Even though some of them have been in the AYSO Under-six and Under-eight divisions in the past. We break and meet in a circle some time later. He looks down at Meryl and says, "When you are finished this season your legs will look like hers," and he points out a little girl half Meryl's height and size. COMPARING IN FRONT OF THE GROUP! Then he says, "They will be pure muscle." I assume he is trying to recover. The following day before the first practice I take him aside and tell him that with girls it is not a good idea to comment about their bodies. Meryl is particularly self-conscious about her body and her legs (she doesn't like to wear shorts even). I assumed that he slipped up, but instead he said that he had no idea that what he said might be offensive and he took my comment well. I, of course, was outraged (inside). It may be incorrect to assume that women are more sensitive to these female cultural issues on body image, problems with anorexia, etc. in our society.

Reflected in this story is the mother's recognition of the kinds of issues that girls and young women face in a world that teaches them to be ultra-critical of their own bodies, and of how this self-surveillance can contribute to eating disorders and related health problems. Cognizant parents hope that sports will help their daughters develop healthy habits and positive body images, but this mother's story suggests that an insensitive male coach's words can possibly undo this positive potentiality in sports, and she wonders whether women coaches might be more "sensitive to these female cultural issues on body image."[7]

Women Coaches Teach Girls and Boys to Respect Women

Rosa Ramirez does not think it's particularly important for boys to be coached by men. To the contrary, she thinks it's "a bad thing" that so many kids assume that women should just be team moms, and she would like to see more women coaching girls and boys. Jessica Torres agrees: "Oh yeah, definitely, I think a lot of kids would like to see their moms out there. You know, I think it would add a little bit of heightened respect for the woman, you know. Because they're used to seeing them in a homemaker role or just—you know, not that women don't work nowadays, but it's just not in that athletic role, you know. I think it would give them a newfound respect for women in general." Norma Delgado also said that she thinks it's important for more women to coach boys: "I would love more, yeah, I think that's important. I think it breaks gender stereotypes. I think it's important for boys to see women outside of the tradition of the roles [like] the team mom that they're used to seeing them in. I think that they don't realize that a lot of women have a competitive fire that can inspire them as much if not more than the dads who are yelling at them, you know. I think it'll go a long way to, you know, perceiving women in terms of equal . . . for boys to see women coaching boys."

A small number of the men also went beyond simply saying it's desirable to have "balance" between women and men. For instance, Bill Munson said that his ideal for AYSO would be "to have half women and half men coaching," because, "I think it's real good for boys to see women in a coaching experience, and frankly I think it's good for girls to see women in a coaching experience—for all kids to see moms or wives or women in a role of leadership, particularly in athletics, where you know historically women have not been." And one of the more stridently feminist statements on this topic was made by soccer coach Carlos Ruiz, who said that it's important for there to be women coaching girls and boys:

> I think that social positions for boys and girls are still different in our society. I think there are things that happen in society that are much more destructive of girls, especially at this age, from beginning about age ten to about age twenty that have very serious consequences. So to have them experience their own power as women, I think, is helpful to have strong women in their lives that are not their mothers.
>
> [Do you think it's important for boys to be coached by women?]
>
> Yes, I do. I think that the benefits would be that they stop associating all women that they know with the women's portrayal in mass culture or even the role of their own mother in their own lives, and that they broaden their experience of who women are in society. And that that could be achieved by having a strong, a good female coach.

"THEY'RE JUST DIFFERENT": THE NATURAL DIFFERENCE THREAD

Coaches' essentialism—their belief in natural differences between boys and girls—tends to run up against their commitment to equality for girls and boys. And, as I shall show, it tends to be stronger when they are talking about boys than when they are talking about girls. When asked whether there are good reasons for boys to be coached by men, soccer coach Michael Ortiz said yes, especially for older boys:

> At U10, because the level of play is a lot more rigorous, the kids are a lot more demanding—you're starting to get some prepubescent boys here and, just the energy level and that type of thing . . . . I think the boys respect more a male figure at that point. I've noticed it particularly for some of the players that have single moms. I think boys need interaction with men. There's some studies that have been in England showing that boys who become homosexuals tend to have a very poor relationship with their father between the critical ages of three or four years old and seven. So, I think there's a real important time to have a good role model, whether it's a father or coach or whatever at that point in time. Beyond that, I think there are certain things that you need to teach boys, and I think men can model that. Um, I don't think that women, because we're wired differently, you know, can. I think women have something to offer boys. I don't necessarily think that it has to be a coach. It could be a Cub Scout leader or whatever that could provide a female influence, but I think at some point I think there needs to be a male interaction.

Ortiz's statement shows some of the common strains in conservative essentialist thought about gender. He believes that women and men are "wired differently," but this hard-wiring is clearly not enough, in his mind, to ensure that boys become properly masculine and heterosexual. At the heart of his argument is the belief that boys and girls need "appropriate modeling of womanliness and manliness, you know, femininity and masculinity," and that one way to model this is through coaching. When asked if he thought it was good for girls to have women coaches, his response revealed a common way that gender essentialism is played out in adults' narratives about youth sports:

> Um . . . is it important? I know that there's a lot of dads that coach soccer for girls and that's fine. Because again, you need appropriate modeling of womanliness and manliness, you know, femininity and masculinity, I think, regardless of whether you have boys or girls. I want my daughter to know how a man should act appropriately as well as I want my sons.

Put simply, despite the presence of girls in sports—which he supports—Ortiz still views adult leadership in sport as a primarily male realm, a place where men can model "appropriate" forms of masculinity for boys *and* for girls. Thus, while it's okay for women to coach girls, it's not necessary. But it *is* necessary for men to coach boys, in order to model masculinity and to prevent homosexuality. Albert Riley, who coaches girls' softball, held a similar view:

> I think it's much more important for men to coach boys than it would be for women to coach boys. Again the respect issue, and I just think from a perspective of a dad, like a dad with a son or whatever, um, you know, moms are so important in the growing up and the maturing process and all that, [but] I just don't think that they would get the response as a coach of boys that a man would get from boys.

As we have seen, most women coaches do not complain of a lack of respect from kids, but they do feel pressure from parents, especially from fathers. And it's fathers' essentialist views—especially as they relate to their sons—that help to create and maintain the glass ceiling on women coaches in boys' sports, especially baseball. Joan Ring said, "Well, my experience in general is that parents are happier to have a female coach coach girls than they are to have a female coach coach boys." And Barbara Jones said that a woman coach has to deal with the parent who thinks, "Who's this woman coaching my son?" Indeed, George Starr told me a story, his voice betraying his incredulous disapproval, of a man who did not want his son coached by a woman:

> A couple of years ago, there was this lady moved to town, and she volunteered to coach a Little League team. She had experience, so I backed her, and she was approved by the board. That year we were having trouble getting enough coaches, and I had tried and tried to get Kirk Babcock to coach, but he said no, he'd rather not coach that year; he'd rather just run the league. Well, come draft day, Kirk's son is drafted by this lady. Immediately, Kirk announces that he's decided to coach, and takes his son off her team. He just didn't want his son to be coached by a woman.

Somewhat ironically, coaches' narratives about girls sometimes served as a basis for arguing for the value of women coaches. For instance, Albert

Riley—probably among the least "feminist" coaches we interviewed—sees value in having more women coaches, especially as girls get older and go through puberty. When asked if he thinks it is important for women to coach girls teams, he replied:

> I do. I do. I wish more did, and I wish more qualified women would step up and take that on, because I think it would be better, because, you know, girls can relate to women better. I mean, I had a situation this year where my [male] coach and I are playing catch and all of a sudden these girls are talking about a girl at school [whose] period started. And now they're all talking about this. I said, "G-Girls, Coach Seth and I don't need to hear this stuff!" [*He laughs.*] And what do they do?—Next thing you know they're all around one of the moms who's my scorekeeper, talking about it, you know. And those types of things [women] can relate to, you know, and if a girl's having a prob—an issue or something.

THE EQUITY-WITH-DIFFERENCE THREAD

How do adult coaches simultaneously make sense of their belief in natural differences between the sexes and their commitment to equality for girls and boys? How are these apparently contradictory beliefs woven together in their narratives about kids and sports? Several themes emerged from the interviews that can be seen as ways that adults attempted to navigate the complicated terrain of thinking and talking about kids and gender in this era of increasing opportunities for girls. First, most coaches believe that it is necessary to have sex-segregated sports for boys and girls because of what they assume to be the natural differences between the sexes. Second, rather than talking about "equality" for women and men coaches, many spoke of favoring a "mix" of women and men that would benefit kids by providing them with the different traits they assumed men and women bring to coaching. Third, many coaches talk (approvingly) about how sports participation can stretch girls *away* from their presumably softer and cooperative nature and *toward* more individualistic, competitive, and aggressive traits that will benefit them, while assuming (often implicitly) that playing sports

is already fully consistent with boys' aggressive and competitive natures. And fourth, many coaches view boys as having a singular simple
natural essence, yet seem also to assume that they are vulnerable to feminization if they are not hardened by the leadership of adult men.

Sex-Segregated Sports

In 1973, when Little League Baseball was fighting their legal battles to exclude girls from baseball, LLB president Dr. Creighton J. Hale, who held a
Ph.D. in physiology, drew on biological arguments to make the case
against girls' inclusion. "There are differences between the male and female, in spite of the trend now to say there aren't any differences," he argued, adding that boys had more muscle fibers and "power units" that
made them faster and stronger than girls. It is indicative of the sea-
change brought about by girls' movement into sport that by the year
2001, this same Dr. Hale had changed his views. He now says that girls'
inclusion in sports is "one of the best things that's happened," and he
speaks proudly of one of his granddaughters in Ohio: "This year she became the first girl ever selected to play on the Little League [Baseball]
tournament team there." Referring to his own transformation, he wryly
adds, "What goes around comes around."[8] Like many adults interviewed
in my study, Dr. Hale no longer holds categorically essentialist views that
would bar girls from playing certain sports. And it's notable that he, like
many men of his generation, has had his eyes opened not so much by
medical science, but by seeing with his own eyes how his daughters' or
granddaughters' athletic abilities blossomed, once they were given the
opportunity to play.

While girls' movement into sports has challenged essentialist assumptions, most adults still seem to believe that sports should be sex-
segregated. This continued sex-segregation of kids' sports creates a
context within which essentialism can still be constructed, albeit in a
somewhat different form. One common way that youth sports coaches
bridged their belief in opportunities for girls with their belief in natural
difference was to talk less often in terms of *equality* (a condition within
which boys and girls are fully equal in status, rights, and opportunities),

and more in terms of *equity* (a condition within which every individual is treated fairly and impartially). For many people, the idea of treating girls "fairly" coexists straightforwardly with the idea that their essential difference from boys requires that they be separated into different sports activities. As we have seen, AYSO separates girls and boys from the very youngest ages, while Little League allows sex-integrated T-ball for the youngest kids but then herds kids onto separate gendered paths—boys to baseball, girls to softball.

The United States long ago broke away from the "separate but equal" idea that underlay race relations during the Jim Crow era, acknowledging ultimately that separate schools, drinking fountains, restaurants, buses, and other public facilities are inherently *un*equal. By contrast, most advocates of gender equity in sports in the United States have explicitly argued for *equitable but separate* athletic funding, leagues, and facilities for girls and women. Recently, though, political scientist Eileen McDonagh and journalist Laura Pappano have argued provocatively that there is no good reason for our routine separation of girls' and boys' sports, and that this institutionalized sex-segregation disadvantages girls and women—in short, they argue that "separate is not equal in sports."[9] What are the implications of the ways that we routinely sex-segregate children's sports? How do adults balance this separation of boys' and girls' sports activities against their commitment to equity for all kids? Though nearly all of the coaches seem implicitly to accept sex-segregation, some ask critical questions about it. Soccer coach Kathi Ralston brings a feminist sensibility to her criticism of sex-segregation in Little League, while also neatly weaving together her belief in natural difference with her commitment to equity for girls and boys. Boys and girls are just different, she says, but at the same time, she wants opportunities opened up to them that offer them a range of choices:

> The thing I find very funny is, Why is there softball? I mean, it's a sexist sport. Can't girls play baseball? Or why can't boys play softball? It's just sort of a random thing—I guess they thought girls needed a softer ball, and it's a slower and safer game. Why don't they have a girls' Little League [Baseball], you know? It seems like softball was just invented as a dumbed-down baseball. I don't think you would ever hear of a boy

playing softball . . . . I have to say, having had daughters and having had a son, it's made me throw up my arms and say, "Whatever. They're different—and they're *born* different." [But] I think that instead of drawing this line, that boys can only do this and girls only that, we need to draw a path that's broad enough so that they can all do whatever they want.

What Ralston is expressing is a rejection of categorical separation of boys and girls in favor of an opening of choices to kids, and this belief exists alongside her essentialist belief that "They're different, and they're *born* different." Soccer coach Nikki Lopez also favors doing away with sex-segregated sports for kids, because she thinks it would make girls better athletes:

> There probably are a lot of people that don't agree with me: I think the girls and the boys should play together. I know a lot of AYSO regions do play the girls and boys together under-6. But girls would be much better athletes, and I don't think that it would bring the boys down if they play together. I mean our girls play together with the boys at school at recess and in both soccer and basketball. I've seen them play basketball; they beat the boys all day long. I just think overall that women would be much better athletes, much more competitive athletes, and I don't think that it would do any harm to the boys, it won't bring them down a level, if they played together.

Most coaches, however, disagree with Ralston and Lopez, and believe it's best for girls and boys to have separate leagues. Soccer coach Barbara Jones, for instance, fears that putting the kids together might disadvantage the girls, perhaps driving them away from playing sports: "I like it when they're separate. I like having the girls and boys separate. There used to be co-ed at the under-6. But I think it's nice for the girls to have their own teams. You know, I think that you might find a different dynamic—I think you'd find different issues. I think you'd find the coaching was different for the girls than for the boys on the same team. Or the treatment was different. So, to me, I like having them separated."

As Jones's words suggest, the question of what's best for kids—sex-segregated or integrated teams—is complicated, even from a feminist perspective. If one is interested in giving boys experiences that will counter the kinds of sexist attitudes and assumptions that they commonly develop in male-only sports, then one would likely favor co-ed sports. The more boys can learn, early on, that will allow them to fully respect girls' and women's full range of abilities, the better off they will be in their future relationships with women—as classmates, co-workers, bosses, and family members. However, if one is thinking of girls' interests, this seems a more complicated question. As Barbara Jones suggested, she fears that, especially given the fact that coaching is still so dominated by men, sex-integrated teams might create "different issues . . . different treatment" that might alienate girls, pushing them out of sports and thus denying them the many benefits of sports participation. Perhaps a good middle ground at this historical moment would be to do both—to have all-girls' leagues as an option, alongside fully integrated leagues.[10] For the moment, though, the vast majority of kids do play in sex-segregated sports, and this leaves few opportunities for essentialist assumptions to be fully contested. I have written elsewhere of the valuable lessons that young boys can learn when they see with their own eyes that the girls they are playing sports with are every bit as skilled as the boys are.[11] But kids older than age five or six rarely if ever get a chance to play organized co-ed sports. After T-ball, most girls are channeled into playing softball, but they retain a legal right to play Little League Baseball, and occasionally during my years of field research I saw a baseball team with a girl on it. What kind of impact does this have on kids' and adults' assumptions about gender? Consider the following field note, taken during a 13–14-year-olds Little League Baseball game:

> It's a playoff game, with everything at stake. The winner goes on to play another game; the loser is done for the season. Tight game, late innings; you can feel the tension in the air with every pitch. James hits a sharp grounder down the third base line, just fair. Their third baseman darts quickly to her right, backhands the ball well behind the bag, her momentum carrying her into foul territory. She plants her right foot and makes the long throw, a laser to first base, just nipping the runner. A very tough play on this full-sized field. What's remarkable to me is that nobody in the dugout (or behind me in the stands) remarks that it was the only girl on either team that made this play. A kid in our dugout just says, "Damn. Great play!" and the game goes on.

What struck me about this moment was just how unremarkable it was that the kid who made this "great play" was the only girl on the field. Perhaps since the boys had already been through many seasons where there was a girl here, a girl there playing baseball with them, it was simply no big deal that a girl had made such a good play. Does this kind of moment in some fundamental way challenge essentialist ideas the boys might otherwise be learning through sex-segregated sports? I can't answer this question definitively, as I did not interview the kids. But what I can say is that the boys on both teams, and the adults in the stands— some of whom had earlier that same day watched their daughters play softball—saw this girl make that nice stop and the perfect throw. The mere presence of a highly skilled girl competing effectively with the boys creates a different dynamic that makes the creation of hard, categorical essentialism less likely. On the other hand, perhaps this moment was unremarkable precisely because the girl who made this great play is *not* viewed as representing the category "girls." Rather, perhaps the girl is a single "token," who instead of challenging assumptions of natural differences between the sexes becomes a kind of "honorary," or "fictive," boy, like the girls who cross gender boundaries in Barrie Thorne's classic study of children and gender on grade school playgrounds?[12] Despite the occasional girl "crosser" into boys' sports, the dominant fact about how we structure kids' sports is (near) categorical sex-segregation.

A "Mix" of Women and Men is Good for Kids

A second way that adults bridge a belief in equality with a belief in natural difference is to talk not about creating equal opportunities for women coaches, but to speak in somewhat more vague terms of the benefits of there being "balance," or a "mix" of women and men, in coaching youth sports. Soccer coach Dave Chadwick said: "I don't think there has to be one gender or another [coaching the kids] necessarily. It'd be nice if there were a balance, I guess." Soccer coach Terri Patrick sees boys and girls as having a different, probably biologically based, essence, but he likes the idea that men and women coaches can bring unique and complementary traits to coaching:

I think men and women contribute some very similar things and some very different things. I think men obviously have been raised to be more competitive, women have been raised to be more cooperative—whether that's an inherent, um, genetic difference, I kind of tend to believe that it is. I tend to believe the way that we have evolved as humans have created some inherent gender differences in the way we approach life. There are differences in our brains in the way that they work.

These essentialist ideas, however, do not lead Patrick to conclude that girls should be excluded from sports, or that kids are better suited having men coaches. Instead, she states that with a "mix" of women and men in coaching, kids will benefit from exposure to the range of attributes that men and women bring to the field:

I think women, for boys, will teach them that soccer is a team sport. I think they approach the sport differently, and approach team sports differently, as a cooperative team effort, which is what gets you the results. Men's approach is that it's a competitive thing, and I think they tend to reward superstars more then they do a team effort. [So] I think it's equally important for boys and girls—it's nice for girls to see a woman as a role model; it's nice for boys to see a woman as a role model. I think it's better for the kids to see a mix.

Many coaches spoke of this "mix" or "balance" between women and men in ways that revealed a certain asymmetry in their thinking about boys and girls. For instance, soccer coach Don Clark said that having more women coaches and more male elementary school teachers is desirable because both boys and girls "just crave that balance, that additional dimension of humanity":

I'm traditional in a lot of my views, but not nearly as much as maybe my father or my grandfather, and I really think that there needs to be fluidity between the genders. I think that's very important—the kind of more-fluid nature between the genders in lots of aspects of life. And I think the more young boys and young girls are exposed to both male and female coaches and politicians and parenting and parenting styles, I think it just leads to a better, more multidimensional, probably stronger adult in the future.

As Clark's words clearly indicate, his view may in some ways echo a "traditional" essentialism, but this is not his father's or his grandfather's essentialism. It is an essentialism that recognizes the contemporary blurring (though surely not obliteration) of boundaries between men's and women's separate worlds, and the "fluid nature" of those who move across those boundaries. As he continued to speak, however, his views of boys' and girls' differences suggest that he sees them fitting differently within this world:

> There's a different—girls are very competitive and can be very competitive, but their approach to a lot of sports is different than boys and I think—I think it's probably more pure. I mean, you know, sometimes guys can get so doggone *focused*—myself included—that it's just, it becomes like this *laser,* and I think female athletes see a bigger field a lot of times, see a bigger dynamic, see a more fluid give-and-take situation than boys.

As with other coaches we interviewed, it seems that the "fluidity between the genders" that Clark sees really relates more to the girls than to the boys. The images he invokes suggests girls are "more fluid" and are able to "see a bigger field," while boys are relatively fixed, "focused . . . like this *laser.*" This idea, that girls are flexibly able to move across a broad social field, whereas boys are rigidly focused to a particular path, is a theme that came up time and again in the interviews with coaches. In fact, the more I listened to the coaches—both men and women—the more I concluded that feminism has given adults a clear vocabulary with which to talk about girls' lives as a *socially contextualized field of choices.* By contrast, we still don't have very sophisticated ways of thinking about boys, beyond assuming that everything they do is driven by "testosterone" and by their natural predisposition to be active, aggressive, and competitive.

Sports Stretch Girls and Are Natural to Boys

Many of the parents who held essentialist views of boys and girls saw sports participation as a way for girls to learn more conventionally masculine traits that would benefit them in public life. These adults seemed to see boys' aggressive and competitive traits as a simple expression of nature, played out within (but not constructed by) sports, while girls were viewed as malleable, their softer natures reformable through sports participation. Research on children and families has shown, in fact, that parents tend to push sons to conform to culturally valued conceptions of masculinity more strongly than they push their daughters to conform narrowly to feminine traits. Parents also tend to reward boys more than girls for gender conformity.[13] This gender asymmetry reflects the long-standing cultural valuation of masculinity and the devaluation of femininity: it's acceptable to many parents—even highly valued—for girls to adopt some masculine traits—to become "tomboys" and to strive for educational and career success;[14] but the boy who values or displays culturally defined "feminine" traits is still too often stigmatized, ridiculed, viewed as a failure. This asymmetry has likely been amplified as contemporary professional-class families have increasingly absorbed feminist-inspired ideals of girls and women having access to public life. For example, Gilbert Morales, who has coached both girls and boys at various age-levels, suggested that sports participation creates aggressive traits in girls that make them more like boys:

> They're very, very different in style . . . . The girls tend to form a team much easier than boys. Boys seem to have a much more competitive streak in them and a much more aggressive streak in them than the girls do—sometimes to the detriment of the team. They are individuals playing together, not a team working together, which I think is one of the significant differences that I've seen between the boys' team and the girls'. I think that changes a little bit as the girls get older and become more trained or conditioned into behaving in a more aggressive manner—the girls 19-and-under, 16-and-under teams were much more similar to the boys' teams in terms of aggressive behavior, in terms of the way they played the game—even in the showboating and even in some of the taunting that can occur, like when they would make a nice tackle and knock somebody down, glaring at the player on the ground. So, over time, girls who would have been aggressive, to some extent, and competitive, to some extent, I think learn to be more so. And I think what happens is, as they grow older, those who are willing to be like that—be more similar to boys, I think—stay in the sport. And I think that's where the similarities—they become more similar. So, I think as that happens,

as they get older, I think the differences tend to get a little bit more blurred.

Morales, like many coaches we interviewed, assumes that girls are naturally cooperative and group-oriented, but he concludes that with athletic experiences, they can become aggressively competitive individuals, "more similar to the boys." Boys, though, are still viewed categorically by Morales, whose unspoken assumption seems to be that boys are naturally aggressive individualists, and that this essential nature is played out in sports. Boys and girls become more similar, "the differences . . . a little bit more blurred," when girls play sports and become more like boys. These sorts of assumptions made me think about my own two sons, who are very different from each other. My younger son Sasha, whom I have mentioned in this book, enjoys sports, plays baseball and runs cross-country. My older son Miles, now eighteen years old, never took to organized sports, having dropped out of AYSO and Little League by the time he was eight or nine years old. Miles was the kind of kid who, when the soccer ball came within striking distance, would not automatically go after it; instead he'd hesitate, until another, more aggressive boy went after the ball, and then he'd just move along with the pack of kids, rarely touching the ball. His gentleness and lack of aggressiveness—traits which, incidentally, I see as major attributes that make him a kind and good person—did not serve him well in sports. So, like many boys who don't fit the mold, he opted out of sports early on, thus avoiding the discomfort or even public humiliation that so many boys face as marginal or poor athletes.[15] Coaches' narratives rarely recognize this kind of range among boys, tending instead to assume that all boys have a natural affinity with sports. This assumption—especially when compared with the common view of girls as flexible, complex, and fluid—speaks volumes to our one-dimensional and still largely unreconstructed views of boys.

Boys Need Male Coaches

Adults' common view of boys as destined by their nature to compete in public life seems almost to occur by default, as they just don't seem to think that much about boys and gender. Baseball coach Mitch Flores said that it was fine for girls to be coached by either men or women, but when we asked him about whether it mattered for men to coach boys, he seemed stunned by the question:

> Men to coach boys? My, I never even gave that a thought. I—I, um, that seems—it seemed pretty natural. There aren't—there are no women coaching boys' baseball or men's baseball.
>
> [Do you think it's good for boys to see women as coaches?]
>
> Um. I don't think, I don't know, I don't—I don't know. I wouldn't . . .

When we asked soccer coach Mark Daly what he thought about women coaching girls, he replied quickly and clearly: "I think it is good for the girls to see girls as coaches—I think it is important to see women, in coaching roles, 'cause it does teach them that [sports] doesn't all just stop. I mean could be a life long thing." But when asked what he thought about women coaching boys, he said, "Um, and for the guys I—I really don't have an opinion. I mean, I—I never had any female coaches, but I never thought about it, um, I just never thought about it."

Many coaches—men and women—struggled similarly to find words to talk about boys and gender. Soccer coach Al Evans, when asked if it was important for boys to be coached by women or by men, confessed confusion and ambivalence:

> I don't know, uh, I don't get—um, I think I really don't know. I mean I'm really of two minds. In one sense, there's all of that, you know, they learn how to behave like men kind of blah-blah-blah, but you know girls don't learn how to behave like men by watching. I don't know, there's such a debate about that going on in everything I've read that I—I'm still not of a mind on it. I think in the final analysis, for instance, uh, I—I really don't know. I suspect that it probably doesn't make much difference. I think that there—there—oh boy, I don't know. See I really am—I'm completely conflicted.

His confusion and ambivalence about boys and gender, however, contrasted sharply with his sense of clarity about whether it matters for girls to have women coaches:

Uh, that I'm a little more clear about. I think at some point, because of, like, self-esteem issues and stuff like that, I think it is. I think that when my daughters are able to coach it'll be important for them to coach. I do think that for women one of the components is to have someone that they can look up to, and that's a motivator, that's a cool thing. So it's important.

Many coaches similarly struggled and stumbled around to weave a coherent narrative about boys and gender, and eventually many settled into one or more of the three following themes that are familiar in cultural discourse: boys—especially older boys—respect men's leadership and respond better to men's voices than to women's; boys need to be toughened by men; boys need men in their lives because of the predominance of women in their lives as teachers and mothers (especially in single-parent families). I will illustrate these three themes briefly below, but I want first to note an irony here. On the one hand, adults' narratives tend to view boys as driven by a fairly straightforward natural drive to be competitive, individualist actors in sports and other aspects of public life. But on the other hand, underlying these essentialist constructions of boys are vaguely articulated fears that boys are vulnerable, that they may fail to develop into proper men without adult male role-modeling and leadership. These fears of the instability of boys' and men's "nature" reflect long-standing "fears of social feminization" of boys, especially prevalent among middle-class fathers.[16]

Soccer coach Barbara Jones says that as long as they were in the younger age brackets, she was certain that it was a good thing for her to have coached both her two sons' and her daughter's soccer teams: "I like being their coach so I can make sure they're not with a guy who's gonna just win at all costs. So, I think for me, I'm contributing to them: a coach who will emphasize all the right things. And I also think it's good for them to see, you know, a mom able—*their* mom is able to coach their team. It's not just dads. Women can do it, too. And I think, in those very subtle ways, they will carry that throughout their life." Jones believes that as the girls get older, it's fine to have either women or men coaches: "Either one would be effective. If they're good, they're gonna be effective—it doesn't matter what their gender is." However, as the boys get to about age eleven or twelve, she's no longer certain what's best, and as she spoke about older boys, it seemed that her feminist sensibilities were wrestling with her hunch that perhaps there's something "instinctual" about older boys needing men coaches:

> That's kind of when they start getting a little bit more rowdy, a little bit more physical and I almost wonder if at that age they need sort of a more physical threat—like a man's bigger, louder voice, or some instinctual kind of thing. And I almost kind of wondered whether about that age is when should they have a male coach to just even, kind of—you know what I mean? Right about that eleven-twelve age. But, on the other hand, then I think, 'I don't know.' I'm not sure about that, actually. I'm still sort of figuring out whether it's important to have a man when they're like eleven-twelve years old. But, on the other hand, I was considering coaching [my son], and I think I could have done it. So, I have mixed feeling about that.

Gilbert Morales, a divorced father, articulates his fears about boys primarily within a discourse of contemporary family breakdown. He thinks it's good role-modeling for girls to have women coaches, but thinks that boys benefit from having men coaches, because contemporary family changes create a breakdown of what he sees as complementary male and female family roles: "I think that in the non-nuclear family now, with a lot of single parents—I think it's difficult for children to get modeling for both male and female roles. And I think that is creating possibly some conflicts in the future where it's gonna be a bunch of individuals living together, not a cooperative effort, because now both the male and the female have to assume responsibilities for what would have been traditional opposite-gender roles." Many coaches who said that boys need men, like Little League coach Nina Ramos, couched their narrative in a similar discourse of family breakdown: "I think guys, boys, need that [male] figure in their life, you know, because there's a lot more divorces and they just don't have that fatherly figure, and I think that helps out." Though herself living in an intact family, Nancy Morrison spoke of the boys' problems in single-parent families almost as though it was hearsay: "I happen to hear, like, parents—like, single parents, for example—if there's a single mom with a son, she is really counting on her son having a male coach to kind of have an influence in his life. Especially if the father is deceased or not around."

And Pam Burke first noted the relative stability of families in South Pasadena, but then broadened her analysis to thinking about the general lack of adult male role models in boys' lives: "Although this is a pretty *stable,* kind of *family-oriented* community, there are still boys that have no dads at home, and I think that it is important for them to have male role models, too. And if they don't have a dad at home, 90 per cent of the elementary school teachers are women, you know."

In this context of a perceived absence of adult males in boys' lives, many people see male coaches as surrogates for missing fathers. Soccer coach Eric Caldwell suspects that boys already receive more than ample "mothering" from adult women, and need more men in their lives:

> I have a tendency to say [that it's more important] for men to coach boys than it is that women coach girls. I just kind of have a feeling that boys get so much mothering that its part of their normal activity from their teachers and moms that they need the boy-to-boy time that they are going to get with a male coach. My son has had, I think, two women coaches, and I don't know if they were extremely good or extremely bad, they were just regular coaches. Very talented women, but I kind of had a feeling that they would have maybe benefited a little bit more if they would have had a male coach. You know, like I said, I want that coach to be a little bit of a drill sergeant. The boys get the drill sergeant from the mom and the teacher occasionally, and I think they need the time off from the women drill sergeants and they need a man drill sergeant. So I want them to not only experience the drill sergeant mentality from me and from my wife and from their teacher, but also from another source, which would be a male coach.

It's not only men who feel that boys need male coaches. Shelley Parsons coaches her son's soccer team, but as he has started to get a bit older, "I've been telling my husband, 'You know, I'd like to turn this over to you.' [*She laughs.*] I said, 'I really think [their son] needs you to coach him.' I don't know why I think that, but I really think that at a certain age boys really need a guy. Not that I'm inferior, but I think that that when boys get older, I think they're more influenced by males. I think it has to do with male dominance that—that low voice, you know. I think boys as they get older respond better to a male. That's my own thinking. So I may turn this over to him next year." This assumption about older boys' needs for men—held by many men and some of the women we interviewed—is another component of the age-based "glass ceiling" on women coaches, which I discussed in chapter 3.

What exactly is it that adults believe boys can get from men that they don't get from women? Mark Daly, who has coached both girls' and boys' soccer, says that boys respond well when he yells at them: "The under-19 boys, we had practice last night, and you know I found myself yelling at a couple of them. Whereas when I coached the high school girls, I never—I won't say never, but almost never—scream at them. That's just, I find that they kinda of go into themselves and its kind of, uh, it doesn't work out. Whereas the guys you can yell at him, tell him that he's going to do fifty laps and, and they don't hate you. There's no problem, do you know what I mean?" Mitch Flores has coached both girls' softball and boys' baseball, and he takes a "very different approach" to coaching them:

> When I coached boys baseball, it was totally, it was a total different style. The boys are a little more rough around the edges, and you can talk to them a certain way and they take it and it just rolls right off 'em, but the girls, no way. I'm boisterous, I have a deep, big voice; I can yell at a kid across [the field]. I had some nine-year-olds on the team and I did *"Come on,"* you know, and you see the little girls' faces and you're thinking, I hurt this little girl's feelings. I'm sorry, you know: "Are you all right?" And they're standing there and they're quivering, and you're going, "Oh my gosh," and it, but it's a different, it's a different style.

As these coaches' statements show, and as the vignette that opens this chapter illustrates, coaches tend to treat boys and girls differently. To the extent to which they are conscious of this different treatment, they believe it to be a reasoned response to the different natures of boys and girls. Research on kids and gender suggests, however, that the coaches' behaviors are in fact helping to *construct* these differences. Mark Daly's and Mitch Flores's belief that when a coach yells at boys, "there's no problem," that "it just rolls right off 'em," is based on an assumption that boys are emotionally invulnerable, compared with the emotional vulnerability that seems so visible in girls. What they do not recognize, perhaps, is the many years of gender socialization that nine-year-old boys have already endured—from families, peers, popular culture, and sport—that has taught these boys to hide or repress their emotional and physical pain and not to show their vulnerabilities. Rather than simply responding to some natural ability that boys have to "take it," coaches who yell at boys are simply adding another layer to what psychologist William Pollack calls "the hardening of boys."[17] Adults—more often men, but sometimes women as well—too often use emotional separation, shame, and fear to toughen boys in ways that prepare them for the cutthroat competition of public life but that simultaneously stunt their ability to engage in the kinds of mutual intimacy that is the foundation of close relationships and happy family lives. My observations and interviews suggest that fathers are often openly approving of instances where their sons are toughened by other men. When we asked Tony Barnett if there might be some value in women coaching boys, he leapt from thinking about AYSO, which he coaches, to high school football: "Particularly in a sport like football that's so demanding, that's so hard, there's something about, uh, the sort of, the male authority, to have your kid be yelled at by some man who's not your father, that's part of growing up."

In my years of observing boys playing baseball, I've noticed that in the younger age-groups, when a boy gets slightly injured, strikes out, or gets yelled at by a coach for a bad play, he will get visibly upset. Some of these younger boys cry—often privately, pulling their caps over their faces in the dugout—and the other boys and coaches usually don't look at or speak to them, respectfully giving them private space to express feelings that are not considered fully appropriate. With the older boys—especially by age eleven or twelve—these tears and displays of vulnerability are few and far between. Instead, boys' most common response to injuries, to making a bad play, or to getting criticized by the coach, is a short burst of anger—like a thrown helmet after a strikeout—followed by a posture of sullen, determined silence in the dugout.[18] The hardening of boys teaches them to transform any feelings of hurt, pain, or sorrow into the more "appropriately masculine" expressions of contained anger or stoic silence.

To what end do we continue to toughen boys? I believe that we toughen boys because we continue to assume that they are destined for public lives, with jobs and careers, and that their most important responsibility in families will be primarily as breadwinners. Will Solomon, who is very supportive of women coaches and who agrees with the more general idea of gender equality, nevertheless seems to see the value of sport for his sons as partly in the realm of socialization that will toughen them for future competition in a public world of men. For that reason, he said, it's good for his sons to have male coaches, "because part of it is that whole learning how to deal with the other guys. There are guys' ways of dealing with other guys. Now that doesn't mean you shouldn't know [also] some of the more sort of sensitive ways to deal with it. But you gotta also learn how to, you know, talk trash and do all that. Uh, it's—it's just one more piece of survival. And I think there's another side to it too, which is kids have to learn how to deal with assholes growing up. And I think that a good piece of that are things like sports coaches and shop teachers, you know [laughs]."

Coaches consistently stated that boys and girls are very different emotionally and interpersonally. Alan Lindgren noted, "Girls are a lot more complex, [while] the boys tend to be—if you go to a boys' game, its very quiet—you can hear a pin drop almost, you know there's just—there's just not much going on . . . . With the boys it's—it's *subtler*—they don't really push back very much, they just kinda do it. They keep their thoughts more to themselves, I think." This discourse on emotional differences between girls and boys seems to a certain extent to be institutionalized in youth sports. Little League coach Ted Miller says that he has read articles on coaching that say that when coaching boys, "male coaches can, you know, come up and grab the face mask and shake 'em and yell at 'em, 'Rah-rah!' " But Miller has learned from these articles that girls "don't seem to respond to that very well, the yelling and screaming." These kinds of comparisons are based on real observations by coaches who work closely with boys and with girls, and most likely they do reflect some real differences. However, the question we should ask is to what extent the coaches' different treatment of boys and girls simply serves as an add-on to differences that have been socially constructed through a myriad of gendering processes that shape boys and girls at deeply emotional levels. In turn, the coaches' actions and discourse about kids serves to *naturalize* these differences, thus helping to reestablish an ideology of gender essentialism.

THE EMERGENCE OF SOFT ESSENTIALISM

Research by sociologist Emily Kane shows that parents are much more supportive of gender nonconformity among young girls than among young boys. Moreover, Kane found that heterosexual fathers are more likely to strongly enforce gender conformity in their sons than are mothers or gay fathers.[19] To put it a different way, fathers tend to enforce a harder essentialism, while mothers tend toward a softer essentialism. And this contemporary essentialism is harder when it comes to boys, and softer, more flexible when it comes to girls. Boys, it seems, are more defined in parents' views by their presumed nature. Driven by testosterone and genes, boys are seen as fairly simple creatures, "hard-wired" to think, act, and respond competitively and aggressively. Girls, by contrast, are viewed as complex, able when given the proper opportunities to combine their supposedly natural nurturant and affective traits with more competitive goal-oriented and aggressive traits.

This idea that boys are defined by their nature, while girls are complex and malleable within shifting social contexts, seems to be an interesting inversion of a long-standing tendency to define women as close to nature and men as aligned with culture. In a highly influential 1974 article entitled "Is Female to Male As Nature Is to Culture?" anthropologist Sherry Ortner wrote that "woman's body seems to doom her to mere reproduction of life; the male, in contrast, lacking natural creative functions, must (or has the opportunity to) assert his creativity externally, 'artificially,' through the medium of technology and symbols. In so doing, he creates relatively lasting, eternal, transcendental objects, while the woman creates only perishables—human beings."[20] Through much of the nineteenth and twentieth centuries, this association of women with "nature" and men with "culture" justified a gender-dichotomized world that confined women to the domestic, private sphere of supportive and procreative activities, while viewing the public world as men's domain.[21]

It is perhaps the hallmark of the contemporary emergence of soft essentialism that boys and men are now seen as defined by their biology—
"all that testosterone"—while girls and women, when given a range of
opportunities, are seen as capable of exercising "choice." This view of
girls allows for us to imagine them as adult women straddling two
worlds—the world of family, home, and hearth, where their true nature
presumably draws them, and the public world of education, sports, and
work, which they will have a right to choose to participate in, or to opt
out of. By contrast, this view of boys continues to see the competitive
public world of sports, work, and careers as their natural destiny. Since
their inflexible biology presumably predisposes men to the public
world, they are not viewed as able to "choose" alternative (especially
stigmatized, feminine) paths.[22] Ironically, fears that their sons just may
"fail" to develop properly lead many adults to engage in (or at least toler-
ate) a "hardening" and "toughening" of boys that makes it difficult for
boys to develop their full emotional potential (empathy, caretaking skills,
etc.), something they will need in order to become healthy adults, good
partners, and effective parents. Unchallenged, this socially constructed
emotional deficit in boys will leave the responsibility on women's shoulders to, through their "choices," straddle both the public world and that
of domestic labor. Clearly, essentialism is alive and well in the ways that
we think about children. But this is not our grandparents' essentialism. It
is an emergent, "soft" essentialism that accommodates the reality of girls'
and women's presence in sports, and in public life more generally. The
ideology of soft essentialism views girls as "pre-choice," while positioning boys as "pre-career."

Youth sports is an ideal site for the construction of soft essentialism. As
an institution that's premised on making visible people's bodily abilities
and limitations, sport, more that most other institutions (the military is
perhaps equivalent), has historically created and conveyed cultural assumptions and values about essential differences between women and
men. Though clearly contested by girls' and women's movement into
sport, this is still a place where essentialism is constructed through sex-
segregated bodily practices. And there is plenty of evidence that most
adults are not only "comfortable" with thinking of boys and girls as nat-

urally different—they in fact revel in the pleasure of shared talk about the ways that girls and boys differ. We live in an era of dramatic changes in gender relations, in education, families, workplaces, and professions—changes that may be confusing and disconcerting to many, resulting in what sociologist Barbara Risman calls "gender vertigo."[23] Given this turbulence in gender relations, perhaps people look for places that reaffirm comfortable ideas of natural difference. As sex-segregation breaks down or disappears in many areas of social life, perhaps the institutional homes of essentialism, because of the psychological security and pleasures it brings, tend to migrate to particular social sites, like youth sports, where continued sex-segregation of bodily practices makes gender difference particularly salient. Perhaps contemporary youth sports, rather than being a context in which gender inequalities and differences are challenged and changed, has instead become a kind of "gender comfort zone," with soft essentialism as its main ideological product.

SIX "It's a Safe and Fun Place for Kids"

YOUTH SPORTS, FAMILIES, AND
THE GOOD COMMUNITY

While walking on the street on a sunny fall day in 2007, I run into a soccer coach whom I interviewed some time ago. She asks if I have finished my book yet, and I say no, somewhat apologetically, but add optimistically that I am writing steadily. She replies, "Well, you'd better hurry up and finish your book. Things are really changing fast. I think there are a *lot* more women coaches this year." She tells me that I should come to the annual AYSO opening ceremony next Saturday, to see for myself.

A few days later, I arrive at the opening ceremony early so I can walk around on the infield with my camera and notepad to observe and talk with people. There's a feeling of familiarity from past opening ceremonies, with one difference being that this year's is held for the first time at the San Marino High School field, because South Pasadena AYSO has recently merged with San Marino and South Pasadena High is currently renovating its football/track field. There are lots of people I've never seen before, and some familiar faces too, though it's hard to tell by eyeballing it whether there are more women coaches than last year. As I wade through hundreds of boisterous, soccer-uniformed children and adults talking in friendly tones, I admire the always artistic and humorous team banners (my favorite this year is a boys' team called the Exploding Eyeballs). I'm struck by how this familiar annual ritual creates a collective feeling of a good kid-friendly community. I am warmed by this feeling, even though my own kids are now too old to play. Suddenly, I run into Joan Ring. She's coaching again this season, and her team of under-8 boys is coalescing around her. She tells me in a mildly incredulous tone that when she arrived at the field this morning and attempted to enter the special coaches' entrance, a guy barred her way, saying, "This is for coaches only." Laughing, she tugs the front of her T-shirt forward with both hands and says, "I showed him my shirt that says right here, 'AYSO Coach,' so he let me in. And did you notice? The shirt's too big again this year. They ordered mediums. They said that they ordered smalls, but only three of them, so I had to get this medium. I wasn't going to wear it, because it's so long, but oh well—I guess it got me in the gate! And do you notice it's see-through!?" She pulls up the bottom of the shirt to show me that she's worn a cotton T-shirt underneath. "If I didn't' wear this, you could see my bra. I guess the men don't have to worry about that!" (*She laughs.*)

Community rituals like the annual AYSO opening ceremony speak more to continuity than to change. I was excited when the coach told me she thought things were changing rapidly, that "there are a *lot* more women coaches this year," and indeed, I later found that the percentage of women coaches in this AYSO region had continued its three-year upward rise, nudging up to 19 percent in 2007 (see chapter 1, figure 1). If this gradual increase in the number of women coaches in AYSO (though not in LLB/S) can be thought of as "two steps forward," my conversation on the field with Joan Ring suggested "one step back" in terms of progress for women coaches; the common gendered assumptions and informal interactions that I described earlier in the book continue to marginalize women coaches. And in all other ways things looked pretty much the same to me at the opening ceremony—it was 2007, but it seemed no different from the 1997 opening ceremony. Honored speakers, including the national chair of AYSO, spoke glowingly of the ways that AYSO helps to create strong families and kid-friendly communities, and praised the many local adults who made this possible through their volunteer labor, as hundreds of people cheered.

In this book, I have pointed to some signs of change, but mostly this has been a story of continuity. In chapter 2, I showed how informal interactions between adults create a "sex-category sorting process" that channels most men into the coaching pipeline, and most women into becoming "team moms." In chapter 3, I focused on the experiences of women coaches and illuminated the informal processes of marginalization that lead many women coaches to quit, to cycle back to coach the youngest kids, or in a few cases, to develop successful strategies that help them survive for several years as coaches. In chapter 4, I examined the experiences of men coaches, and I argued that at each age-level of the kids' teams there is an unspoken norm for a preferred style of masculine leadership, each of which creates strains and tensions. The gender strategies that the men deploy in response to these strains create a "gender-sorting process," resulting in a professional-class-based masculine style that I call the "CEO" coach. In chapter 5, I considered how adults' beliefs about gender difference, along with the ways that they treat boys and girls in youth sports, creates a professional-class-based gender ideology that I call "soft essentialism." Unlike the "hard," categorical essentialism created by sports in the pre–Title IX era, soft essentialism sees sport as a viable choice for girls, whose participation teaches them competitive values and physical skills that counter the limitations of their supposed feminine nature. Boys, by contrast, are simply assumed to be competitive and aggressive, their natures consistent with the values of sport.

In this final chapter, I will broaden the scope of my analysis to examine how these gendered processes and beliefs within youth sports connect with peoples' lives in workplaces, families, and in the community. I will argue that soft essentialism—especially the idea that women can *choose* how they want to straddle careers and family life, while men are simply *expected* to have professional careers—is part of a historical moment of class-based family formation, just as hard essentialism was during the middle decades of the twentieth century. And I will suggest that the resulting hegemonic professional-class family-type is foundational in building a community that residents experience as a "safe, kid friendly" place, in which youth sports serve an integrative role for kids and adults. However, I will show that to those who live outside South Pasadena, this "good community" is sometimes viewed as an unfriendly place, characterized by class- and race-based boundaries that exclude others.

YOUTH SPORTS AND THE GOOD FAMILY

Carol Morris's husband is a successful professional, and she describes herself as a "full-time mom." She says "it's good to have fathers out there coaching," because "in this community where it's pretty traditional daddy goes to work and mom is at home and not working, to have that time with your father doing volunteer things, that is a good thing for them to see." People in South Pasadena often remark that many families in town have a high-earning male breadwinner and a "stay-at-home mom." At first glance, this does seems to be true: of the fifty people interviewed for my study, forty-six are married or cohabiting, and twenty of these forty-six families include a mother who is exclusively or primarily identified as a full-time homemaker. However, twenty-three of the families include two parents who both hold down full-time jobs. Nearly all of those interviewed were currently in heterosexual marriages (only one identified as lesbian or gay); two others were cohabiting, and five were divorced. The social class and race of the interviewees is also fairly homogenous: nearly all were college-educated professionals, and two-thirds were white. Though this sample seems fairly accurately to reflect the class and race composition of those who coach youth sports in South Pasadena, it does not cleanly reflect the population of the city, which is only 44 percent white, and with a substantial proportion of working-class and lower-middle-class people (see appendix 2).

In short, the range of family types, as well as the class and race composition of youth sports coaches in South Pasadena is less varied than that seen in the city as a whole. The dominant family type among those in South Pasadena youth sports leadership is a married, heterosexual, professional-class couple with two or three children. This family is disproportionately white, proportionally Hispanic, and Asian Americans are underrepresented (given the local demographics).[1] Numerically, roughly half of these are dual-career families; but judging by what people *say* about the typical family in South Pasadena, the most *publicly visible* family type is one composed of a male professional-class primary breadwinner and a college-educated female who has opted out of a full-time career to become a homemaker and who often is an active volunteer in community activities.

In fact, I will argue in this final chapter that despite the societal growth in types of families, gentrifying suburban enclaves like South Pasadena often attest to the continued power of a unitary ideal of "the family."[2] The creation of gender divisions of labor on youth sports teams creates a potent public symbol of an ideal family headed by a man and supported by a team mom. The symbolic power of this heterosexual nuclear family lies partly its nostalgic appeal to an idealized "traditional family" of the 1950s.[3] But there's more to it than simple nostalgia. The ideal family symbolized in South Pasadena youth sports is a contemporary professional-class family that has incorporated the reality of women's movement into public life. This family type is not numerically predominant; however, it is the highly visible hegemonic ideal. Most people live in real families, not hegemonic ideals, and real families are characterized by strains and challenges. I will next examine how youth sports coaches talk about gender divisions of labor in their families, and I will then turn to an examination work, families, and community volunteer work.

FAMILY DIVISIONS OF LABOR

Sociologist Scott Coltrane observes that married couples with children tend to fall into two patterns.[4] "Main provider families" are those in which the women earn 20 percent or less of the overall family income. In these families, the women, whose primary commitment is seen as home and kids, do most of the family labor. Men's primary commitment is providing an income, while family work is seen as secondary. In "co-provider families," men and women spend approximately the same amount of time in paid work. While some co-provider husbands try to become equal co-parents, many still expect their wives to do most of the family labor, resulting in what sociologist Arlie Hochschild called a "second shift" of family work for employed women.[5] This second shift was evident in many of my interviews with South Pasadena parents. Lisette Taylor, a mother of two with a full-time job, is in a co-provider family. It works for her to be an assistant coach for her daughter's softball team, or even to be a team parent, because "it's a juggle" she can manage. But, she says, it's logistically hard for her and for other women to be head coaches, because so many of the dads are either unavailable or unwilling to share with the day-to-day childcare:

> If you have more than one child, what are you gonna do with that extra kid? And so, I think, logistically, unless the man, the husband, is willing to swoop down and say, "Okay, you go coach, I'll be home," you know, you have that logistic thing that, that prevents you from serving in that role. That probably wouldn't happen in my house: "Yeah honey, I'll be home so you can go do that coaching thing." No, that probably wouldn't happen here.

In contrast to the second shift described by employed mothers in my study, many of the men coaches in my study have wives who handle all or most of the family labor. Albert Riley and his wife both have jobs, but he says she handles the "logistical stuff" at home and for his softball team:

> I'll be honest—I think most men rely on their wives or girlfriends or whatever to do those types of things, you know, whether the wives wanna . . . . [My wife] does a great job with that. You know, she doesn't particularly *want* to do it [*slight laugh*], but you know what?—she does it. And she's kinda the logistical coordinator of our house [*slight laugh*], you know, so she does that better than I do it. I—I don't do that very well. Uh, thank the good Lord for that [*laughs*].

Some women in "main provider families" experience a disadvantage as coaches, one that is grounded in family labor inequities. Tracy Nash, a divorced mother of three who recently secured a part-time job, directly compares herself to Albert Riley. She manages her daughter's softball team, and even during the previous years, when she was married and not employed outside the home, she was aware of a privilege enjoyed by many of the men coaches:

I joke with [fellow softball coach] Albert Riley that he has a *wife,* so he can go out and coach and his wife can have dinner ready and everything else. I go out and coach and *I* am the wife, so if dinner isn't ready before I leave to go do my coaching, I come back in and things slide, and I think that's why a lot women don't coach. They're doing so many other things. Those years that I coached my daughter were very fun, but they were—I mean it was hard. I mean it was not easy, because during those softball seasons, there was practices three or four days a week. I was out from three to five, or four to six, I mean, right when my little kids should be doing homework, the other kids are coming home.

Tracy Nash's discussion of why things are often so hard for her is a vivid description of the gendered negotiation of time across three realms of workplaces, families, and community volunteering (including youth sports), an issue to which I will next turn.

WORK, FAMILIES, AND COMMUNITY VOLUNTEERING

When men coaches were asked whether they did any additional volunteer work besides coaching, a couple of them said yes and listed an impressive array of community, church, or school services they provide. But most of the men said no, that coaching was the main, or in some cases, the only volunteer activity they did. Many men—especially those in main provider families, saw their wives' heavy volunteer activity as a logical extension of their family division of labor: I earn money and coach soccer; she takes care of family and home and volunteers in schools and the community. Several men, like Bill Munson, spoke with pride of their wives' activities: "She's very much that kind of a hands-on, day-to-day volunteer, you know, directly in the things that our kids get involved in."

Many of the women responded initially to the question about volunteer work by downplaying the amount of time they devote and importance of what they do. But then—especially those who were not employed—they would list a dizzying array of contributions they make to their kids' schools and to other community organizations. Joan Ring said that in addition to coaching, she volunteered in other areas, "Well, on and off, I was on the PTA executive board for three years at [her kids' elementary] school, and for two years I ran the prizes for the fun fairs at the all-city carnival—which may sound silly but it was actually a huge job. AYSO—I'm on the AYSO board. No, that's really it—you know, little things in the classroom. I'm their room parent." Pam Burke is also an AYSO league official, but she does many other things, most of them connected to her children: "I helped to organize the jog-a-thon; I go on field trips and stuff with them. I've helped organize the book fair; I've helped with my daughter's Girl Scout troop, going on campouts and overnights. Whatever they need, I'll do whatever they ask. [At her church], I did help out this year with vacation bible school . . . and I helped decorate the sanctuary for the kids' play."

While it may be understandable that women like Joan Ring and Pam Burke, in "main provider families," would do the lion's share of volunteer work, I found that even in "co-provider families," in which women were employed full-time, women tended to do a wide range of volunteer activities. Shelley Parsons is an employed mother of two, and she says her job makes it hard for her to volunteer as much as she'd like to in her kids' schools, but she still manages to do more than her husband: "I'm probably the volunteer in the family." Lillian Mohr is an elementary school teacher and mother of two. She coaches virtually all year long: soccer, baseball, and basketball. At first she said that her job made it hard to volunteer very much, but then as she thought about it, her list of volunteer activities blossomed: "Hmm—I'm sure I've done volunteer work. I'm trying to think. I don't know. I mean, I think it's wonderful when people do that, but I have to say I usually find that life is so full, it's hard to do. I mean, like, I was on the board at my child's preschool, and I've done things like that, but not a tremendous amount—oh, like actually, for two years running, I've coordinated four book fairs for my school. That was a big volunteer thing." When I asked her if her husband, a scientist, does any volunteer activities, she replied simply, "No, I would say I'm the main one."

The vast majority of men, by contrast, said that their volunteer activity is primarily or exclusively in youth sports coaching. Eric Caldwell is a corporate manager whose wife is a stay-at-home mom. When asked if he does volunteer work for his kids' activities, he first said no, that his wife does lots of things but that he doesn't have the time. But then he described a large amount of work he does with his kids' sports: seven years as AYSO coach; coaching at "every level" of Little League, and also YMCA kids' basketball. It seems that men with busy careers tend to leave most or all of the community volunteer work to their wives, *except* for sports. Al Evans and his wife are both employed, and he initially responded to the question about volunteering by saying, "I get volunteered a lot—we're kind of a volunteer family. What else have I done? I'm gonna draw a big blank on this—you gotta ask my wife [*laughs*]—um, what else have I done with the girls? Gosh, I guess a lot of soccer." Evans went on to list a huge array of volunteer activities that his wife does, but when she tries to draw him in to PTA work, he says he tells her, " 'But I'm coaching, dear.' [*He laughs.*] See, that's why I coach, 'cause I know I'm gonna get volunteered, so if I coach, I can go, 'I'm coaching, don't ask me to do more.' "

PLUG-IN DADS AND STRETCHED MOMS

When people talk about how they negotiate the tensions between work, family, and community volunteer work, they describe what I have come to think of as the *gendered organization of time.* For instance, when asked why she thought there were so many more men coaches than women, and why team moms are women, Carol Morris spoke of how men's careers constrain their time, and of how family work constrains women's time:

> It's probably that it's a Saturday commitment, and in this community, women do so much volunteering during the week for the schools that I think by Saturday [*laughs*] we don't want to volunteer. And so it's something that you can send Daddy to do it. So I think that might be, in this community, in the bigger picture, it's probably because if you were to give the men a choice, if you said on Saturday you know we're gonna have reading at the library if we can find enough dads to read, I bet they wouldn't do it. It would be harder to get them to do that than it would be

to get them to go coach. So it probably is the activity itself, as well as the timing for the availability.

Sociologists have shown how "time binds" that cut across work and family life tend differently to constrain women and men.[6] My research shows how these time binds connect to a third realm: community volunteer work. Workplaces, families, and community organizations like youth sports all have their own internal divisions of labor and power—or gender regimes. While people might experience each realm as a separate space with its own set of internal relations that variously constrain and enable their choices, the decisions that adults make about how to allocate their time in any one realm (say, youth sports) is also constrained and enabled by their relations in the others (careers and/or families).[7] Within these overlapping sets of institutional constraints, individual women and men negotiate with each other and develop gender strategies for dealing with time binds.

One gender strategy is to form a strict division of labor, where the man simply defines volunteer work (with the exception of coaching) as his wife's job. For instance, Mitch Flores has a managerial job and is a father of three with a homemaker wife: "I don't volunteer—coaching right now, that's pretty much it, you know. Not much volunteer work. Not at schools, no, I don't get involved; my wife does a lot of that. She has more time—the whole day to do that, where I don't. I do have to work [*laughs*]." A gender strategy expressed by attorney Carlos Ruiz is to define his *job* as a form of community volunteer labor: "I think to some extent my job is a volunteer activity. I mean, I talk to victims every day. I do try to go the extra step, if I can get somebody into a shelter or help them deal with a particular situation. But no, I can't think of any other, I think that probably soccer is the major voluntary activity I do."

Like Flores and Ruiz, most dads say that, besides coaching, they have little time to do other volunteer work. For example, Gilbert Morales's managerial job leaves him little flexibility to volunteer in his kids' schools: "You know, if there's things that I can help with at school or they need to go on a trip or whatever, I volunteer to go if they need parents. I don't have the time right now to actually spend, for example, a day at school. I wouldn't mind doin' that, in a classroom, but it just always worked out that way. I just don't have the time." Like Morales, many employed men end up doing what sociologist Paul Lichterman calls "plug-in volunteer work," in which the dad shows up for a single event, like a field trip or a book fair, and contributes a few hours of labor.[8]

The "plug-in" pattern of volunteer work is the most common gender strategy through which men (and a few women) with full-time careers negotiate their time binds. Paul Leung is a father of two with a professional-class job, and his wife is a former schoolteacher who left her job to become a stay-at-home mom. His description of his volunteer work in his kids' school epitomizes the plug-in pattern:

> If they need someone to drive, if they need someone to escort them, I'm usually like the only father—everybody else is the mothers that come. But this is something that—my only way of connecting with my children would be that. That's if you call that volunteering, yes, I do volunteer. But nothing on a regular basis, like my wife would go to the school and do it on a regular basis, like every other week she would do volunteer work at the school inside the classroom. I—I don't have time for that.

When he notes that "I'm usually like the only father," Leung's words also hint at another aspect of fathers' volunteer labor in schools: when men do show up, even just to plug-in for a few hours in an elementary school, they commonly find themselves working in a women's volunteer space (and primarily in a women's workplace).

Plug-in work is the major form that my own volunteering took during the years my kids were in elementary school,[9] and when I did this kind of work, I was frequently struck by the unearned kudos I would receive, for being such a "good dad" that I would give up my supposedly valuable work-time to accompany a field trip, or to work for a few hours at a school holiday fair. Arlie Hochschild has noted that there is a publicly recognized "going rate" for how much childcare and housework a father is expected to do, and that the bar of expectations is actually quite low.[10] I find that it works this way in community volunteer work, too: when a man does something, he is often rewarded with a disproportionate amount of positive attention. Men's own knowledge of the low "going rate" on men's volunteer work can be used as a resource in negotiations with our spouses, and it allows us to congratulate ourselves for the little things we do. Will Solomon said that neither he nor his full-time employed wife do much volunteer work, due to their busy work schedules. But then, as an afterthought, he added, "I do things, like I've gone on field trips this year with each of the kids—which I guess there aren't many dads that do, so I guess you know, little things like that."

Curiously, most of the men coaches said that they were too busy with work demands to engage in anything other than plug-in volunteer work, *except* when it came to youth sports. To be sure, some men coaches talked of the strain it put on their work to consistently find the time for practices and games. But what was striking to me is that many of them said that they were somehow able to "find" the time to do this. In fact, their words revealed that many of them consciously *managed* their time in ways that allowed them to prioritize a commitment to coaching their kids' teams. Attorney Alan Lindgren, for instance, is a father of four with a wife who left her professional-class job to be a homemaker. When asked if he volunteers at his children's school, he replied:

> Not really, no I haven't—uh, I'm—I'm a lawyer and [it's a] very, very demanding job, time-wise. And to get any time off is a trick, and I kind of use it for the softball coaching, but other than that, I really don't do anything else. My wife is pretty involved in that.
>
> [So is softball actually what fits best with your work schedule?]
>
> I wouldn't say it necessarily fits best—it's the thing I have the most interest in, and therefore I make it work. I'm more interested in this, and therefore I do it more.

Lindgren's words illustrate his conscious management of his time as a specific gender strategy that prioritizes coaching as his singular volunteer contribution, while defining other volunteer work and family labor as falling within his wife's realm. This patterned division of time and labor is expressed most sharply in main-provider families, like Lindgren's, but also to a somewhat lesser extent in many co-provider families. The structure of this family division of labor and time is illustrated in figure 2.

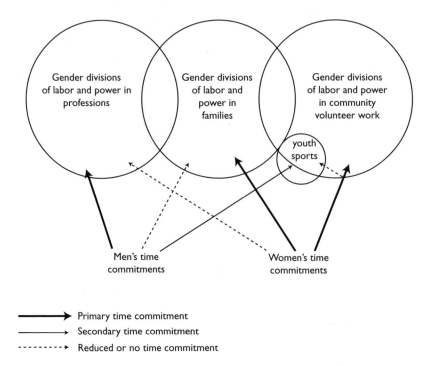

Fig. 2. Professional-class men's and women's common gender divisions of labor in "main provider" families, across three gender regimes.

Some employed women do plug-in volunteer work too, but these women frequently compare themselves with the not-employed mothers who are doing huge amounts of day-to-day work in the schools and the community, and they conclude that they are not doing enough. The bar of volunteer expectations is simply higher for mothers than for fathers, so employed women are less likely to give themselves much credit for occasional plug-in work. One gender strategy utilized by some women in co-provider families is to pursue a career that allows more time flexibility than do other professional careers. In my study, I found it striking how several of the employed women who managed to be active in their kids' worlds were school teachers. A couple of these women had even left more "high-power," demanding jobs (one, for instance, had been an attorney) to work as school teachers, a job that allows much greater time flexibility when one has school-aged kids. In fact, for women who can't or don't want to opt out of full-time careers, taking a teaching job can be seen as a gender strategy that allows these moms a bit more time flexibility with which to negotiate the strains that are built into straddling work, family, and volunteer labor. The strains felt by mothers in co-provider families lead some women to adopt a more extreme gender strategy: opting out of professional careers in favor of less-demanding part-time work,[11] or becoming full-time "stay-at-home moms."

THE INVISIBLE LABOR OF *ÜBER*MOMS

As I have shown, women's work as team moms, their often unacknowledged work as informal assistant coaches, and their proclivity to be the ones ferrying the kids to and from sport practices and games (what sociologist Shona Thompson refers to as "mother's taxi"), amounts to a large amount of invisible labor in support of youth sports.[12] This work, for many women, is woven together with volunteer activities in schools and other community organizations. In her pioneering studies of women's volunteer work, sociologist Arlene Kaplan Daniels argued that women's "invisible labor" performs the valuable function of creating community solidarity.[13] Research shows that women and men tend to do roughly the same amount of volunteer community labor, but there are common gender divisions within volunteer organizations, with men doing the instrumental work of public leadership and women doing the behind-the-scenes support work.[14] In volunteer work, just as in the home and in many workplaces, women are expected to do the work of caring for others' emotions and daily needs.[15] Women's volunteer labor is routinely devalued in much the same ways that housework and childcare are devalued in the home and women's clerical support work is devalued in the professions.[16] As a result, Kaplan Daniels observes, even women volunteers sometimes come to see their own work as less important than the work being done by men.[17]

People are often motivated to volunteer partly out of self-interest, to further their own kids' concerted cultivation. A younger coach who did not live in South Pasadena told me that she was uncomfortable with the community's "gender role separation," and she said she remembered "sitting there just dreading these conversations with these moms because they were just *obsessed* with being, like, the perfect mom." I have heard South Pasadena parents over the years joking about the "*Über*moms" that we see racing around town in their minivans or SUVs, from soccer match to girl scouts to PTA to church events to school book fairs and numerous other volunteer-based community events centered around the kids. "It's all for the kids," people joke, implying that perhaps it's *not* all about the kids—it's about the parent's (usually the *mom*'s) sense of self-importance, and her attempt to elevate her child to a position of public prominence. But people also tend to see another side to this picture: these are moms with huge amounts of education and expertise who are shifting their energies away from high-status careers and toward non-paid, undervalued labor that, yes, supports their own children, but that also supports all of our children.[18] Adults benefit, too. The added "value" of public schools in a place like South Pasadena is based on monetary contributions made by well-to-do parents,[19] and on a wealth of volunteer labor from highly skilled and educated parents, mostly moms. In turn, the reputation for high quality that South Pasadena public schools enjoy is a major factor in amplifying the inflated property values of privately owned homes in the town.

WOMEN'S NARRATIVES OF CHOICE AND THE RISE OF SOFT ESSENTIALISM

Employed mothers, as I have shown, often find that involvement in their children's activities, like youth sports, amounts to a *third* shift, particularly if they don't have a husband who shares childcare responsibilities. Pam Burke dealt with the pressures of these overlapping demands by leaving her job as a teacher a few years ago, after her third child was born. Now she coaches soccer, and she mused about how things are different for her and for the men coaches she works with:

> Just this weekend we had picture day, opening ceremony, the parade. I was out there at 5:30 helping to set up—5:30 in the morning. And I was

thinking, what's the difference between me and a man coach? How is our day different? Well, I know one thing: I came home, and between my two soccer games, I did two loads of laundry and made the kids' beds and make lunch for everybody. And I'm sure that's not the, the same routine for the men coaches. They don't have the same, um, expectations on them at home.

Burke's decision to leave her job, at least for a few years, is indicative of a major pattern in South Pasadena family life: college-educated women who opt out of their professional careers to become full-time moms and who become very active volunteers in their children's schools, churches, sports, and other activities. Although it is not the numerical norm, the family with a high-earning father (a professional, manager, or business owner) and a highly educated mother who has opted out of the career track is the singularly visible hegemonic ideal in South Pasadena.

Why do such accomplished professional women sometimes opt out of their careers to focus on family life? Popular explanations often point to a supposedly natural biological "tug" that mothers feel toward home and hearth. Critics of this view see opting out as a strategy that some women develop in response to a cacophony of demands on their time from multiple sources: their high-power jobs, their mounting "second shift" of childcare at home, and a looming "third shift" of volunteer work as their kids enter schools, Scouts, and sports.[20] In order to reflect on this process, I will present the story of soccer coach Barbara Jones, whose words offer a valuable case study of opting-out. Jones's husband is an attorney, and she gradually opted out of her own career as an attorney once her three kids starting arriving. In speculating about why she, and not her husband, ended up sacrificing her career to do the lion's share of family work, she vacillates between social constructionist claims ("This is not innate to me") and essentialist explanations ("Maybe it's instinctive"). Eventually, she bridges these two opposing views with a discourse of choice. When her first daughter was born, like many women, a second-shift descended on her:

My husband and I were both at law firms. We both were associates working really hard. I kind of used to laugh when I had [my first child]: the equality just flew out the window. I mean, there's so much that just somehow comes your way. And I remember saying to my husband, you know, "Yeah, I didn't [already] know [about] sickness or illness. I mean, I got a *book*, you know, about, like, What's wrong with her." I used to say, "It did not come on the extra X chromosome, okay? So, this is not innate to me." But for some reason, it seems to—maybe because you're the one who had the baby, maybe it's instinctive. I think mom's sort of a little bit more aware of what's going on with the child. So, you automatically kind of assume that role. Or your husband automatically just kind of all of a sudden says, "Oh, well, that's your problem."

Like many career women who become mothers, Barbara Jones was hit head-on with the demands of an unequal family division of labor: "the equality just flew out the window." Despite these second-shift burdens, Jones was determined to continue with her career, but she soon found that working part-time wasn't *really* part-time, and her job became a kind of mommy track that would preclude her career advancement to becoming a partner in her firm. Neither work nor family felt fully satisfying to her:

> So, if I was going to go back to work, *I* was going to find the childcare. You know, he was somewhat involved, but I figured out which agencies to call. I figured out who the doctor was going to be, I took her to the doctors appointments. And then I kind of said, "You know, the way I want to parent my kids, I just don't want both of us to be full-time lawyers at law firms." So, I actually started part-time, which is fifteen hundred billable hours, which is not *really* part-time, but that's a different story. So it immediately kind of hit me right away: my career was immediately changed, but yet it was a choice that I was willing to make. It's going to be my career that kind of goes on hold during the child-rearing phase. And then I got pregnant with my second child, and they were saying, "Oh, but you can stay here part-time forever." And I'd say, "Yeah, but that's like treading water. I mean, you're basically saying no partnership."

When her third child arrived, her two older children were approaching the age where they were entering school and participating in other activities. Jones then felt the pull of what might become a third-shift of volunteer labor:

And then I had another one, and I'm like, "Oh my God." And then they get older, and they're doin' eight thousand million things. And I suppose I could still go back to work. I mean, I could. My husband would support it. I could do it. But, four years ago, [for] the first time ever, I felt like— let's just call it a day. My company got sold for the third time and I was, like, "Okay, I've had enough."

Barbara Jones then shifted her energies away from career and toward what sociologist Sharon Hays calls "intensive mothering on behalf of the sacred child," an ascendant professional-class cultural ideal that views children as needing highly involved mothers who dedicate themselves to guiding their children away from danger and toward success.[21] Women like Barbara Jones direct their considerable talents toward what sociologist Annette Lareau calls the "concerted cultivation" of their own kids and into a range of volunteer activities with kids in the community.[22] The result of this shift is what sociologist Pamela Stone calls "the professionalization of domesticity, manifested in two arenas: motherhood and volunteerism."[23] As Barbara Jones described it:

I think it's a luxury to be able to not work. But I'm still doing a heck of a lot of stuff. I think that there's a lot of professional women—and that's what they do. And I think that's what happened in the fifties. You had all these very intelligent women—some who were educated—who couldn't get jobs. And that's why the volunteer core was so strong back then, because you had these incredibly talented women doing all these things, because they couldn't work. Now, I think people are *choosing* not to work, and so now you're kind of getting a group of people who can do the volunteer work. I do a lot of volunteer activities. Now [that] my youngest is in school full-time, I've filled my days with volunteer work.

Jones's comparison of her life with the lives of women in the 1950s—the college-educated women discussed in Betty Friedan's classic 1963 book *The Feminine Mystique*—is telling. Half a century ago, these women were prevented from having careers, and they focused their energies toward family labor and community volunteer work. Today, women like Barbara Jones see themselves not so much as *prevented* from pursuing careers, but rather as *choosing* to opt out of careers. But just as women's choices to become team moms are constrained and enabled by social contexts, these career-family choices are also contextualized. A woman's choice to opt out of her professional career is, first of all, usually enabled by the fact that her husband has a high-powered, high-paying career of his own. Not all women can do this: one mother in a dual-career family told me, "Sometimes I'd like to quit working for a while, or cut back to part-time, so I could be more involved in [my son's] activities. But that's just not possible. We need my income."

Women's career-family choices are also constrained by gendered belief systems that view childcare as primarily women's (natural) responsibility; by workplaces that still do not create family-friendly policies; and by husbands who still too often see their own careers as primary, thus placing a disproportionate burden on their wives to handle the day-to-day running of the household and care of the children. Barbara Jones's story typifies all of these constraints, as well as illustrating the enabling factor of ample financial resources provided by her husband's career. And her explanatory focus on *choice* rather than constraint—especially the way she contrasts her generation as different from that of the 1950s—is a hallmark of soft essentialism. Viewed through this ascendant ideology, men are seen as naturally suited to the public world of work and careers, and as inept at housework and childcare. Women are viewed as having the choice to pursue their careers, but when they opt out, this is often interpreted as their natural motherly inclinations tugging them homeward, rather than as a result of the time binds that women experience at the nexus of professional careers, families, and communities.[24]

Soft essentialism is the dominant ideology underlying the hegemonic professional-class family pattern, and a key component of the language of soft essentialism is women's narratives of choice.[25] In these narratives, women do not describe themselves as forced to do family work and community volunteer labor; rather, they choose to this for the good of the kids and out of their nature as mothers. Soft essentialism in youth sports, as I showed in the previous chapter, mirrors (and ushers the kids into) this hegemonic work-family form.

Though some of them use the term, it is a misnomer to call these women "stay-at-home moms." In fact, they all have very public lives—in sports, in PTA, in Scouts, churches, etc.—it's just that *career* is no longer a part of this public life. For them, public life is directly linked to their roles as primary caretakers of children, but they also bring an enormous amount of expertise and self-confidence from their previous lives as career women to these community activities. Their volunteer labor is a major foundation in making South Pasadena the kind of community that most people want their children to grow up in.

THE GOOD COMMUNITY

The adults in my study almost unanimously say that they love living in South Pasadena and feel fortunate to have their kids growing up there. And many say that they appreciate youth sports for the ways it integrates their families into the community. Eric Caldwell said, "I think we've met a lot of people through Little League that now we call friends that we probably might not have met at church or other organized function, so I think that its beneficial for us as parents, as well as for the kids." And Alan Lindgren likes participating in Little League Softball especially for the way it seems to integrate people across lines of social class:

> There's overall just incredible positives associated with this—the community feeling and interaction—it's just a way to meet all kinds of people from different walks of life. I mean in this town you've got everything from the rich investment bankers down to the most modest housekeepers. There certainly is economic diversity, and I run into people here who I really like, who I really would be unlikely to otherwise run into, I think, and develop relationships that are very positive with them—which is very nice—a very strong community feeling, and that's a big part of it.

Coaches frequently expressed this idea that youth sports in South Pasadena serve an integrative function in a diverse community. Albert Riley spoke of this not so much in terms of social class but in terms of what he sees as racial/ethnic integration. Speaking of his softball league, he said:

We do have a couple of families that speak Spanish with their kids. We don't have very many African Americans that play—a couple. There's probably a little bit more influx of Asians over the last couple of years, but Hispanic and White primarily, and then followed by Asian and Black. But you know to me that's just the melting pot that we're in. I mean, I think it's pretty cool. I mean there's just a lot of interaction with everybody and it seems pretty healthy stuff. I don't really see any parents having any issues, you know. I think it's good to have, you know, all the different cultures involved.

It seemed to me that it was one thing for a white attorney in South Pasadena to laud the relationships that develop across "economic diversity," or for a white man in a managerial career to remark how "cool" it is to experience youth sports as a kind of cultural "melting pot." But even some others who were not white professional-class men said that they appreciated the community feeling that they got from having kids in youth sports in town. Elena Rosas works as an elementary school teacher in the Los Angeles Unified School district. When I asked her to discuss her experience in South Pasadena as an employed Latina mother, she replied:

When I talk to my colleagues in education who work in East Los Angeles—of course the majority of students out there are Latinos, and you have a lot of professionals that are Latino—when they mention they are looking for a home, I say "How about South Pas? It's a great city." And why do I say this to them? So that we can outnumber whites? [*laughs*]— No. It's because of the families—I've had nothing but positive experiences with the families—and yes, it's mostly white, [but] it's a great, cohesive little town."

This internal cohesion in the community is created largely through the tireless labor of volunteers. Ted Miller coaches softball, he says, not just to help his daughter but also out of "a commitment or a desire to contribute to the community. I feel like the program has two thousand kids and if parents don't volunteer to do these things, the program doesn't exist. So it's sort of my community involvement, my community contribution." And Nancy Morris describes her coaching and her other considerable volunteer work as contributing to the kind of community that drew her and her husband to the town in the first place: "Part of the uniqueness in South Pasadena is the involvement of parents, and my husband and I moved to South Pasadena keeping in mind that our children would be going to public schools and knowing that would mean involvement in the schools and volunteerism—and that's what makes this community."

But why is organized youth sports such a major part of so many peoples' ideal of the good community? In chapter 1, I outlined some of the broad social trends that have led to the boom in youth sports. One of these trends, especially evident in professional-class suburbs, is the dramatic over-organization of kids' activities by adults. Bill Munson was born and raised in South Pasadena, and happily returned there after med school to raise his own family because it gives his kids family connections and because it's "a special community—it's a safe and fun place for kids to grow up." But South Pasadena has changed, he says. When he was a kid, "there was a lot more time and space to just be a kid and just play—either organizing your own games or kind of unstructured play." Much of his unstructured play, he said, was down in the semiwild Arroyo, where the Little League fields are:

> We spent a lot of time in the Arroyo playing in those hills that run up from the fields. We dreamed up a thousand games, and the Arroyo was our home, our sanctuary. Now those hills for the most part are fenced off and you're discouraged from going in there. Well, now, of course, you'd get nervous having your kid playing around down there if there wasn't a soccer coach around to keep an eye on him or a Little League coach, because somebody might come in from someplace, or some weirdo, you know, who knows? Our world has changed a lot in that respect, so what we've got now is the more structured parts of when we were kids.

Munson's description of the transformation of the Arroyo—which sits directly on the border of South Pasadena and the more working-class and Latina/o Los Angeles neighborhood of Highland Park—illustrates how parents' fears that "somebody might come in from some place . . . some weirdo" and harm our children—has led communities literally to fence off areas previously used by children for creative, self-organized free play.[26] Instead, adults now drive their children to the Arroyo, where they are organized into adult-supervised sports, after which they are driven home or to the next activity. Youth sports are, among other things, an organized response to a culture of fear for our children's safety. The excellence of the South Pasadena AYSO and Little League programs is an important part of what makes parents feel like South Pasadena is a "safe and fun place for kids to grow up."

Thinking about a community like South Pasadena as an internally cohesive, safe place for kids is premised on the usually unspoken assumption that neighborhoods outside the town are less safe. Feeling one's family to be part of a good, internally cohesive community has a logical flip-side: the idea of "inside" presupposes an "outside." If "we" are a good community, then that suggests that "they" are not. The Arroyo is a visible geographic boundary that divides one side of South Pasadena from its working-class and predominantly Latino/a neighbor. Such geographic boundaries are physically permeable, but communities-as-imagined-by-people also involve the creation of *symbolic boundaries*, inside of which "we" reside, and outside of which "they" reside. The markers of symbolic boundaries are not physical fences, but in this case take the form of peoples' shared expressions of cherished family and community values that mark differences between us and them.[27] My study was not set up initially to gain insight into this issue, but my observations and interviews gave me two provocative windows into how symbolic boundaries based on social class and race/ethnicity are constructed through South Pasadena youth sports: first, people sometimes projected negative gender characteristics onto coaches of teams from other communities; and second, people from other communities who participated in South Pasadena youth sports sometimes had a very different view of how inclusive and cohesive the South Pasadena community is.

Projections onto Neighboring Others

One opportunity to observe how people in South Pasadena feel about others in neighboring communities was when the town's baseball, softball, or soccer teams got into regional tournaments of champions. These high-stakes tournaments match up the top teams from each community to compete for regional championships. In the baseball playoff games I observed, the coaches of non–South Pasadena teams—frequently from Alhambra, Highland Park, or Temple City—were nearly always Latino men, many of whom had very different styles than the South Pasadena coaches. Will Solomon described the coaches from Temple City: "I think they are a bit harder core; I think they are a little bit more into it." Indeed, when I observed the 13–14-year-old boys' Little League playoffs, the difference in the coaches' styles was striking. The South Pasadena coaches conformed mostly to what I called in chapter 4 the "CEO" coaching style, characterized by restrained, quiet managerial control. The men from surrounding communities tended to be more verbal on the field— usually not in a negative way, but continually utilizing loud verbal instruction and encouragement. For instance, a Latino third base coach from Temple City paced continually back and forth clapping his hands, and when he had no specific instruction to yell out, he would frequently just yell to the batter, "Okay, Oscar, see it and hit it, see it and hit it. C'mon now!" As he did so, a parent from South Pasadena chuckled and said to the other parents in the stands, "Wow. That guy is *too serious!*"

There was also a striking difference in the ways that coaches dressed, as indicated in this field note from a playoff game between South Pasadena's team and a team from Highland Park:

> The South Pasadena team has driven maybe four miles to get to the ballpark that sits in a gorgeous park atop a bluff overlooking L.A.'s Dodger Stadium. The game is about to begin, and as "The Star-Spangled Banner" plays over the P.A. system, the South Pas team stands, hats over hearts, along the third base line, while the team from Highland Park stands along the first base line. I'm struck by how home plate seems a kind of ethnic divide: the Highland Park kids appear to be all Latino, as are all three of their coaches. The South Pas team includes two Asian American boys, one boy whose dad is Indian, and the rest are white boys. The coaches then meet with the umpire at home plate to discuss ground rules. Our three coaches—two of them white, one a dark-skinned Indian man— are all professional-class men in their mid-forties with closely cropped hair and fit bodies. They are dressed almost identically: white tennies with short white socks, knee-length shorts, red team shirts tucked in, topped by team hats and sunglasses. The Highland Park coaches offer a

real contrast. The three Latino men appear to be slightly younger than their South Pas counterparts—maybe mid-thirties to forty—all with heavyset frames. All three wear dark tennies, short white socks and shorts, but two of them wear baggy shorts that extend far down their calves, baring only a few inches of leg. Their untucked team shirts stretch tightly over their large upper bodies. Only one of them wears shades; all three are wearing team hats. One of the coaches sports an earring and a ponytail that extends halfway down his back. It strikes me that not only do the South Pas coaches look uniformly "professional"; in my memory, I have never noticed any South Pas Latino coaches appearing so *cholo* as some of these coaches from our neighboring community.

The more working-class Latino men's style of dress, along with their tendency to be more verbal on the field, often led South Pasadena parents to jokingly comment while watching games that those men were "more serious . . . more intense" than our coaches. Mark Daly, a white South Pasadena soccer coach, said that his occasional games with some of the "Spanish-speaking" teams from neighboring Alhambra had led him to conclude that "South Pas AYSO, I get the feeling, it is a lot more gentle than a lot of the other AYSO's."

As I have shown, the South Pasadena "CEO" coach is a masculine style that is hegemonic in the context of this professional-class community; however, it is no less "serious" or "intense" than other styles of masculinity. The more restrained, quiet control displayed by the CEO coach, however, leads some people in the town to project negative characteristics of masculinity—such as over-aggressiveness and over-competitiveness—onto the more working-class styles of masculinity embodied by some Latino coaches.[28] I never heard South Pasadena people make outright racist comments about others; to the contrary, they seem happy that youth sports gives their kids opportunities to interact with the broader diversity of Southern California's population. My point is that class- and race-based symbolic boundaries are created not through discrimination or hate talk, but subtly, through "innocent comments" that mark differences. The off-the-cuff comments about others that often included a subtly coded projection of the negative characteristics ("That guy's too *serious*," "He's *intense*") of supposedly atavistic styles of masculinity onto Latino men is part of a larger social process of symbolic boundary formation: the (supposedly) kinder, gentler CEO form of masculine leadership connected to a hegemonic professional-class family form becomes part of what creates a distinction between "us" and "them."

South Pasadena as Seen by Outsiders-Within

A second way that I glimpsed the creation of class- and race-based symbolic boundaries in South Pasadena youth sports came to me through the stories of coaches who are not insiders in South Pasadena. I will next highlight how four coaches talked about South Pasadena. Three of these coaches are women of color; one is a Latino man. Three of the four reside in predominantly Latina/o L.A. neighborhoods just outside the boundaries of South Pasadena. Their words offer us a different standpoint on "diversity" and "inclusiveness" in South Pasadena. They are, to borrow a phrase from sociologist Patricia Hill Collins, "outsiders-within."[29] Collins argues that people who straddle different social worlds based on race, social class, and gender tend to have different understandings of those worlds—understandings that often, though not always, include a heightened awareness of processes of exclusion or marginalization that "insiders" may not even see.

Delores Quintero—a mother of four and a teacher with a deep sports résumé—managed softball teams in South Pasadena for four years and won several championships. It is not lost on her that a well-hit baseball from the Arroyo might land in Highland Park, many of whose residents live closer to the ballparks there than many South Pasadena residents. But as a Mexican American woman with a dark-skinned Mexican American husband serving as her assistant coach, and as a resident of neighboring Highland Park, she said she "always felt like an outsider":

> My husband is darker, more Indian—and I can tell you, without a doubt, when I introduced myself to the team on the first day and then he showed up—it was amazing. I would meet 'em, greet 'em, speak to them. And [then] my husband would show—his appearance was so powerful on the field that I guess without knowing him, a lot of parents would shy away, they wouldn't speak—and he would tell me, "Gosh, you know what?

Some of these guys can't even look me in the eye! I don't know what they think I'm gonna do." [*She laughs.*] And we have found that to be true. It's real interesting.

After coaching in South Pasadena for a couple of years, her team won a championship, and though it was conventional for the champion manager to became the league's All-Star manager, there were attempts to squeeze her and her husband out:

It was horrible—my team took first [place] and there was a longtime coach who tried to play a card that I was not a resident of South Pasadena, therefore I should not be eligible to manage that team. We worked it out with a couple advocates within the system hierarchy, [but] my husband they really squeezed out . . . . They didn't wanna let him in. I finally had one guy who actually stepped down to let my husband [coach]. It was the best thing for the team. It was really obvious. But I—I always felt like an *outsider,* working with the hierarchy. My feeling now is this [Highland Park] is my community. So, I intend to work now in coaching here with [my daughters]. Maybe put a team into the Little League. And—I will *never* coach in South Pasadena.

In the end, Quintero concluded that although Highland Park borders South Pasadena, "We might as well be fifty miles apart! It's—it's amazing."

Jessica Torres has experienced some similar feelings of marginalization. A Hispanic mother of three, Torres works as a secretary, and her husband holds a working-class job. She coaches softball in South Pasadena but lives in nearby El Sereno.

Sometimes I hear [El Sereno] people say, "Everybody hates South Pas," and even people I work with will say, "Do you ever go to South Pas? People are really mean there." I guess there's a—it's a prejudice, I think. It's because you're not from the town, you know, it could be because I'm Mexican, it could be because we're not in the same schools or we don't have the same type of money. I think it's a lot of things. I choose to—well, I can't say ignore it, because I know it exists, but I just don't let it affect me as much, you know. I say, "Oh my daughters still wanna play, I'm not gonna not let them play here simply because one person made me feel uncomfortable," you know. I think my little one feels that she's shunned by everyone, but I'm not sure she understands why. She thinks that it's

just because she doesn't go to school with these girls—but then you realize that a lot of the girls don't go to school together, some go to private
school, and yet she's still not in that same group, you know, so to speak.

Though South Pasadena Little League has a policy of including kids
from the bordering neighborhoods of El Sereno and Highland Park, Jessica Torres says that some South Pasadena parents don't know that:

> There was this couple [who said], "Why do you play here?" You know,
> "Don't you live in L.A.?" And [I said], " 'Cause we're [in] the district."
> And I don't understand why that has to be questioned. *I* don't know—
> maybe they were worried that all of El Sereno and Highland Park was
> gonna be [*laughs*] playing soon.

> [Do you think that South Pasadena is really trying to keep Highland Park
> out of . . . ?]

> Yes, yes. Originally, when I first started playing, they would advertise more
> in the area; they don't advertise at all anymore. *At all.* So we have very few
> girls from our area. In fact [*pause*], I think [my daughter's] the only one.

Another outsider-within, Michael Duran, is not a South Pasadena resident, and as a bilingual coach and member of the AYSO board, he is trying to bring more Spanish-speaking kids from L.A. into the league. He
said that about 10 percent of the kids in South Pasadena AYSO did not
live in the town. His words hint at the existence of a small cluster of
outsiders-within who are working to diversify the league:

> I think that more kids in L.A. should play in this region. I would think
> that would be good for them and good for the region. That I speak Span-
> ish is a big plus; when I call my team for the first time, if there's a parent
> or a grandparent who doesn't speak English but does speak Spanish, I
> can speak to them. And that's a function that I think is helpful if I'm do-
> ing outreach to the city of L.A. There are a number of coaches who are
> also bilingual, and referees, so sometimes when we're sort of kidding
> around we'll sort of talk in Spanglish to each other—sort of saying, you
> know, "We share something here even though we live in different cities."

When he was asked if he believed that ethnic diversity is something that
the AYSO board actively encouraged, his response suggested that the effort to diversify is more likely an effort of a small subset of people:

No, I don't think it was ever articulated. [But] I know that another board member who's part of the inner circle, who's also bilingual, has said to me the importance of having visibility within this organization and helping everybody understand it's not all upper-middle-class white people who are interested in this organization, or interested in what we're doing. I remember him saying something after my first board meeting: "I'm really glad we have someone, another one of us."

Running counter to these kinds of sincere efforts to build bridges to Spanish-speaking kids and families in Highland Park or El Sereno is the structural fact of the recent merger of South Pasadena AYSO with the even more class-privileged community of San Marino. June Park, a biracial mother, is very critical of the claims of South Pasadenans to "diversity," and she sees the recent merger of South Pasadena and San Marino AYSO as a kind of class alliance against neighboring poor and brown communities. When Suzel told her that others we had interviewed see South Pasadena as a "very diverse community," she scoffed and said:

Yeah, well they're not [laughs]. We're very um, tokenly diverse, yeah, we are. There are like a handful of gay and lesbian parents maybe at the most. This whole place is—very nice veneer. I mean, we say things like, "Oh we're gonna reach out to L.A." I mean it's what, a block away, literally. From where we play soccer, if you walk across the street, you'd be in a part of L.A. that should be included in our region probably, and we should invite those kids to come over and play. But you know, I mean you cross that street and all of a sudden you're talking about apartments, single-family homes, people from Mexico. You know, we're very careful to say how inclusive we are and how we have this open registration, which means that everybody from San Marino can come over here and play with their buddies here. The San Marino people don't want to go to San Gabriel to play 'cause then they'd have to play with the other people over there—and it makes sense that they should be with us, because, like, socioeconomically we're so tight [laughs]. And these people think that they're doing their children a favor by keeping them with other children that are just like them somehow. And some of them are really just downright racist; they are really just mean. And these are the same people that come across as saying, "Oh, we're a very diverse community." I mean they're as diverse as they wanna be.

As I said above, I never witnessed or heard any "downright racist" words or actions in the years I participated in and watched youth sports in South Pasadena. But as I listened to the voices of these outsiders-within, it made me think about the limitations of my own standpoint as a white, male, professional-class homeowner in South Pasadena. I experience, and my family benefits from, the warm and gentle feelings of inclusion that come with the insider status our family enjoys in the community. Exclusion and marginalization of others may sometimes happen, due to outright racist, sexist meanness or class exclusiveness. But I don't see that. What I do see, however, is marginalization and exclusion being created routinely (and probably less visibly and thus more perniciously) beneath a veneer of self-congratulatory celebrations of "diversity" and "inclusiveness."

These narratives of inclusiveness in privileged communities, I believe, are usually sincere, but they fail to acknowledge the routine ways that class, race, and gender privilege creates insiders and outsiders. This, in fact, is the most common way that privilege normally operates: rarely through meanness or intent to exclude; more often through a kind of in-group civility that creates internal cohesion and external boundaries. I never saw and rarely heard of sexist men trying to bar women from coaching; yet the institutional structure and routine interactions of youth sports did channel women and men into different directions. I never saw and rarely heard racist comments or crass class bias directed at outsiders; but the routine expressions of a professional-class culture of families and community created symbolic boundaries that illuminated who is inside, and who is outside.

CONCLUSION: YOUTH SPORTS, FAMILIES, AND COMMUNITY

I began this study several years ago with a simple question: why are there so few women coaches in youth sports? The answers to this question are not simple. My explorations of the internal dynamics of youth sports revealed the ways that everyday gendered interactions, shaped and constrained by the gender regimes of youth sports organizations, lead most men volunteers to become coaches and most women volunteers to become team moms. To many people, this gendered division of labor seems to occur almost naturally, because it affirms long-standing beliefs in natural differences between women and men. But this old ideology of difference takes a new form in today's professional-class communities: a belief system that I call "soft essentialism." To understand the significance of soft essentialism, we need to think of youth sports not simply as a standalone institution, but as one that is intricately intertwined with peoples' lives in families, workplaces, and communities. Professional-class women, through the lens of soft essentialism, *choose* to pursue or to opt out of careers; *choose* to do the lion's share of housework and childcare; *choose* to do community volunteer work; *choose* to be team moms; *choose* to coach only the youngest kids' teams. Men, through the lens of soft essentialism, do not choose: they are destined to be breadwinners, with high-profile careers in public life. Since their time and energy is constrained by their careers, their contributions to family work are understandably minimal; their community volunteer work is relegated to occasional, plug-in tasks. Coaching youth sports, though, becomes a singular, highly visible, non-career-related commitment, through which some men connect with their children and with their community. And this is in large part because despite girls' and women's massive movement into sports, the institution is still saturated with masculine meanings.

I have argued that youth sports used to be a place that constructed a hard essentialism, based on categorical separation. Girls' and women's movement into sport created a massive historical challenge to this construct, making sport a terrain of contested gender meanings. But we are still far short of having accomplished a feminist revolution that has created equal conditions for boys and girls. Instead of social equality, we see in sports a sex-segregated (and still often unequal) field within which girls are believed to have, not *equality*, but rather, *equity* or *equal opportunity*.[30] Supporting this liberal system of equity-with-difference is the ascendant ideology of soft essentialism, as revealed in the gendered narratives and actions of the adult volunteers who run youth sports. Soft essentialism is consistent with dominant professional-class family forms that are based on the idea of women's right to choose to opt in or out of the workforce. This hegemonic professional-class family becomes a powerful symbol that marks and polices the symbolic boundaries that separate a community like South Pasadena from its less privileged neighbors. Soft essentialism, in short, helps to sustain "hard" inequalities.

Youth sports is an ideal site for the construction of soft essentialism. As an institution, sport carries cultural assumptions and values about natural differences between women and men, more so than most other institutions (the military is perhaps equivalent). Twenty years ago, I wondered to what extent the movement of girls and women into sport would challenge gender hierarchies, and in what ways that would contribute to the feminist movement for equality. I now believe that many people have a deep emotional and psychological commitment to the idea of natural difference between the sexes. As women move into previously all-male realms of life, this commitment to difference is challenged. But essentialist ideas do not disappear. Instead, because of the psychological security and pleasures it brings, essentialism tends to migrate to particular social sites, like sports, where gender is made especially salient through sex-segregation and the different engendering of male and female bodies.

My observations in this study thus suggest a paradoxical conclusion about the role of youth sports in today's contested terrain of gender relations. Yes, girls' and women's movement into sport created a stunning challenge to categorical assumptions underlying beliefs in natural male superiority. However, the combination of sex-segregation, routine gendered interactions, and the ascendant ideology of soft essentialism has stripped youth sport of much of its revolutionary possibilities. Instead, especially for parents, youth sports has become a kind of gender comfort zone.

My study points primarily to ways that peoples' agency is reproducing gender difference in children, families, workplaces, and communities. However, countertendencies exist, and change is possible. We can see hints of such changes in AYSO, though not in Little League. Due largely to its different history, AYSO is a gender regime that affords women more elbow room. Indeed, the number of women head coaches in South Pasadena's AYSO, while still small, has been inching up in recent years. And there is evidence that the number of women coaches in AYSO is now large enough that they are beginning to connect, support each other, and recruit other women coaches. By contrast, men still appear to "own" Little League—especially boys' baseball. The number of women managers in LLB/S has not budged, and the few who exist suffer from token status, usually having to rely on male "sponsors" who recruit and support them.

Social change operates on many levels. If leaders in youth sports organizations want to move toward supporting more women to become head coaches—and they say they do—then they need to act affirmatively to recruit and encourage women to enter the coaching pipeline. They need also to raise awareness of how routine interactions—for instance, the first team meeting of the season and regular practices—tend (usually non-intentionally) to discourage women from coaching, instead channeling them toward becoming team moms, and placing a glass ceiling on existing women coaches that keeps most of them from coaching in the higher age-levels or for boys' teams. Conversely, routine gendered language and informal interactions actively route men away from taking on the team parent roles.

Raising awareness about these routine interactions, and changing them, can contribute to a more equitable sharing by women and men of various tasks in youth sports. However, this study has also shown how youth sports is connected to other institutions, so trying to bring about changes within the gender regime of youth sports presupposes that we also consider the need for changes in other realms. The gender separation of male head coaches and female team moms makes sense in light of normal gender divisions of labor in families. As long as people continue to assume that women are naturally suited to housework and childcare, leaving men excused from participating substantially in this family work, then it will continue to seem natural for men to be leaders and women to do the invisible support work for their children's sports teams. Fathers need to see that it is fair to our spouses, and it is life-enhancing for us and for our children, to be fully involved in the daily care of our children and our homes. And if more-equitable family divisions of labor are to emerge, we also need changes in the organization of workplaces and professions, many of which are still characterized by hierarchical sex-segregation. Even professions that have begun to desegregate—like law or medicine—continue to organize career paths based on the assumption that the professional is a male with a stay-at-home wife who takes care of the home and children, thus giving him time to put in sixty-hour weeks in his climb to career success.

Underlying these inequalities within youth sports, families, and occupations are stubbornly persistent assumptions that it is women, not men, who must make the tough work-family choices in response to the time binds that come with parenthood. Institutions need to be reorganized to minimize these time binds, and to the extent that time binds are inherent for parents, men must share equally in the tough choices that have to be made about who sacrifices time and labor. These kinds of changes are important if we care about fairness and equality among adults; they are also important because relations between women and men are part of the context within which our daughters and sons are currently shaping their values and future expectations about gender. What kinds of work-family and community lives will they value and create?

Participation in youth sports, I am convinced, can be a positive activity for parents and for kids. However, if youth sports is to live up to its full potential as a fun and healthy activity for kids and families, and as an institution that builds strong, cohesive communities that are committed to equality and diversity, then people need to become more conscious of the ways that youth sports—despite many peoples' better intentions—help to create sex difference, racial inequality, and class distinction. If we become conscious of these matters, and commit ourselves to making the necessary social changes to support values of social justice, then youth sports can truly be "a fun and safe place" for all of our kids.

APPENDIX ONE Demographic Description of Interview Subjects

Pseudonym (Sport)*	Ethnicity†	Age	Occupation	Family**	Occupation of Spouse‡
WOMEN					
Isabel Bacad (AYSO)	Filipina	37	Family physician	M, 1 child	PROF
Pam Burke (AYSO)	W	36	Homemaker	M, 3 children	PROF
Norma Delgado (LLB)	Asian/Pacific Islander	41	Homemaker/Part-time writer	C, 2 children	PROF
Barbara Jones (AYSO)	W	43	Full-time mom	M, 3 children	PROF
Kate Kaplan (LLS)	W	23	Graduate student	S	
Veronica Leonard (AYSO)	W	34	Elementary school teacher	D, 2 children	PROF
Ellen Lessing (AYSO)	W	52	Professor	M, 3 children	PROF
Nikki Lopez (AYSO)	Hispanic	37	CEO, promotions agency	D, 1 child	MGT
Wendy Lytle (AYSO)	W	39	Self-employed in home	M, 2 children	MGT
Lillian Mohr (LLB)	W	35	Elementary school teacher	M, 2 children	PROF
Carol Morris (AYSO)	W	41	Mom	M, 4 children	PROF
Nancy Morris (LLS)	W	41	Full-time mom/Realtor	M, 2 children	PROF
Tracy Nash (LLS)	W	50	Teacher's aide	D, 3 children	BUS
June Park (AYSO)	Mixed race	44	Elementary school teacher	M, 2 children	PROF
Shelley Parsons (AYSO)	W	44	Elementary school administrator	M, 2 children	PROF
Terri Patrick (AYSO)	W	45	Self-employed writer	C, 3 children	PROF
Delores Quintero (LLS)	Mexican American	46	Middle school teacher	M, 4 children	WK
Nina Ramos (LLS)	Hispanic	21	College student/ Part-time job	S	
Kathi Ralston (AYSO)	W	43	Homemaker	M, 3 children	BUS
Rosa Ramirez (LLS)	Other/Biracial	37	Homemaker/Part-time administrative assistant	M, 2 children	MGT

(continued)

Joan Ring (AYSO)	W	40	Homemaker/Writer	M, 3 children	PROF
Melissa Rosas (LLB-TP)	Latina	40	Elementary school teacher	M, 1 child	PROF
Lisette Taylor (LLS- Asst.)	W	48	Speech pathologist	M, 2 children	MGT
Jessica Torres (LLS)	Hispanic	39	Legal secretary	M, 3 children	WK

MEN

Tony Barnett (AYSO)	W	50	Attorney	M, 4 children	PT PROF
Doug Berger (AYSO)	W	41	Real estate manager/Investor	M, 3 children	HOM
Eric Caldwell (AYSO)	W	45	Vice-president, sales	M, 5 children	HOM
Dave Chadwick (AYSO)	W	40	Self-employed writer	M, 2 children	PROF
Don Clark (AYSO)	W	42	Property management	M, 3 children	HOM
Mark Daly (AYSO)	W	33	High school coach	M, 2 children	HOM
Al Evans (AYSO)	W	49	Screenwriter	M, 2 children	PROF
Mitch Flores (LLS)	American Mexican	47	Sales manager	M, 3 children	HOM
Jon Gaines (AYSO)	W	47	Physician	M, 2 children	PROF
Roger Hall (AYSO)	W	48	Real estate broker	M, 2 children	HOM
Gerard James (AYSO)	W	47	Construction developer	M, 2 children	MGT
Dick Jordan (LLB)	W	48	Police officer	M, 2 children	HOM
Paul Leung (AYSO)	Chinese	49	Architect	M, 2 children	HOM
Alan Lindgren (LLS)	W	51	Attorney	M, 4 children	HOM
Ted Miller (LLS)	W	45	Senior real estate manager	M, 3 children	MGT
Lenn Molina (AYSO)	½ Mexican, ½ Japanese	30	Manager	S	
Gilbert Morales (AYSO)	Mexican	45	Manager	D/C, 3 children	WK
Bill Munson (AYSO)	W	48	Physician	M, 3 children	HOM
Michael Ortiz (AYSO)	Latino	46	Attorney	M, 3 children	HOM

Oscar Rice (LLS)	W	45	Store manager	M, 2 children	HOM
Albert Riley (LLS)	W	49	Regional sales manager	M, 2 children	PROF
Carlos Ruiz (AYSO)	Latino	44	Prosecutor	M, 2 children	PROF
Will Solomon (LLB)	W	48	Business CEO	M, 3 children	PROF
George Starr (LLB)	W	47	Grocery store cashier	M, 2 children	WK
Campbell Weber (LLB)	W	54	Professional writer	D, 1 child	
Brian Yu (LLB)	Chinese American	48	Real estate manager	M, 2 children	HOM

* I list interviewees here as either AYSO, LLB, or LLS, based on my initial identification of their coaching positions. However, several of the interviewees revealed that they had coached both AYSO and LLB/S, and some had also coached other youth sports like YMCA basketball. The interviewee who is listed as "LLS-Asst." was not a head coach but served as an assistant coach. The one listed as "LLB-TP" served five years as a boys' baseball team parent and one year as an assistant coach.

† Self-identified ethnicity; "W" is used for "White" or "Caucasian" responses.

** M = currently married; D = divorced; C = currently cohabiting; S = single. All individuals listed here as married or cohabiting are in heterosexual couples, except for one woman who is cohabiting with a woman partner "until [gay marriage] is legalized."

‡ To help ensure confidentiality, I have generalized the spouses' occupations under the following categories: PROF (professionals); MGT (managers); BUS (business owners); WK (working-class jobs); HOM (homemakers); PT indicates part-time employment. Occupations of the spouses of women coaches included, under professionals: two physicians, a police officer, a teacher, two film industry professionals, a newspaper editor, a research scientist, a college sport trainer, three attorneys, and two college professors. Management jobs included bank manager, insurance manager, and stock manager. Under business owners, there were two small-business owners and an insurance broker. Working-class jobs included salesman and delivery driver. Occupations of the spouses of men coaches included twelve homemakers; under professionals, a part-time pediatrician, an accountant, a nurse, two teachers, an attorney, and a librarian; under managers, a money manager and an advertising manager; and under working-class jobs, a cook and an administrative assistant.

Racial/Ethnic Composition of
South Pasadena LLB/AYSO
Coaches and of the City of South
Pasadena, by Percent

Racial/Ethnic Group	Coaches Interviewed (N=50)	Coaches in AYSO LLB/S Yearbooks (N=240)*	City of South Pasadena (2000 Census)
White	68	73	44.2
Hispanic	18	14	16.1
Asian American	4	7	26.6
Asian/Pacific Islander	2	0	5.2
South Asian/Indian	0	2	0
Filipino American	2	0	0
Black	0	0	3.4
Biracial/Other	6	4	4.5

* I estimated these numbers by looking at one year of each of the South Pasadena AYSO and
LLB/S yearbooks and assigning coaches to racial/ethnic categories based on their names and
photos. Thus, these numbers should be seen as a rough estimate of the racial/ethnic composition
of the coaches, rather than as an exact count that would result from people's actual responses to
questions about their racial/ethnic identification.

Proportion of AYSO and LLB/S
Women Head Coaches in
Communities Surrounding
South Pasadena

	Teams with Women Head Coaches	Teams with Women Assistant Coaches	Under-10 Teams with Women Head Coaches	11 & older Teams with Women Head Coaches	Girls' Teams with Women Head Coaches	Co-ed Teams with Women Head Coaches	Boys' Teams with Women Head Coaches
AYSO Region 2* (2006)	11/175 (6.3%)	n/a	8/76 (10.5%)	3/99 (3.0%)	9/77 (11.7%)	n/a	2/98 (2.0%) (1 in U7, 1 in U10)
AYSO Region 13 (2007)	21/269 (7.8%)	n/a	18/196 (10.9%)	3/73 (4.1%)	15/109 (13.8%)	n/a	6/160 (3.8%) (4 in U10 or lower)
AYSO Region 40 (2007)	5/57 (11.4%)	n/a	4	1	3	n/a	2 (1 in U6, 1 in U8)
AYSO Region 60 (2006)	11/94 (11.7%)	8/94 (8.5%)	9/65 (13.8%)	2/29 (6.9%)	6/40 (15.0%)	n/a	5/54 (9.3%) (all in U6 or U8)
AYSO Region 88 (2006)	28/287 (9.8%)	n/a	19	8	19	n/a	8 (all in U10 and younger)
AYSO Region 214 (2007) South Pasadena	**41/211 (19.4%)**	**n/a**	**34/156 (21.8%)**	**7/55 (12.7%)**	**19/100 (19.0%)**	**n/a**	**22/111 (19.8%) (2 in U6, 16 in U8)**
LLB/S East Altadena (2006)	1/18 (5.5%)	2/36 (5.5%)	0/10 (0%)	0/7 (0%)	0/2 (0%)	1/5 (20%)	0/11 (0%)
LLB Santa Anita (2006)	0/25 (0%)	1/54 (1.9%)	0/13 (0%)	0/12 (0%)	n/a	0/8 (0%)	0/17 (0%)

LLB San Carlos (2006—in SF Bay Area)	1/83 (1.2%)	n/a	1/46 (2.2%)	0/37 (0%)	n/a	1/23 (4.3%)	0/60 (0%)
LLB/S South Pasadena (2007)	**3.5/60 (5.8%)**	**n/a**	**2/26 (7.7%)**	**1.5/34 (4.4%)**	**1.5/14 (10.7%)**	**1/11 (9.1%)**	**1/32 (3.1%)** **(7–8-year-old team)**

* AYSO Region 2 covers Arcadia, Monrovia, Sierra Madre, Bradbury, and Duarte; Region 13 is Pasadena, Altadena, and La Cañada; Region 40 covers San Marino, San Gabriel, and Rosemead; Region 60 is Alhambra and Monterey Park; and Region 88 is Glendale and La Crescenta.

APPENDIX FOUR In the Field

For this study, I deployed multiple research methods. The nine years of numerical data that I collected from the AYSO and LLB/S annual yearbooks tracked the number of women and men coaches and their placement in different age-groups or with boys' and girls' teams. These numbers gave me a descriptive picture that illuminated the question: *What* is the state of play of the gender division of labor among adults in South Pasadena youth sports? The in-depth interviews helped me to probe peoples' shared beliefs and their meaning-making processes, specifically the question: *Why* do people believe that gender divisions of labor exist and persist? Finally, my participant observation allowed me to make direct observations of social processes, giving me insight into the question: *How* are gender divisions of labor created (and occasionally resisted)? Any one of these three methods, taken alone, would have had severe limitations. By putting them into play together, I found these three methods to be very useful in pondering the *what, why,* and *how* questions about the social construction of inequality.

While doing this study, I gained an appreciation for the ways that researchers can create productive "dialogue" between different kinds of qualitative data. I will give two brief examples here. First, while I was in the field, I was reading the interview transcripts, some of which alerted me to look for—and begin to see—processes of social exclusion or marginalization. Several women coaches spoke of the ways that men coaches' loud voices and their use of their usually larger bodies on the space of the playing fields served to silence or intimidate women coaches. After hearing this in the interviews, I began more consciously to listen to voices during games, and to observe the ways that coaches used space on the fields. This interview material sensitized me in ways that enriched my field observations.

It worked the other way, too. After observing several years of start-of-the-season team meetings and seeing *how* the gender divisions of labor are created (with women mostly becoming team parents, and men assistant coaches), my research assistant, Suzel Bozada-Deas, and I probed more deeply in our interviews to better understand the ways that people understand *why* these divisions happen. What I observed were ritualized gendered interactions that differentiated women and men; what most people we interviewed understood to be happening was a sorting of women and men into different roles that resulted from individuals' choices. As my research progressed, I increasingly mined this give-and-take between interview data and observation data.

While using the quantitative data from the annual yearbooks as a descriptive backdrop, I deployed primarily qualitative methods: participant observation and in-depth interviews. My field observations included participation in many practices and countless games, taking part in a daylong training workshop for Little League coaches, observing several annual tryouts for baseball and softball players, attending several annual opening ceremonies for AYSO or LLB/S, and having many informal conversations with people at all of these events. As would any field researcher, I took notes when I saw something of interest. And over time, as I began to see recurring patterns that revealed hidden social processes, I took more extensive notes from which I could create thickly descriptive examples. I did not intend originally to spend seven years doing this study, but in retrospect I can see that this amount of time in the field benefited me greatly in identifying recurring patterns in peoples' informal interactions.

My position as a researcher rarely caused any problems, as far as I am aware. At the start of each season, I would notify the head coach of my son's team that I was doing a study of adult volunteers in youth sports. Once, about four years ago, when I failed to speak right away with my son's new coach, I received an e-mail from him saying that he had heard "a rumor" that "a USC professor is doing research on Little League." I admitted that I was the researcher, and apologized for not yet having told him. This incident suggested to me that there was knowledge of my study within the coaches' network, and it reminded me always to talk to a new coach about the study well before the start of the season. Most of these coaches, as well as the AYSO and LLB/S league officials with whom I discussed the study, were supportive of the research, and said that they were keen to see what my research would reveal.

It is my impression that, like many who conduct participant observation, my role as researcher was frequently "forgotten" by others, and I was most often seen as a father, an assistant coach, or a scorekeeper. The scorekeeper job put me into an invaluable position of observation in the dugout, near the field and the coaches. Though the actual business of scorekeeping kept me quite busy, when necessary I could also jot a short field note on a pad that I kept in my pocket. Once, driving home from a game, my son Sasha asked nervously if my study was about the kids. He worried that I might be jotting down the conversations of the boys in the dugout. I assured him that, although I loved overhearing the often hilarious conversations of thirteen- and fourteen-year old boys, my field notes were focused on the adults. Since my son was playing baseball, my field observations are skewed toward that sport. I did on occasion go over to the girls' softball field, and to the soccer fields, to observe games there, too.

I benefited over several years from the help of two women soccer and softball coaches who served as informants for my research. Their insights alerted me at times to new women coaches I might interview, and they identified the men whom they saw as particularly supportive or obstructive to women coaches. They also provided tidbits of information that gave me an insider's feel (this was especially helpful with AYSO, since my son stopped playing soccer years ago, whereas I had continued a close connection to LLB/S). And they read and commented on some of my chapter drafts. These two women have particular points of view—they are especially active in their attempts to promote women coaches—so I would not say that my having them read parts of my manuscript gave me some sort of "objective" insider's take on my analysis. Still, I found it very helpful to receive their feedback, and I respected their willingness to read my work as yet another dimension of their commitment to improving women's position within youth sports. I fully expect that some of the people I interviewed and observed will disagree with some of my interpretations of gender, race, and class dynamics in South Pasadena. I can only say that I have tried to accurately convey the words of those we interviewed, and to fairly describe the things I have seen. The interpretations of what these words and observations mean, of course, are mine.

My "insider" role as a community member and a father of kids in these sports leagues allowed me easy access, and my position as a USC sociologist seems to have given me instant credibility with my research subjects. However, as observers of the ins and outs of research methods have often pointed out, insider status can also create blind spots in the researcher. Sometimes an outsider will ask "naïve questions" that lead them to see things that in insider might miss; familiarity can breed a kind of blindness. In the text of the book, I note at times how my eyes were opened during this research by listening to the voices of "outsiders." For instance, in the final chapter, I speculate on how my own status as a white, professional-class homeowner in South Pasadena has encouraged me to see the town as a safe, accepting, warm-and-fuzzy place for my family, and to assume that it must also be so for others. But listening to the voices of a handful of others—women and men who are not white, who are not homeowners in the community but who have participated with their kids in South Pasadena youth sports, I heard stories of race- and class-based marginalization and exclusion. Due to my experience as a privileged community insider, I simply did not see some of the informal social processes that create exclusionary boundaries based on race and class.

The fifty interviews—with twenty-four women and twenty-six men—were nearly all with head soccer coaches or baseball managers. I conducted the first three interviews together with my research assistant, Suzel Bozada-Deas. Suzel conducted thirty-eight of the subsequent interviews, while I did nine. Interviewees were given the standard consent form to sign, informing them that they had the right to refuse to answer any questions or to end the interview at any time, and telling them that they would be assigned pseudonyms in any publication of their words. As I wrote the book, I occasionally changed details, such as a person's specific profession, when I felt is was necessary to protect anonymity.

We interviewed slightly more men than women. Given the overwhelming proportion of coaches who were men, these interviewees were easy to locate and the interviews easy to arrange. Women coaches (and especially women baseball or softball managers) were fewer and farther between. We located women coaches through the yearbooks and also by going to opening ceremonies or tryouts and approaching them about interviews. Thereafter, we asked women whom we were interviewing to nominate other women coaches that they knew of.

Though we were by no means trying to collect a scientifically representative sample, we made an effort to interview people who reflected various forms of diversity that we saw among coaches—particularly racial/ethnic diversity (see Appendix 2). We also sought to interview both high-profile members of the AYSO or LLB/S organizations and those who were not "insiders" in these organizations but who had simply decided to coach their kids' teams. We attempted to interview an even number of coaches from AYSO and managers from LLB/S; however, we soon found that this distinction did not hold up, as many had coached both sports (and other sports) at one time or another.

When I conducted interviews, I used my insider status as a member of the community and as a parent of kids who had played in the local youth sports leagues to establish trust and rapport with interviewees. I have little doubt that my status as a white male college professor with a deep background in sports also gave me instant credibility with many of those I interviewed. Suzel Bozada-Deas, by contrast, was an outsider in most ways. She is a Latina graduate student who has never lived in South Pasadena, so of course she did not have children playing in local youth sports. Moreover, she had almost no sports background. Suzel closed the social distance between herself and her interviewees in a number of ways. First, she mentioned in the interviews, when appropriate, that she is the mother of two (then-) teenaged daughters. Second, before doing interviews on her own, she enrolled in a coaching clinic and a refereeing clinic to learn more about soccer. Third, she observed several practices and games in order to better understand the role that coaches play with the kids. In the interviews, Suzel judiciously used her knowledge from these clinics and her observations of practices and games to ask knowledgeable questions and sharp follow-up probes. This strategy created rapport, and it also allowed Suzel to demonstrate knowledge of sports and coaching, thus bridging what might otherwise have been a credibility gap between herself and some of her interview subjects with deep athletic experience and knowledge. Suzel's outsider status was sometimes a benefit, as she was able to ask "naïve" questions about the particularities of South Pasadena that might have sounded disingenuous coming from a known insider like me.

Notes

PREFACE

1. See Eitzen and Sage 2008, chapter 4.

2. Shields et al. 2005. Interestingly, *self-reports* from youth coaches indicated extremely low levels of coaches encouraging kids' cheating or intentional rule-breaking, or advocating violence against an opponent, and moderate levels of arguing with a referee or yelling at a player for making a mistake. By contrast, the kids' perception is that their coaches engage in much higher levels of these transgressions than show up in the self-reports of the coaches (ibid.).

CHAPTER 1

1. For simplicity's sake, I use the term "coach" or "head coach" throughout to designate the on-field adult leader of the youth soccer and baseball teams.

However, I acknowledge that in baseball this person is referred to as the "manager," while baseball "coaches" are always assistants to the manager.

2. All interviewees throughout the book have been assigned pseudonyms, and in some cases, I have changed other aspects of an individual's identity (e.g., his or her specific occupation) to ensure anonymity.

3. For an earlier ethnographic study of an AYSO opening ceremony, see Messner 2000.

4. Glazier 2003.

5. U.S. Census Bureau, "United States Census 2000," www.census.gov/main/www/cen2000.htm

6. The racial/ethnic breakdown of South Pasadena and its neighboring communities is reflective of the Los Angeles area's often extreme patchwork residential segregation patterns. The more working-class bordering town of Alhambra is 47.5 percent Asian American, 38.7 percent Hispanic, and only 11.2 percent white; the more affluent bordering town of San Marino is 49.7 percent Asian American, 44.4 percent white, and only 4.4 percent Hispanic. To the north, the much larger city of Pasadena is 53.4 percent white, 14.4 percent black, 14.4 percent Hispanic, and 10 percent Asian American (U.S. Census Bureau, "United States Census 2000," www.census.gov/main/www/cen2000.htm).

7. For a discussion of recent research that explores these kinds of connections between sport and other institutions, see Messner 2005.

8. When I say "youth sports" in this book, I am referring not to school-based sports, but to community-based sports for kids (usually from ages 5 through the mid-teens) that are linked to national organizations. Organizations like AYSO and LLB/S begin from an "everybody plays" ethic of participation: any child who meets the age requirements can sign up. Each child must pay a participation fee ($120 per year for AYSO; $135 for Little League) which pays for most of the child's uniform and other costs associated with running and maintaining the league. Both leagues have financial support available for families who can't afford to pay the fee. Most of the rules that govern these local community sports are set by the national AYSO and LLB/S organizations. Local field care, coaching, and other activities that sustain the leagues are supplied entirely by adult volunteers. Head coaches in AYSO and managers in Little League are selected by the local board of directors. Most coaches and managers are parents of kids playing in the leagues, though anyone can volunteer to be considered as a coach.

9. For a discussion of post–World War II fitness concerns in the United States, and its connection to organized sports, see Montez de Oca 2005.

10. Glassner 1999. See, especially, chapter 3, "Youth at Risk," 51–84.

11. For a thoughtful analysis of the midnight basketball phenomenon, see Hartmann 2001. Sociologist Jay Coakley (2002), responding to midnight basketball as well as to other efforts to use sports to solve youth problems that are grounded

in larger, systemic problems like poverty and institutionalized racism, urges caution, and suggests that we look to sports for the kinds of positive things that they really can deliver to kids, rather than seeing them as a panacea for social problems.

12. See Hochschild 1989.

13. See Hays 1996.

14. Lareau 2003, 82.

15. See Coakley 2006, 153–63. Coakley, a sociologist, argues that today middle-class families and communities are permeated with the "prevalence of the conservative and neo-liberal view that parents must be accountable for the behaviour and whereabouts of their children 24 hours a day and seven days a week. . . . Under these conditions, the achievements of children in an activity as visible and highly publicized as sports come to symbolize proof of one's moral worth as a parent. Talented child athletes, therefore, become valuable moral capital in neighbourhoods, communities, and subcultures associated with high-performance youth sports programmes. This leads many parents to feel obligated to 'invest' in their child's sport participation" (159–60).

16. Moreover, the study found that an additional 16 percent of kids had at one time participated in an organized or team sport, leaving only 17 percent of respondents who said that they had never been involved in an organized or team sport. The "never participated" rates are still higher for girls, at 21 percent, than they are for boys, at 13 percent (Sabo and Veliz 2008).

17. This pattern continues as youth move from community sports into school sports. A national study of high school sports participation rates found that though Title IX has benefited girls widely, the benefits of increased participation rates have been disproportionately reaped by girls from economically privileged families (see Stevenson 2007, 486–505).

18. Many parents hold these beliefs about the positive outcomes for kids who play sports, but the research reveals a more complicated picture. In several national studies of youth, adolescence, and sports, spanning the late 1990s through 2006, Kathleen Miller and her colleagues found differences between teens who played some sports and those who were "highly involved" in sports. Teenaged boys and girls appear to derive some health benefits from playing sports: they are statistically less likely than non-athletes to use illicit drugs, drink alcohol, smoke cigarettes, or attempt suicide. In addition, girls who played sports were found to have a more positive body image than girls who did not play sports, and were more likely to use seatbelts when riding in cars. On the other hand, "highly involved athletes" were found to be *more* involved in dangerous risk-taking and unhealthy practices: they were more likely to use anabolic steroids, more likely to binge drink, and twice as likely to be suicidal. Highly involved girl athletes were also more likely than non-athletes to use dieting and exercise to control their weight, and to use extreme forms of weight control like vomiting and/or laxatives

(see Miller et al. 1999; Miller et al. 2001; Miller et al. 2005; and Miller et al. 2006). For this reason, I believe that parents, teachers, coaches, media, and sports organizations should carefully consider the extent to which—for girls and for boys—*playing sports*, which can be a very good thing, can differ from becoming a highly involved *athlete*, which may not be a very good thing.

19. The 2008 national survey of families found that parents report high levels of involvement, as measured by talking with their kids about their sports, driving their kids to and from games and practices, attending games or performances, and practicing sports skills and exercising with their children (Sabo and Veliz 2008). Unfortunately, the survey did not ask about more official kinds of participation, such as volunteer coaching, team parenting, or refereeing.

20. I list these as the main national organizations for youth sports in the United States, though in some communities youth sports leagues are organized instead by local or regional organizations that may or may not be affiliated with these big national organizations. Pop Warner used to be devoted only to youth football, but its Web site claims that in 2004 Pop Warner organized 6,300 tackle football teams, 883 flag football teams, and 5,400 cheer and dance squads, with a total number of over 380,000 participants. USA Hockey's Web site claims 585,000 ice and inline hockey players, coaches, officials, and volunteers for the year 2007. I was told by the national YMCA office that they do not keep track of the numbers of kids who participate in their youth sports programs, but they did inform me that of 2,682 YMCAs, 63.6 percent have youth basketball programs, 54.7 percent have youth soccer, 43.6 percent have youth T-ball, 38.9 percent have youth flag football, 30.3 percent have youth baseball, and 25.4 percent youth volleyball, while a smaller percentage of YMCAs offer youth sports programs in gymnastics, field hockey, golf, lacrosse, racquetball, softball, tackle football, and tennis.

21. See Connell 1987. For applications of Connell's concept of gender regimes to analyses of sport, see Boyle and McKay 1995; McKay 1997; and Messner 2000.

22. Kimmel 1990.

23. For a good general history of Little League Baseball, see Van Auken and Van Auken 2001.

24. Little League Museum, "A Piece of Little League's Past: Little League Softball Uniforms," May 2006, Little League Online, http://littleleague.org/museum/pop_may_06.asp.

25. Berlage 1994; Gregorich 1993.

26. David Nielsen, "Sports Key to Breaking Down Gender Barriers," *South-Coast Today*, August 20, 1999.

27. Girls are legally allowed to play Little League Baseball. In fact, at the entry level of T-ball, girls and boys play together. In South Pasadena, this usually translates into between one and three girls on each T-ball team. At age 8, nearly

all of the girls are routed into girls' softball, though they retain the right to play on the baseball teams with the boys.

28.   Yablonsky and Brower 1979, 36–37.

29.   Theberge (1989) argues that early– and mid-twentieth century physical educators and women's colleges organized "adapted" sports for women, based on essentialist notions that girls and women benefited from exercise but were harmed or endangered by strenuous exercise, physical stress, and the body contact characterized by men's sports. Still today, adapted sports allow for an incorporation of women into sport while perhaps creating a kind of ghettoization process that lessens the challenge that women athletes might otherwise pose to men's entrenched interests in sports organizations, or to ideologies of male superiority that have traditionally been bolstered by men's control of sport (see Messner 2002, 138–42).

30.   Personal communication from LLB/S media relations manager Christopher Downs, June 17, 2005.

31.   I have made no effort to systematically sample other communities beyond those immediately surrounding South Pasadena. But the 2006 LLB yearbook of the Northern California community of San Carlos provides further anecdotal evidence that South Pasadena's gender division of labor among coaches is not unique. Of eighty-three baseball teams (San Carlos Little League does not have a girls' softball league), eighty-two (98.8 percent) are headed by men head coaches.

32.   AYSO Region 214—South Pasadena—San Marino Web site, http://www .ayso214.org/ (accessed January 11, 2006).

33.   See Dworkin 2001; Wachs 2002; Acosta and Carpenter 2000; and R. Wilson 2007.

CHAPTER 2

1.   See England 2006.

2.   Thorne, Kramarae, and Henley 1983. For an application of theories of gendered language to sport, Messner, Duncan, and Jensen 1993.

3.   Barrie Thorne, in her groundbreaking ethnographic research on children and gender in schools, argues that sociological studies that attempt to discover "why" gender divisions occur fall into the trap of searching (fruitlessly) for "origins." Instead, the ethnographer should seek to describe "how" gender divisions are created, and under what conditions gender divisions become salient, become less salient, or are dissolved (see Thorne 1993, 61).

4.   Pioneering work on understanding the ways that social spaces are gendered can be found in Henley 1977; see also Massey 1994.

5. See Dworkin 2001.

6. See Messner 1988; Montez de Oca 2005. See also sociologist Timothy Curry's fascinating analyses of the gendered space of men's locker rooms and sports bars (Curry 1991; 2000).

7. See Martin 2001.

8. Thorne (1993, 133) notes that "successful crossers" of gender boundaries are usually persistent and have certain skills that make their crossing acceptable to members of the dominant group.

9. Thorne 1993, 133.

10. The term "second shift" was made popular by sociologist Arlie Hochschild, whose study of two-career, heterosexual families showed that women were still doing the vast majority of the housework in these families (Hochschild 1989; see also Hochschild 1983).

11. Using minimum ($6/hour) and medium ($10/hour) hourly wage multipliers, Grasmuck estimates the market cost of this volunteer labor at between $215,976 and $359,963 (Grasmuck 2005, 62).

12. See Chafetz and Kotarba 1999, 46–54; quotes on 48–49. Boyle and McKay (1995) and Thompson (1999a) also examine how women's supportive labor helps to sustain adult men's sports.

13. See Petrzelka and Mannon 2006.

14. Ollilainen and Calasanti (2007), in their study of self-managing teams that are intended to break down gender divisions in the workplace, show how team members' use of "family metaphors" tends to maintain the salience of gender, and thus helps to reproduce a gendered division of labor.

15. Charles and Grusky 2004, 336.

16. Patricia Martin's work has been foundational in showing how gender works in organizations in informal, non-reflexive ways that rely on peoples' "tacit knowledge" about gender (2006). In particular, she points out "how and why well-intentioned, 'good people' practise gender in ways that do harm" (255). See also Martin 2001; and Martin 2003.

CHAPTER 3

1. Grasmuck 2005, 14.

2. In chapter 1, for the same period, 1999–2007, I weighted teams that had both a woman co-manager and a man co-manager as being headed .5 by a man and .5 by a woman. Using that method of counting, I came up with a total of 31.5 LLB/S teams that were headed by women between 1999 and 2007. Here, I am referring to the total number of LLB/S teams that had either a woman manager or co-manager; the unweighted number, then, is 36.

3. See Thorne 1993

4. Paul Lichterman (2006) notes that there are different "camps" of social capital theory, with each camp having its own distinct roots and varying meanings applied to the concept. My usage here is closest to the tradition of Pierre Bourdieu, whose concepts of "field and habitus" exist in dynamic relation to each other. Fields may be thought of as "spaces of objective relations that are the site of a logic and a necessity that are *specific and irreducible* to those that regulate other fields. For instance, the artistic field, or the religious field, or the economic field all follow specific logics" (Bourdieu and Wacquant 1992, 102). Habitus "consists of a set of historical relations 'deposited' within individual bodies in the form of mental and corporeal schemata of perception, appreciation and action" (16). The "rules" of the field tend to condition and structure the habitus of agents who pass through the field. Habitus thus becomes "the embodiment of the immanent necessity of a field [and thus] contributes to constituting the field as a meaningful world" (127). Habitus is a socialized subjectivity, an embodied set of dispositions, strategies, and actions that agents have adopted to help them survive, or perhaps even thrive, within the context of a given field. Bourdieu demonstrates how an upper-class habitus becomes a kind of social capital that allows a person to thrive in upper-class fields, while those lacking this habitus do not "fit." Applying this idea to the present study, I would argue that an embodied athletic masculine habitus allows athletic males to fit in, thrive in (and reproduce) athletic fields. But what happens when women enter this masculine field? What I am arguing here is that women youth coaches often mobilize the embodied set of dispositions, strategies, and actions—or habitus—that they have developed in other fields, such as mothering, elementary school work, and various other forms of care work with children. While this form of capital (which I calling "kids-knowledge") is a valuable resource for women entering the youth sports field when coaching very young teams, it becomes a liability if the coach does not absorb and embody sports habitus (which I am calling "sports-knowledge")—particularly the local forms of knowledge that the existing groups of men coaches have.

5. Research on women and coaching has focused almost exclusively on elite-level and college coaching. Still, this research can be useful when thinking about the constraints faced by women volunteer coaches in youth sports. Nancy Theberge (1990; 1993) studied women coaches in Canadian national sports teams and found that the women coaches were keenly aware of their "token status" in trying to build a profession in a man's world. She found that the women struggled with an attempt to bring an alternative conception of power to the experience. Women's representation in the college coaching profession in the United States has been tracked for many years by Vivien Acosta and Linda Jean Carpenter, whose research shows how, during the post–Title IX explosion of women's

athletic participation, the proportion of women's sports teams coached by women has declined precipitously. In 1972, over 90 percent of women's teams were headed by women coaches; by 2008, that number had declined to 42 percent, the second-lowest percentage of women coaches in the thirty-one years of the study. By contrast, only 2–3 percent of men's teams are coached by women. What this means is that, in 2008, only 20.6 percent of all head coaches are women (see Carpenter and Acosta 2008). In a recent survey of coaches of women's college sports, Deborah Rhode and Christopher Walker (2008) explored the continuing barriers and problems that women coaches face, including unequal institutional budgets and salaries, perceived gender preferences of athletes, work/family conflicts, perceptions that women are less-able leaders than men, and problems with an "old boys' network" that reinforces favoritism for men in hiring decisions. There is a dearth of research on women and youth coaching. Weiss and Sisley (1986) studied why volunteer youth coaches quit, but they focused only slightly on gender. Still, their study did suggest that women coaches tended to quit coaching more for reasons related to perceptions of "lack of ability/success," whereas male coaches' number one reason for quitting had to do with conflicts with administrators and officials.

6.   Paula England (2006), Eva M. Meyerson Milgraom and Trond Petersen (2006), and Laurie A. Morgan and Karen A. Martin (2006) have all written about the persistence of sex-segregation in the professions.

7.   Yablonsky and Brower 1979, 128–29.

8.   Messerschmidt 2004, 43.

9.   Messerschmidt 2004, 49–50.

10.   See Kanter 1977.

11.   Theberge 1993, 303. Annelies Knoppers (1994) also draws from Kanter's ideas of proportionality in her study of women and coaching.

12.   Theberge 1993, 303–4.

13.   See Deutsch 2007.

14.   I do not want to suggest here that large numbers of women coaches would bring radical change to youth sports, due to women's having some essentially different nature from men. However, I do think that there is evidence that women's experiences—especially as mothers and caregivers—create a somewhat different standpoint for them, a standpoint that they bring to non-family contexts (e.g., the workplace, where a critical mass of women employees can often push for more family-friendly policies for workers). I find evidence for this differently gendered standpoint in the interviews, especially in the women's and men's discussions of what I am calling kids-knowledge and sports-knowledge.

CHAPTER 4

1. Sabo and Veliz 2008.

2. The Positive Coaching Alliance is a national organization formed in recent years in response to the frequent negative stories in the news media about adults' negative, even violent behavior as coaches and parents in youth sports. The PCA is partnered with many national and local youth sports organizations, including AYSO and LLB/S. The PCA mission, as stated on their Web page, is "to transform youth sports so sports can transform youth. PCA was created to transform the culture of youth sports to give all young athletes the opportunity for a positive, character-building experience. We have three national goals: (1) replace the 'win-at-all-cost' model of coaching with the Double-Goal Coach, who wants to win but has a second, more important, goal of using sports to teach life lessons; (2) teach youth sports organization leaders how to create an organizational culture in which Honoring the Game is the norm; and (3) spark and fuel a 'social epidemic' of Positive Coaching that will sweep this country" (http://www.positivecoach.org/subcontent.aspx?SecId=107).

3. "Little League International, Positive Coaching Alliance Partner to Enhance Educational Offerings to Volunteers," Little League Online, http://www.littleleague.org/media/pca_announcement.asp.

4. Yablonsky and 1979, 112.

5. For my purposes here, I overdichotomize what Grasmuck shows to be a more complex picture. Coaches vary, she says, in terms of how much technical sports knowledge they have, in whether they emphasized skill-building or winning, in whether they use positive or negative forms of reinforcement with the kids, and in how they manage their own and their kids' emotions. She finds, for instance, that there are some Newcomers who display a "tough" masculinity, and some Fairmounters who display a "tender" masculinity. However, she does find that the men fall into the general patterns that I discuss here (see Grasmuck 2005).

6. From Machine-Pitch through Juniors, there were occasional individual girls on a few teams; however, nearly all of these teams were made up exclusively of boys. Nearly all of the girls, beyond the Coach-Pitch level, are playing softball.

7. I conducted similar observations on the South Pasadena girls' softball field as well, but the context was not as ideal as on the baseball fields. There is only one softball field on which games are played, so essentially there is only one game being played at any given time, and thus only one age-group to observe at any given time. I also conducted a few observations of soccer matches. My observations of softball and soccer coaches are therefore less systematic and more anecdotal; nevertheless, my observations of these sports tend to support, rather than contradict, my typology for baseball coaches.

8. Drawn from the ideas of the sociologist Max Weber, an "ideal type" is an analytical construct taken from many empirical observations but not necessarily conforming to any particular empirical manifestation. The construct is useful for making descriptive generalizations about particular social contexts.

9. A masculine style is "hegemonic" to the extent that a considerable amount of public consent coalesces around it, which in turn serves to stabilize power in the hands of a small group of men. Hegemonic masculinity, by definition, is not something to which all—or even most—men conform. Some men fail to conform, some refuse to conform, and others achieve some degree of success in conforming to hegemonic masculinity. What my research illustrates—even within a single institution like Little League Baseball—is that hegemonic masculinity shifts across contexts, and that as men move across and through these contexts a noticeable amount of strain and tension results. For major theoretical statements on hegemonic masculinity, see Connell 1987 and Connell and Messerschmidt 2005.

10. The percentages I use in this chapter to describe the "tilt" of the balance between kids-knowledge and sports-knowledge are my own estimates based on my observations, on what I was able to glean indirectly from the interviews, and on an informal survey I gave to about twenty youth-sports coaches in which I asked them to plot their own balance between these two kinds of knowledge when coaching different age-groups of kids.

11. For discussions of how gender subordination and superordination are reflected and reproduced in everyday talk and bodily conventions, see Henley 1977; Thorne, Kramarae, and Henley 1983; Messner, Duncan, and Jensen 1993.

12. Sociologist Scott Coltrane's research on fathers suggests that many fathers are more comfortable interacting with children as they get older—after they can walk, when they are verbal, when they can joke and play games (see Coltrane 1996).

13. Messerschmidt 2004, 43.

14. See Knoppers and Anthonissen 2005.

15. See Levin 2001. Levin quotes one trader: "It's like when you make an error when you're playing baseball. I played sports my whole life, and whenever I made an error, you sat there and moped about it, chances were next time . . . the ball was hit to you, you're going to make the error again. So you, it's like, so key to just forget about it. And how weird is that, that you say to yourself, O.K., forget about the fact that I just lost $12,000 for that guy, let's go back to work" (121).

16. Pierce 1993, 9.

17. Lareau 2003. Lareau argues that this middle-class "cultural repertoire" passes on to children a set of skills that teach them to understand " 'the rules of the game' that govern interactions with institutional representatives" (6).

18. See Connell and Messerschmidt 2005.

19.   For an excellent collection of essays on studying privileged groups, see Kimmel and Ferber 2003.

20.   I utilize a "feminist standpoint" approach more as a sensitizing methodology than as a complete "theory of knowledge." It's important to understand, I think, that marginalized and subordinated people do not have a "complete" or fully "correct" view of social reality (nor does anyone; everyone's understanding of social reality is partial). But I take it as axiomatic that women, gay, lesbian, and queer people, as well as poor people, people of color, or colonized people, are positioned in systems of power in ways that consistently put them in situations where certain kinds of knowledge—certain patterned standpoints—are created. And these standpoints tend to offer researchers useful points of entrée into understanding how systems of power and inequality are produced and contested. They also offer to those of us who are doing "sociology of superordinates"—that is, studies of groups who are central to systems of power (like, in this chapter, men coaches)—new points of departure for asking critical questions about how power works. For elaborations on taking a standpoint approach to understanding gender and power, see Enloe 2004; Harding 1991; Messner 2005; and Messner 1990.

CHAPTER 5

1.   This same survey found that families in which kids play one or two organized team sports report higher levels of family happiness than do families of kids who do not play sports. Interestingly, this family happiness benefit seems to reverse itself—dramatically so in single-parent families—when kids play on three, four, or more teams (see Sabo and Veliz 2008).

2.   This is not to say that girls and women did not play sports before the 1970s. In fact, there was a boom of female athletic participation that corresponded with the "first wave" of feminism, in the first two decades of the twentieth century. Following a backlash against feminism and female athletics in the 1930s, however, girls' and women's sports were either eliminated or ghettoized. Although working-class communities, and especially those made up of African Americans, continued in some ways to support women's sports through the middle decades of the twentieth century, white middle- and upper-class women no longer played organized sports in great numbers (the exception being some very limited programs within women's colleges) (see Cahn 1994).

3.   By the mid-1980s, this idea of sport as a terrain of contested gender meanings was well established in the scholarly literature. See Messner 1988; Willis 1983.

4.   In a highly influential article, Mary Jo Kane argues that women's participation in sport has exploded the idea of a natural gender binary and has instead

revealed that men's and women's bodily capacities are scattered on a "continuum of difference" (M. Kane 1995; see also Lorber 1993).

5. Sargent 2001.

6. I have written elsewhere about the implications of the socialization of boys, and of institutions, like sport, that systematically teach boys (and reward them) for suppressing their capacity for empathy for self and others (see Messner 2002, chapter 2).

7. Though research suggests that girls generally experience bodily empowerment through their experiences in sport, girls in certain elite-level sports sometimes experience the opposite. Journalist Joan Ryan's research on girls in gymnastics and figure skating revealed frightening stories of eating disorders and injuries, too often enforced by emotionally abusive coaches whose only aim was to create champions (see Ryan 1996).

8. Van Auken and Van Auken 2001, 148.

9. McDonagh and Pappano 2008. Similarly, political scientist Jennifer Ring argues that girls have been denied the opportunity to play baseball because the sport has been a key locus in the United States for the construction of a masculine national identity: "When it was evident that girls and women *could* play and *wanted* to play, their history with the sport was denied and ignored and they were ushered into a 'separate but equal' sport that could be more readily reconciled with femininity without undermining the manliness of American national identity" (Ring 2008).

10. If we fully supported girls to play on integrated teams with boys while maintaining parallel girls-only leagues, it could create some of the same sorts of dynamics that led eventually to the disappearance of baseball's Negro Leagues, after the integration of Major League Baseball in 1947. Rodney Fort and Joel Maxcy argue that "the unabashed talent raiding by MLB killed African American Baseball a couple of years after integration began . . . . Competitive baseball was lost to countless thousands of fans throughout the South and Midwest, profitable businesses were lost to African American and White AAB team owners, and hundreds of African American players were denied a 'big league' livelihood as the result of integration" (2001, 35; see also Lanctot 2004). Though girls' youth sports are not a profit-generating business, like the professional Negro Leagues were, it is reasonable to expect that the rapid sex-integration of youth sports might result in a similar "talent drain" from all-girls' leagues as most of the most talented and motivated girl athletes gravitate to the integrated leagues. With the all-girls' leagues consisting mostly of the less athletically talented or less-motivated girls, it is an open question whether or in what manner these girls-only leagues would survive.

11. See Messner 2002, 142–46.

12. See Thorne 1993.

13.   See Adams and Coltrane 2005; Lytton and Romney 1991.

14.   To be sure, especially starting with the age of puberty, and stretching through adulthood, girls and women still find that they are subjected to a double standard. It's okay to express "masculine" traits of competitive individualism and goal-orientation, but a woman will also often be judged negatively if she's seen as less than "feminine."

15.   This is certainly not a new insight. A good deal of feminist-inspired writing by men about sports—much of it personal, autobiographical, or journalistic, rather than scholarly—blossomed in the 1970s and early 1980s. And much of this work focused on the pain and humiliation that nonathletic boys had experienced in organized sports and physical education. For the first important collection of these works, see Sabo and Runfola 1980.

16.   See Kimmel 1987, in which he argues that urbanization and changes in the organization of middle-class work led, during the turn of the twentieth century, to fears of social feminization and a "crisis of masculinity." The rise of organized sports among educated elite white men was one response to this crisis of middle-class masculinity (see Messner 1992).

17.   See Pollack 1999.

18.   The common silence in the dugout that surrounds an individual boy's sadness or pain may in one way be seen as a masculine form of collective respect and caretaking: since it's not acceptable to cry, the group gives the boy space to do it, looks away, and does not thus shame him for it. On the other hand, Sherri Grasmuck concluded from her research with boys' Little League Baseball that teams that had a boy who did "emotion work" in the dugout—empathizing with teammates who were upset or injured, staying positive when one or more teammates get down about losing a game—that these teams tended to be more cohesive and thus more successful (see Grasmuck 2005). In my son Sasha's last three years or so of Little League, I was frequently proud of him when, in the dugout, he would play this kind of empathetic, upbeat sort of role for his team, in the face of often more highly skilled boys' anger at their own failures. Coaches can model this kind of emotional caretaking behavior for boys, but in my experience they rarely do.

19.   Kane 2006.

20.   Ortner 1974, 75. This historical inversion of the gendered nature/culture dichotomy does not imply an inversion of the hierarchical ordering of male over female; to the contrary, I am suggesting that since the definition of men's narrow nature seems to predestine them for competition in public life, it continues to leave domestic-care work for women. Feminism is, in part, a claim by women not to be defined in terms of their natural bodies, but instead to be part of and to help to shape culture. The contemporary equation of girls and women as complex and able to make choices is a partial incorporation of feminism that has

broadened women's ability to participate in public life. However, since it leaves boys and men largely untouched, this view ultimately leaves women to deal with the constraints of bridging public and domestic life. When they "choose" to not coach, to become team moms, to opt out of full-time careers and shift their energies toward domestic life, this choice then reaffirms the idea that their "nature" as nurturers and caretakers has pulled them back—but now, not because they are forced to do so, as was the case for the post–World War II college-educated women in Betty Friedan's *Feminine Mystique,* who were forced to be mothers/housewives; today's professional-class women move toward the domestic sphere because they supposedly *choose* to.

21. Historically, this gendered separation of public versus domestic spheres for men and women was a dominant part of the ideology that supported modern versions of patriarchy. However, it has never been an absolute empirical "fact" that social life was so divided in "Western" industrial or post-industrial nations. In the United States, working-class women and poor women of color were present in the paid labor force in huge numbers from the outset of industrialization and even during times of backlash against women's public lives, like during the post–World War II era (see Sharistanian 1987).

22. Sociologist Martha McCaughey argues convincingly that misunderstood evolutionary ideas are now circulating as an essentialist ideology (about men, but not so much about women) that she calls "the Caveman Mystique . . . that sense of one's manhood as inherently productive, protective, aggressive, and heterosexual" (McCaughey 2008, 23). According to McCaughey, the Caveman Mystique has become a "grand narrative, a totalizing theory explaining men's experiences as though all men act and feel the same way, and as though the ideas of Western science provide a universal truth about those actions and feelings" (17).

23. Risman 1998.

CHAPTER 6

1. I speculate that the under-representation of Asian Americans in youth sports coaching is partly due to their immigrant status. A large number of Asians in South Pasadena are first-generation immigrants, many of them Chinese who are still learning English and who did not grow up with firsthand experience with U.S. youth sports. By contrast, most of the Hispanics in South Pasadena are second-generation (or more) Mexican Americans who grew up in the Los Angeles area speaking English (often along with Spanish) and immersed in U.S. youth sports.

2. Feminist scholars, for at least the past thirty years, have shown how unitary, idealized conceptions of "the family" place constraints on peoples' choices

and also tend to impose white, professional-class, and heterosexual family norms on the rest of society. One of the most important scholarly interventions by feminist scholars is the reconceptualization of the academic field, as one that studies "families," rather than "the family" (see Thorne and Yalom 1992 [1982]). The idea of family multiplicity is now built in to the ways that sociologists teach about families; see, e.g., Baca Zinn, Eitzen, and Wells 2008.

    3.   Family historian Stephanie Coontz demonstrates that nostalgic yearnings for an idealized "Leave it to Beaver" or "Ozzie and Harriet" "traditional family" of the 1950s are based on a simplistic and distorted view of history, since even in the 1950s there was a diversity of family forms. To the extent that this type of nuclear family did predominate in the 1950s, there was nothing "traditional" about it. Rather, it was "a historical fluke, based on a unique and temporary conjuncture of economic, social, and political factors" (Coontz 1992, 28).

    4.   Coltrane 1996.

    5.   See Hochschild 1989.

    6.   See Hochschild 2001; Jacobs and Gerson 2005.

    7.   Put another way, gender regimes have their own internal states of play that variously constrain and enable action. But every day, people move in, out, and across two, three, or more gender regimes: when a coach goes to the ball park, he or she is not simply constrained by the gender regime of youth sports; the constraints of one's family and/or career work responsibilities are carried right into youth sports, and vice versa.

    8.   See Lichterman 2005.

    9.   My wife Pierrette and I have a "co-provider family"; we both have equally demanding careers. We have tried to create an equal division of labor in the home. When it comes to volunteer work however, she was more likely to volunteer for ongoing things in the kids' elementary school classrooms, and I was more likely to "plug in" to individual events like field trips or the annual holiday craft fair. When Miles was younger, I served as assistant leader in his Cub Scouts den, and when Sasha started Cubs, I was the den leader. But truth be told, I was only an adequate den leader during the year I was on sabbatical from my university position. Thereafter, I was not very good at it, and in the third year I was demoted to assistant, as a father with more time took over. As I have said earlier, when it came to youth sports, I never volunteered to be a head coach. My volunteering to help out landed me several times in assistant coach positions, and in the final three years, in the position of scorekeeper. For the most part, though, I always felt a much stronger tug toward work and family than to community volunteering. Like all other parents who volunteer minimally, I benefit enormously from the labor of those parents who pour hundreds of hours of their time into sports, schools, and other activities that my kids have participated in.

10. See Hochschild 1989.

11. For a recent analysis of how women's part-time jobs connect with family divisions of labor, see Webber and Williams 2008.

12. Shona Thompson observes that women do a lot of invisible labor to support the sport activities of their children and their spouses. Her time-usage survey of Australian fathers and mothers reveals that fathers' and mothers' work in support of their children's sport activities differed in quantity and type. Mothers were more involved than fathers. Fathers' involvement was more sport-related, such as playing with the child or attending a match, while mothers' involvement was "more everyday, private and related to childcare, such as food, laundered clothing and serviceable equipment. Furthermore what fathers did for their children's sport tended to be fitted around their other commitments, whereas the mothers tended to fit their other commitments around their children's sporting needs" (Thompson 1999a, 114; see also Thompson 1999b).

13. See Daniels 1985; Daniels 1987.

14. In his overview of research on volunteer work, sociologist John Wilson concludes that women volunteers "gravitate, or are steered, toward 'women's work,' more of the caring, person-to-person tasks and fewer of the public, political activities, and [they] are less likely to be found in leadership positions" (Wilson 2000, 227–28).

15. Sociologist Arlie Hochschild has written extensively of the ways that women in the home (even when they are also employed outside the home) and women in the workplace are often expected to do the "emotion work" for others; see Hochschild 1989 and Hochschild 1983.

16. In all three of these spheres—paid work, family work, and volunteer work—there is a high level of what Jennifer Hooks calls "gendered task segregation" (see Hook 2004; see also Reskin 1988).

17. Daniels 1985; Daniels 1987. See also McPherson and Smith-Lovin 1986; and Blackstone 2004.

18. For a discussion of community, volunteering, and social capital, see Harvey, Levesque, and Donnelly 2007.

19. For the past three decades, since the passage of the antitax initiative Proposition 13 in California, public funds for education have dwindled. People in wealthy communities like South Pasadena or neighboring San Marino raise private funds through organizations like the South Pasadena Education Foundation (SPEF) to supplement the school budget. This semi-privatization of public schools serves to increase the already existing gaps between schools in poor neighborhoods and those in prosperous suburbs.

20. Though most professional-class women are employed, and those who "opt out" are a numerical minority, their stories have made quite a controversial splash on the cultural landscape (see Vavrus, 2007). An interesting collection of

personal reflections from both stay-at-home moms and career moms can be found in Steiner 2006.

21. Hays 1996.

22. Lareau 2003.

23. Stone 2007, 167.

24. Pamela Stone's study of women who opted out of careers shows clearly that these women commonly experience inflexible workplaces as powerful push factors that are at least as important as any pull toward family life in their decision to opt out (see Stone 2007). Another possible push factor is suggested in an interesting experimental study that found that employed women tended far more often than employed men to be "penalized" for having children (see Correll 2007). These inflexible workplaces contribute to tensions in families, especially those with young children. A quantitative analysis of current population surveys found that the combined work schedules of families with children contribute to work-family conflicts (see Jacobs and Gerson 2001).

25. Women's rendering of their decision to opt out of their professional careers as a "choice," rather than a response to the constraints of inequitable workplaces and families, reflects a broad emergent cultural discourse that philosopher Linda Hirschman calls "choice feminism." Hirschman argues that choice feminism is a middle- and upper-class-based, individualistic, "watered-down version of feminism" that capitulates to the continued constraints faced by women in workplaces and from husbands in their own homes. "Even the most empowered women," writes Hirschman, "do not see how narrow their options are at the moment of 'choice' " (Hirschman 2006, 16–17).

26. Another public park in South Pasadena that my family used to frequent when our children were very young included an overgrown area that the kids called "the Jungle," into which they delighted in disappearing for games of tag or other imaginative pastimes. About a dozen years ago, the city cut down most of the undergrowth in "the Jungle" so that adults sitting at nearby picnic tables could always see clearly into and through the area. The change was apparently made to ensure the safety of children from unknown outsiders who might lurk there. The outcome that I observed was huge disappointment on the part of kids that a realm of semi-autonomous fantasy play had been eliminated.

27. Referring to the common demonization of "welfare mothers," sociologist Sharon Hays writes that "symbolic boundaries thus become *exclusionary* boundaries—simultaneously offering a means to affirm shared values and a means to think of 'outsiders' in terms of individual blame" (Hays 2003, 220). For discussions of symbolic boundaries and race, see Lamont 1999.

28. For a more general discussion of the ways that class- and race-privileged men sometimes construct an honored form of masculinity by projecting negative

characteristics onto the supposedly "traditional" masculinity of working-class and Latino men, see Hondagneu-Sotelo and Messner 1994.

29. See Collins 1990.

30. The Oxford American Dictionary defines *equality* as "the state of being equal, esp. in status, rights, and opportunities." By contrast, *equity* is defined as "the quality of being fair and impartial," a concept that is closer in meaning to *equal opportunity,* defined as "the policy of treating employees and others without discrimination, esp. on the basis of their sex, race, or age." While many people may be committed to the concepts of equity and equal opportunity in sports and in other aspects of public life, this does not imply that they necessarily are in favor of eliminating hierarchical systems of social inequality and moving toward a condition of social equality.

References

Acker, Joan.
　1990.　　Hierarchies, jobs, bodies: A theory of gendered organizations. *Gender & Society* 4:139–58.
　2006.　　Inequality regimes: Gender, class, and race in organizations. *Gender & Society* 20:441–64.
Acosta, R. Vivien, and Linda Jean Carpenter.
　2000.　　*Women in intercollegiate sport: A longitudinal study—Twenty-three year update.* Brooklyn, NY: Brooklyn College.
Adam, Michele, and Scott Coltrane.
　2005.　　Boys and men in families: The domestic production of gender, power, and privilege. In *Handbook of studies on men and masculinities,* ed. Michael S. Kimmel, Jeff Hearn, and R. W. Connell, 230–48. Thousand Oaks, CA: Sage Publications.
Baca Zinn, Maxine, D. Stanley Eitzen, and Barbara Wells.
　2008.　　*Diversity in families.* 8th ed. Boston: Allyn & Bacon.

Berlage, Gai Ingham.
    1994. *Women in baseball: The forgotten history.* Westport, CT: Greenwood.
Bettie, Julie.
    2003. *Women without class: Girls, race, and identity.* Berkeley: University of California Press.
Bird, Joyce.
    1996. Welcome to the men's club: Homosociality and the maintenance of hegemonic masculinity. *Gender & Society* 10:120–32.
Blackstone, Amy Maria.
    2004. Sociability, work, and gender. *Equal Opportunities International* 23:29–44.
Blau, Francine D., Mary C. Brinton, and David B. Grusky, eds.
    2006. *The declining significance of gender?* New York: Russell Sage Foundation.
Bourdieu, Pierre, and Loic J. D. Wacquant.
    1992. *An invitation to reflexive sociology.* Chicago: University of Chicago Press.
Boyle, Maree, and Jim McKay.
    1995. You leave your troubles at the gate: A case study of the exploitation of older women's labor and "leisure" in sport. *Gender & Society* 9:556–76.
Britton, Dana.
    2000. The epistemology of the gendered organization. *Gender & Society* 14: 418–34.
Cahn, Susan.
    1994.h *Coming on strong: Gender and sexuality in twentieth-century women's sport.* New York: The Free Press.
Carpenter, Linda Jean, and Vivien R. Acosta.
    2008. Women in intercollegiate sport: A longitudinal, national study— Thirty-one year update, 1977–2008. http://webpages.charter.net/ womeninsport/2008%20Summary%20Final.pdf.
Chafetz, Janet Saltzman, and Joseph A. Kotarba.
    1995. Son worshipers: The role of Little League mothers in recreating gender." *Studies in Symbolic Interaction* 18:217–41.
    1999. Little League mothers and the reproduction of gender. In *Inside Sports,* ed. Jay Coakley and Peter Donnelly, 46–54. London: Routledge.
Charles, Maria, and David B. Grusky.
    2004. *Occupational ghettos: The worldwide segregation of women and men.* Stanford, CA: Stanford University Press.

Coakley, Jay.

2002.   Using sports to control deviance and violence among youths: Let's
be critical and cautious. In *Paradoxes of youth and sport*, ed. Margaret
Gatz, Michael A. Messner, and Sandra Ball Rokeach, 13–30. Albany,
NY: State University of New York Press.

2006.   The good father: Parental expectations and youth sports. *Leisure
Studies* 25:153–63.

Collins, Patricia Hill.

1990.   *Black feminist thought: Knowledge, consciousness, and the politics of
empowerment.* Boston: Unwin-Hyman.

Coltrane, Scott.

1996.   *Family man: Fatherhood, housework, and gender equity.* New York:
Oxford University Press.

Connell, Raewyn W.

1987.   *Gender and power: Society, the person, and sexual politics.* Stanford, CA:
Stanford University Press.

2006.   Glass ceilings or gendered institutions? Mapping the gender
regimes of public sector workers. *Public Administration Review*
66:837–49.

Connell, Raewyn W., and James W. Messerschmidt.

2005.   Hegemonic masculinity: Rethinking the concept. *Gender & Society*
19:829–59.

Coontz, Stephanie.

1992.   *The way we never were: American families and the nostalgia trap.* New
York: Basic Books.

Correll, Shelley J.

2007.   Getting a job: Is there a motherhood penalty? *American Journal of
Sociology* 112:1297–1338.

Craig, Lyn.

2006.   Does father care mean father share? A comparison of how mothers
and fathers in intact families spend time with children. *Gender &
Society* 20:259–81.

Curry, Timothy.

1991.   Fraternal bonding in the locker room: Pro-feminist analysis of talk
about competition and women. *Sociology of Sport Journal* 8:119–35.

2000.   Booze and bar fights: A journey to the dark side of college athletics.
In *Masculinities, gender relations, and sport*, ed. Jim McKay, Donald F.
Sabo, and Michael A. Messner, 162–75. Thousand Oaks, CA: Sage
Publications.

Daniels, Arlene Kaplan.

1985.   Invisible work. *Social Problems* 34:363–74.

1987.   Good times and good works: The place of sociability in the work of women volunteers. *Social Problems* 32:403–15.

De Lench, Brooke.

2006.   *Home team advantage: The critical role of mothers in youth sports.* New York: HarperCollins.

Deutsch, Francine M.

2007.   Undoing gender. *Gender & Society* 21:106–27.

Drago, Robert, Lynn Henninghausen, Jacqueline Rogers, Teresa Vescio, and Kai Dawn Stauffer.

2005.   Final report for CAGE: The coaching and gender equity project. Funded by the National Collegiate Athletic Association, the National Association of Collegiate Women Athletics Administrators, and the Commission for Women and Athletics of the Pennsylvania State University. Available for download (Word document) at http://lsir.la .psu.edu/workfam/CAGE.htm.

Dreier, Peter, and Beth Steckler.

2007.   Not just for the gentry. *The American Prospect,* January–February, A12–A15.

Dworkin, Shari L.

2001.   "Holding back": Negotiating a glass ceiling on women's muscular strength. *Sociological Perspectives* 44:333–50.

Eitzen, D. Stanley, and George H. Sage.

2008.   *Sociology of North American sport.* 8th ed. Boulder, CO: Paradigm Publishers.

Eliasoph, Nina.

1998.   *Avoiding politics: How Americans produce apathy in everyday life.* Cambridge: Cambridge University Press.

England, Paula.

2006.   Toward gender equality: Progress and bottlenecks. In *The declining significance of gender?* ed. Francine D. Blau, Mary C. Brinton, and David B. Grusky, 245–64. New York: Russell Sage Foundation.

Enloe, Cynthia H.

2004.   *The curious feminist: Searching for women in a new age of empire.* Berkeley: University of California Press.

Ferguson, Ann Arnett.

2000.   *Bad boys: Public schools in the making of black masculinity.* Ann Arbor: University of Michigan Press.

Fine, Gary Alan.

1987.   *With the boys: Little League Baseball and preadolescent culture.* Chicago: University of Chicago Press.

Fort, Rodney, and Joel Maxcy.
    2001.   The demise of African American baseball leagues: A rival league explanation." *Journal of Sports Economics* 2:35–49.

Friedan, Betty.
    1963.   *The feminine mystique.* New York: Dell.

Glassner, Barry.
    1999.   *The culture of fear.* New York: Basic Books.

Grasmuck, Sherri.
    2005.   *Protecting home: Class, race, and masculinity in boys' baseball.* New Brunswick, NJ: Rutgers University Press.

Gregorich, Barbara.
    1993.   *Women at play: The story of women in baseball.* San Diego: Harcourt, Brace & Co.

Glazier, Bill.
    2003.   AYSO Celebrates Community Spirit at Opening Day Event. *South Pasadena Review,* September 17, 2003, 2.

Hamilton, Laura.
    2007.   Trading on heterosexuality: College women's gender strategies and homophobia. *Gender & Society* 21:145–72.

Hanson, Karen V.
    2005.   *Not-so-nuclear families: Class, gender, and networks of care.* New Brunswick, NJ: Rutgers University Press.

Harding, Sandra.
    1991.   *Whose science? Whose knowledge? Thinking from women's lives.* Ithaca, NY: Cornell University Press.

Hartmann, Douglas.
    2001.   Notes on midnight basketball and the cultural politics of recreation, race, and at-risk urban youth. *Journal of Sport and Social Issues* 25:339–71.

Harvey, Jean, Maurice Levesque, and Peter Donnelly.
    2007.   Sport volunteerism and social capital. *Sociology of Sport Journal* 24:206–23.

Hays, Sharon.
    1996.   *The cultural contradictions of motherhood.* New Haven, CT: Yale University Press.
    2003.   *Flat broke with children: Women in the age of welfare reform.* Oxford: Oxford University Press.

Henley, Nancy M.
    1977.   *Body politics: Power, sex, and nonverbal communication.* Englewood Cliffs, NJ: Prentice-Hall.

Hirschman, Linda R.

2005.   Homeward bound. *American Prospect*, December.

2006.   *Get to work: A manifesto for women of the world*. New York: Viking.

Hochschild, Arlie Russell.

1983.   *The managed heart: Commercialization of human feeling*. Berkeley: University of California Press.

1989.   *The second shift*. New York: Viking.

2001.   *The time bind: When work becomes home and home becomes work*. New York: Henry Holt.

Hondagneu-Sotelo, Pierrette, and Michael A. Messner.

1994.   Gender displays and men's power: The "new man" and the Mexican immigrant man. In *Theorizing masculinities*, ed. Harry Brod and Michael Kaufman, 200–18. Thousand Oaks, CA: Sage Publications.

Hook, Jennifer L.

2004.   Reconsidering the division of household labor: Incorporating volunteer work and informal support. *Journal of Marriage and Family* 66:101–18.

Jacobs, Jerry A., and Kathleen Gerson.

2001.   Overworked individuals or overworked families? Explaining trends in work, leisure, and family time. *Work and Occupations* 28:40–63.

2005.   *The time divide: Work, family, and gender inequality*. Cambridge, MA: Harvard University Press.

Kane, Emily W.

2006.   "No way my boys are going to be like that!" Parents' responses to gender nonconformity. *Gender & Society* 20:149–76.

Kane, Mary Jo.

1995.   Resistance/transformation of the oppositional binary: Exposing sport as a continuum." *Journal of Sport and Social Issues* 19:191–218.

Kanter, Rosabeth Moss.

1977.   *Men and women of the corporation*. New York: Basic Books.

Kimmel, Michael S.

1987.   Men's responses to feminism at the turn of the century. *Gender & Society* 1:517–30.

1990.   Baseball and the reconstitution of American masculinity: 1880–1920. In *Sport, men, and the gender order: Critical feminist perspectives*, ed. Michael A. Messner and Donald F. Sabo, 55–66. Champaign, IL: Human Kinetics.

Kimmel, Michael S., and Abby Ferber, eds.

2003.   *Privilege*. Boulder, CO: Westview Press.

Knoppers, Annelies.

1988.　Men working: Coaching as a male dominated and sex segregated occupation. *Arena Review* 12:69–80.

1994.　Gender and the coaching profession. In *Women, sport, and culture,* ed. Susan Birrell and Cheryl L. Cole, 119–34. Champaign, IL: Human Kinetics Press.

Knoppers, Annelies, and Anton Anthonissen.

2005.　Male athletic and managerial masculinities: Congruencies in discursive practices? *Journal of Gender Studies* 14:123–35.

Lamont, Michele, ed.

1999.　*The cultural territories of race: Black and white boundaries.* Chicago: University of Chicago Press.

Lanctot, Neil.

2004.　*Negro League baseball: The rise and ruin of a Black institution.* Philadelphia: University of Pennsylvania Press.

Lareau, Annette.

2003.　*Unequal childhoods: Class, race, and family life.* Berkeley: University of California Press.

LaVoi, Nicole M., and Erin Becker.

2007.　"Where have all the post–Title IX mothers gone? Exploring the scarcity of female coaches in youth sport. Working Paper, Tucker Center for Research on Girls and Women in Sport, University of Minnesota, Minneapolis.

Levin, Peter.

2001.　"Gendering the market: Temporality, work, and gender on a national futures exchange. *Work and Occupations* 28:112–30.

Lichterman, Paul.

2005.　Elusive togetherness: Church groups trying to bridge America's divisions. Princeton, NJ: Princeton University Press.

2006.　Social capital or group style? Rescuing Tocqueville's insights on civic engagement. *Theory and Society* 35:529–63.

Lorber, Judith.

1993.　Believing is seeing: Biology as ideology, *Gender & Society* 7: 568–581.

Lytton, H., and D. M. Romney.

1991.　Parents' differential socialization of boys and girls: A meta-analysis. *Psychological Bulletin* 109:267–96.

Martin, Patricia Yancy.

2001.　"Mobilizing masculinities": Women's experiences of men at work." *Organization* 8:587–618.

2003.　"Said and done" versus "Saying and doing": Gendering practices, practicing gender at work." *Gender & Society* 17:342–66.

2006.   Practicing gender at work: Further thoughts on reflexivity. *Gender, Work and Organization* 13: 254–76.

Massey, Doreen.

1994.   *Space, place, and gender.* Minneapolis: University of Minnesota Press.

McCaughey, Martha.

2008.   *The caveman mystique: Pop-Darwinism and debates over sex, violence, and science.* New York: Routledge.

McDonagh, Eileen, and Laura Pappano.

2008.   *Playing with the boys: Why separate is not equal in sports.* New York: Oxford University Press.

McKay, Jim.

1997.   *Managing gender: Affirmative action and organizational power in Australian, Canadian, and New Zealand sport.* Albany: State University of New York Press.

McPherson, J. Miller, and Lynne Smith-Lovin.

1986.   Sex segregation in voluntary associations. *American Sociological Review* 51:61–79.

Messerschmidt, James W.

2004.   *Flesh and blood: Adolescent gender diversity and violence.* Lanham, MD: Rowman & Littlefield.

Messner, Michael A.

1988.   Sports and male domination: The female athlete as contested ideological terrain. *Sociology of Sport Journal* 5:197–211.

1990.   Men studying masculinity: Some epistemological questions in sport sociology. *Sociology of Sport Journal* 7:136–53.

1992.   *Power at play: Sports and the problem of masculinity.* Boston: Beacon Press.

2000.   Barbie girls vs. sea monsters: Children constructing gender. *Gender & Society* 14:765–84.

2002.   *Taking the field: Women, men, and sports.* Minneapolis: University of Minnesota Press.

2005.   Still a man's world? Studying masculinities and sport. In *The handbook of studies on men and masculinities,* ed. Michael S. Kimmel, Jeff Hearn, and R. W. Connell, 313–25. Thousand Oaks, CA: Sage Publications.

Messner, Michael A., Margaret Carlisle Duncan, and Kerry Jensen.

1993.   Separating the men from the girls: The gendered language of televised sports. *Gender & Society* 7:121–37.

Meyerson Milgraom, Eva M., and Trond Petersen.

2006.   The glass ceiling in the United States and Sweden: Lessons from the family-friendly corner of the world, 1970–1990. In *The declining significance of gender?* ed. Francine D. Blau, Mary C. Brinton, and David B. Grusky, 156–211. New York: Russell Sage Foundation.

Miller, Kathleen, Merrill Melnick, Grace Barnes, Michael Farrell, and Don Sabo.
2005.   Untangling the links among athletic involvement, gender, race, and adolescent academic outcomes. *Sociology of Sport Journal* 22:178–93.

Miller, Kathleen, Merrill Melnick, Michael Farrell, Grace Barnes, and Don Sabo.
2006.   Jocks, gender, binge drinking, and adolescent violence. *Journal of Interpersonal Violence* 21:105–20.

Miller, Kathleen, Don Sabo, Michael Farrell, Grace Barnes, and Merrill Melnick.
1999.   Sports, sexual activity, contraceptive use, and pregnancy among female and male high school students: Testing cultural resource theory." *Sociology of Sport Journal* 16:366–87.

Miller, Kathleen, Don Sabo, Merrill Melnick, Michael Farrell, and Grace Barnes.
2001.   The Women's Sports Foundation report: Health risks and the teen athlete. East Meadow, NY: Women's Sports Foundation.

Montez de Oca, Jeffrey.
2005.   As our muscles get softer, our missile race becomes harder: Cultural citizenship and the "muscle gap." *Journal of Historical Sociology* 18:145–71.

Morgan, Laurie A., and Karen A. Martin.
2006.   Taking women professionals out of the office. *Gender & Society* 20:108–28.

Ollilainen, Marjukka, and Toni Calisanti.
2007.   Metaphors at work: Maintaining the salience of gender in self-managing teams. *Gender & Society* 21:5–27.

Ortner, Sherry.
1974.   Is female to male as nature is to culture? In *Woman, Culture, and Society,* ed. Michelle Zimbalist Rosaldo and Louise Lamphere, 67–87. Stanford, CA: Stanford University Press.

Petrzelka, Peggy, and Susan E. Mannon.
2006.   Keepin' this little town going: Gender and volunteerism in rural America. *Gender & Society* 20:236–58.

Pierce, Jennifer.
1993.   Rambo litigators: Emotional labor in a male-dominated occupation. In *Masculinities in Organizations,* ed. Cliff Cheng, 1–27. Thousand Oaks, CA: Sage Publications.

Pollack, William.
1999.   *Real boys: Rescuing our sons from the myths of boyhood.* New York: Henry Holt.

Reskin, Barbara F.
    1988.   Bringing the men back in: Sex differentiation and the devaluation of women's work. *Gender & Society* 2:58–81.

Reskin, Barbara F., and Patricia A. Roos.
    1990.   *Job queues, gender queues: Explaining women's inroads into male occupations.* Philadelphia: Temple University Press.

Rhode, Deborah L., and Christopher J. Walker.
    2008.   Gender equity in college athletics: Women coaches as a case study. *Stanford Journal of Civil Rights and Civil Liberties* 4:1–50. Available at http://ssrn.com/abstract=922380.

Ridgeway, Cecilia.
    2006.   Gender as an organizing force in social relations: Implications for the future of inequality. In *The declining significance of gender?* ed. Francine D. Blau, Mary C. Brinton, and David B. Grusky, 265–87. New York: Russell Sage Foundation.

Ridgeway, Cecilia L., and Shelley J. Correll.
    2004.   Unpacking the gender system: A theoretical perspective on gender beliefs and relations. *Gender & Society* 18:510–31.

Ring, Jennifer.
    2008.   Waiting for Jackie: Why American girls don't play baseball. Paper presented at the annual meetings of the North American Society for the Sociology of Sport, Pittsburgh, PA, October 31–November 3.

Risman, Barbara J.
    1998.   *Gender vertigo: American families in transition.* New Haven, CT: Yale University Press.

Ryan, Joan.
    1996.   Little girls in pretty boxes: The making and breaking of elite gymnasts and figure skaters. New York: Warner Books.

Sabo, Don, and Ross Runfola, eds.
    1980.   *Jock: Sports and male identity.* Englewood Cliffs, NJ: Prentice-Hall.

Sabo, Don and Phil Veliz.
    2008.   *Go out and play: Youth sport and families.* East Meadow, NY: Women's Sports Foundation.

Sargent, Paul.
    2001.   *Real men or real teachers? Contradictions in the lives of men elementary school teachers.* Harriman, TN: Men's Studies Press.

Sharistanian, Janet, ed.
    1987.   *Beyond the public/domestic dichotomy: Contemporary perspectives on women's public lives.* Westport, CT: Greenwood Press.

Shields, David Light, Brenda Light Bredemeier, Nicole M. LaVoi, and F. Clark Power.
    2005. The sport behavior of youth, parents, and coaches: The good, the bad, and the ugly. *Journal of Research in Character Education* 3:43–59.

Sprague, Joey.
    2005. *Feminist methodologies for critical researchers: Bridging differences.* Lanham, MD: Altamira Press.

Stacey, Judith.
    1997. *In the name of the family: Rethinking family values in the postmodern age.* Boston: Beacon Press.

Steiner, Leslie Morgan, ed.
    2006. *Mommy wars.* New York: Random House.

Stevenson, Betsy.
    2007. Title IX and the evolution of high school sports. *Contemporary Economic Policy* 25:486–505.

Stone, Pamela.
    2007. *Opting out: Why women really quit careers and head home.* Berkeley: University of California Press.

Swidler, Anne.
    1986. Culture in action: Symbols and strategies. *American Sociological Review* 51:273–86.

Talbot, Margaret.
    2002. Playing with patriarchy: The gendered dynamics of sports organizations. In *Gender and sport: A reader,* ed. Sheila Scraton and Anne Flintoff, 277–91. London: Routledge.

Theberge, Nancy.
    1988. Making a career in a man's world: The experiences and orientations of women in coaching. *Arena Review* 12:116–27.
    1989. Women athletes and the myth of female frailty. In *Women: A feminist perspective,* ed. Jo Freeman, 507–22. 4th ed. Mountain View, CA: Mayfield.
    1990. Gender, work, and power: The case of women in coaching. *Canadian Journal of Sociology* 15:59–75.
    1993. The construction of gender in sport: Women, coaching, and the naturalization of difference. *Social Problems* 40:301–13.

Thompson, Shona.
    1999a. The game begins at home: Women's labor in the service of sport. In *Inside Sports,* ed. Jay Coakley and Peter Donnelly, 111–20. London: Routledge.
    1999b. *Mother's taxi: Sport and women's labor.* Albany: State University of New York Press.

Thorne, Barrie.
   1993.   *Gender play: Girls and boys in school.* New Brunswick, NJ: Rutgers
            University Press.
Thorne, Barrie, Cheris Kramarae, and Nancy Henley.
   1983.   *Language, gender, and society.* Rowley, MA: Newbury House.
Thorne, Barrie, and Marilyn Yalom, eds.
   1992.   (1982). *Rethinking the family: Some feminist questions.* Boston:
            Northeastern University Press.
Tucker Center for Research on Girls and Women in Sport.
   2007.   *The 2007 Tucker Center research report, Developing physically active
            girls: An evidence-based multidisciplinary approach.* Minneapolis:
            University of Minnesota.
Van Auken, Lance, and Robin Van Auken.
   2001.   *Play ball! The story of Little League Baseball.* University Park, PA:
            Pennsylvania State University Press.
Vavrus, Mary Douglas.
   2007.   Opting out moms in the news: Selling new traditionalism in the
            new millennium. *Feminist Media Studies* 7:47–63.
Wachs, Faye Linda.
   2002.   Leveling the playing field: Negotiating gendered rules in coed
            softball. *Journal of Sport and Social Issues* 26:300–316.
Wall, Glenda, and Stephanie Arnold.
   2007.   How involved is involved fathering? An exploration of the
            contemporary culture of fatherhood. *Gender & Society* 21:508–27.
Webber, Gretchen, and Christine Williams.
   2008.   Part-time work and the gender division of labor. *Qualitative
            Sociology* 31:15–36.
Weiss, Maureen R., Heather Barber, Vicki Ebbeck, and Becky L. Sisley.
   1991.   Developing competence and confidence in novice female coaches:
            II. Perceptions of ability and affective experiences following a
            season-long coaching internship. *Journal of Exercise Psychology*
            13:336–63.
Weiss, Maureen R., and Susan D. Fretwell.
   2005.   The parent-coach/child-athlete relationship in youth sport: Cordial,
            contentious, or conundrum? *Research Quarterly for Exercise and Sport*
            76:286–305.
Weiss, Maureen R., and Becky L. Sisley.
   1986.   Where have all the coaches gone? *Sociology of Sport Journal* 1:332–47.
West, Candace, and Don Zimmerman.
   1987.   Doing gender. *Gender & Society* 1:125–51.

Williams, Christine L.

    1991.   *Gender differences at work: Women and men in nontraditional occupations.* Berkeley: University of California Press.

Willis, Paul.

    1983.   Women in sport in ideology. In *Sport, culture, and ideology,* ed. Jennifer Hargreaves, 117–35. London: Routledge & Kegan Paul.

Wilson, John.

    2000.   Volunteering. *Annual Review of Sociology* 26:215–40.

Wilson, Robin.

    2007.   Where have all the women gone? *Chronicle of Higher Education,* May 4, A40–A44.

Yablonsky, Lewis, and Jonathan J. Brower.

    1979.   *The Little League game: How kids, coaches, and parents really play it.* New York: Times Books.

Index

Text: 10/14 Palatino
Display: Univers Condensed Light 47 and Bauer Bodoni
Compositor: Binghamton Valley Composition, LLC
Indexer: Sharon Sweeney
Printer & Binder: Maple-Vail Book Manufacturing Group